Economic Transition
and Political Legitimacy
in Post-Mao China

Published by
State University of New York Press

© 1995 State University of New York

Printed in the United States of America

For information, address the State University of New York Press,
State University Plaza, Albany, NY 12246

Production by Bernadine Dawes • Marketing by Nancy Farrell

Library of Congress Cataloging-in-Publication Data

Chen, Feng.
    Economic transition and political legitimacy in Post-Mao China :
ideology and reform / Feng Chen.
        p.   cm.
    Includes bibliographical references and index.
    ISBN 0-7914-2657-2. — ISBN 0-7914-2658-0 (pbk.)
    1. China—Economic policy—1976- 2. China—Politics and
government—1976- 3. Capitalism—China. 4. Communism—China.
I. Title.
HC427.92.C3533   1996
338.951'009'049—dc20   95-8783
                                                         CIP

1 2 3 4 5 6 7 8 9 10

Economic Transition and Political Legitimacy in Post-Mao China

IDEOLOGY AND REFORM

Feng Chen

State University of New York Press

CONTENTS

PREFACE

It is paradoxical to justify capitalist economic policies as means to "enhance" socialism. This is, however, what is happening in today's China. The goal of this book is to explore the origin of this paradox— why and how it occurred—and to analyze its political consequences. In doing so, the book tries to capture and present to readers the major changes in China's ideological landscape since 1978 and to relate these changes to the future social transformation in China.

However, there is one thing to which I would like to alert readers: I began this book project in late 1990 and completed the draft in 1992. Thus, the new round of economic reforms, delayed by the setback after the Tiananmen Incident of 1989 and then inspired by Deng Xiaoping's inspection trip to southern China in January 1992, is not systematically dealt with here. Nevertheless, it is my belief that, despite the emergence of many capitalist practices since 1992, there have been few theoretical breakthroughs since then. While the current leadership has appeared to be more openly encouraging of capitalist economic policies (such as private ownership and stock markets), the main ideas underlying the current reform, were, in my view, largely formulated during Zhao Zhiyang's time. Even the notion "socialist market economy," put forward by Jiang Zeming in his report to the Fourteenth Party Congress of 1993 and highly praised as an unprecedented conceptual innovation, is not entirely new in terms of its basic theoretical components. The concept in fact has incorporated many ideas that were vigorously advocated by liberal intellectuals in different ways before 1989. So I tend to believe that recent changes in economic ideology, if any, have not gone beyond the point they had reached in China before the Tiananmen Incident in 1989. For example, people are now more encouraged to practice capitalism than to (theoretically) justify it. This reflects Deng Xiaoping's tactic of doing whatever can promote productivity while avoiding any debate on theories and "isms," but, as this book suggests, it will certainly deepen the dilemma of socialist ideology versus capitalist practice the Chinese leadership has faced since reform. Although the book's empirical content is limited to a certain period, 1978–91, its analytical framework is designed to provide a better understanding of China's ongoing transformation. It is therefore applicable not only to certain policy issues but also to their long-term political impact.

This book would not have been possible without the generous assistance I have received from many people in the last several years. Though any errors and shortcomings contained within are solely my responsibility, I would like to share credit with those who have assisted me in various ways. I owe a particular intellectual debt to John D. Nagle and Lily H. M. Ling, who rendered unstinting help at every stage of this project, including painstaking reading with extensive comments on every chapter in a long series of preliminary drafts. Their judicious combination of guidance and tolerance made this work possible. Ralph Ketcham, Marwyn Samuels, and Norman Kutcher were also unsparing in giving me encouragement and suggestions, and provided much of the intellectual stimulation behind this book.

I am grateful to Barrett McCormick and two anonymous reviewers who firmly supported the publication of this book while making very important suggestions for its improvement.

I owe special thanks to my brother, Chen Baoping, and my friends Wang Huning, Yang Xiaoxun, and Caroline Tong, who provided valuable insights and materials about changes in China's economic ideology. I would like to express my heartfelt appreciation to Clay Morgan, Bernadine Dawes, and Sherry McCowan at the State University of New York Press for their help in seeing the book through publication.

The Roscoe Martin Fund of the Maxwell School, Syracuse University, provided me with grants that defrayed some of my research expenses.

I am grateful to the following publishers for permission to reprint material from their publications:

Tables 2.1, 2.2, and 2.4 are from Carl Riskin, *China's Political Economy* (New York: Oxford University Press, 1987). Table 5.2 (p. 96), table 5.3 (p. 99), and table 11.6 (p. 257) are reprinted by permission of Oxford University Press.

Tables 4.1, 4.2, and 7.1 are from Mark Selden, *The Political Economy of Chinese Socialism* (Armonk, N.Y.: M. E. Sharpe, 1988). Table 6.4 (p. 170) and table 6.5 (p. 171) are reprinted by permission of M. E. Sharpe, Inc.

Finally, Ting Gong's intellectual companionship and willingness to read more than just one draft lightened my burden enormously. This work is a reflection of our close intellectual and personal partnership.

TABLES

ABBREVIATIONS

BR	*Beijing Review* (Beijing)
CCP	Chinese Communist Party
CR	Cultural Revolution
FBIS	Foreign Broadcasting Information Service–Daily Report-China (United States)
GLF	Great Leap Forward
GMRB	*Guangming Ribao* (Guangmin Daily, Beijing)
HQ	*Hingqui* (Red Flag, Beijing)
HQRB	*Hauquiao Ribao* (Overseas Chinese Daily, United States)
ICS	Industrial Contract System
IHC	Individual Household Contract
JFJB	*Jiefangjubao* (Liberation Army's Daily, Beijing)
JFRB	*Jiefang Ribao* (Liberation Daily, Shanghai)
JJGL	*Jingji Guanli* (Economic Management, Beijing)
JJRB	*Jingji Ribao* (Economic Daily, Beijing)
JJYJ	*Jingji Yanjiu* (Studies in Economics, Beijing)
JJZB	*Jingji Zhoubao* (Economic Weekly, Beijing)

KMT	Kuomintang
LW	*Liaowing* (Outlook, Beijing)
PRC	People's Republic of China
RMRB	*Renmin Ribao* (People's Daily, Beijing)
SHGG	*Shanghai Gaige* (Shanghai Reform, Shanghai)
SHJJ	Shanghai Jingji (Shanghai Economy, Shanghai)
SJJJDB	*Shijie Jingji Daobao* (World Economic Herald, Shanghai)
TGXX	*Tigai Xinxi* (Information of Reform, Sichuan)
XHS	*Xinhuashe* (Xinhau News Agency)
XSYJ	*Xueshu Yanjiu* (Academic Research, Shanghai)
ZGGYJJWT	*Zhongguo Gongye Jingji Wenti* (Issues of Chinese Industrial Economics, Beijing)
ZGJJWY	*Zhongguo Jingji Wenti* (Chinese Economic Issues, Beijing)
ZGTXS	*Zhongguo Tongxunshe* (China News Agency)
ZXYJ	*Zhixue Yanjiu* (Philosophical Research, Beijing)
ZYRB	*Zhongyang Ribao* (Cental Daily, Taiwan)
ZYWX	*Zhongyao Wenxian* (The Collected Important Party Documents, Beijing)

1
Introduction

The Chinese economy is shifting from a socialist one to a capitalist one.[1] By China's transition to a capitalist economy, I mean a process that is producing two phenomenal institutional developments: extensive marketization of the economy and an expansion of private economy. Though few had predicted such a transition at the early stage of the economic reform and many expressed pessimism about it after the Tiananmen Incident of 1989, people are now talking about its irreversibility. Indeed, China's economic reform has reached such a point that any attempted return to the previous centrally planned economy would be economically counterproductive and politically suicidal.

Although few would disagree that the Chinese economy is turning capitalist, questions remain as to why and how this transition has occurred and become consolidated. China's case becomes even more puzzling when compared with that of other former communist states: While the transition to a capitalist economy in Eastern Europe and the former Soviet Union had barely started before communism collapsed in 1989, China's communist state itself is encouraging the transition. In other words, a capitalist economy is taking shape in China prior to a regime transformation.

1

The Role of Ideas/Ideology

According to common explanations, China's economic transition is a consequence of decision makers' rational policy choices, power struggles at the top, or changes in bureaucratic interests. Although none of these approaches is wrong, and hence it is not a purpose of this book to deny the insights they furnish into China's economic transition, this book intends to draw attention to a dimension overlooked by these approaches: the role of ideas. It argues that China's economic transition can largely be attributed to the penetration of capitalist economic thinking into economic policy making. This "conversion," involving both critiques of traditional socialist economic principles and reassessment of capitalist economic ideas, represents a process of reconstruction of the official economic ideology, which has played a key role in redefining the Chinese economic system and bringing about monumental changes in Chinese society.

There are reasons for this book to pay particular attention to the significance of ideas/ideology for China's economic reform. First, contrary to those accounts of Chinese politics that consciously and unconsciously overlook the importance of ideas/ideology, this book argues that China's political system remains an "ideological" one that requires a theoretical basis for all major policies to sustain the system's legitimacy.[2] Ideological constraints on economic policies at the early stage of the reform were significant, and they continue to be relevant as the reform moves on. Of course, in today's China, the ideology remains relevant not because the party still needs to derive policies from it, which happened in the Mao years, but because the party has to present policy changes through the overlay of ideological rhetoric. As what follows will show, the relevance of ideology to China's reform from 1979 through 1991 is reflected in two facts: (1) Economic reforms in this period had recurrently been plagued with ideological controversies; and (2) the party had to define pragmatic (and, later, capitalistic) economic policies in terms of existing ideology. In other words, even a pragmatic policy had to be made ideologically sound. The relevance of ideology remains, even though China's economy has been moving toward capitalism, particularly since 1992. The party's refusal to renounce its ideology, which sharply contradicts its economic policies and its continuing insistence on the concept of "socialism with Chinese characteristics," clearly indicates that ideology still matters. Thus, ideology continues to define a constraint by which the workings of new ideas and policy maneuvers can be comprehended.

Second, in a Leninist one-party system like China's, where decision making on key policy issues is still highly centralized and even personalized,[3] ideas held by top leaders and key policy makers are important for policy change and innovation. Indeed, what Deng Xiaoping thought and what types of ideas Hu Yaobang and Zhao Zhiyang opted for mattered tremendously in China's economic transition. Even though leadership's ideas are influenced by intellectual and policy elites, "ideas from above" perform a significant function of forming and redefining political discourse and ideology in which new policy proposals can emerge.

Third, the role of ideas is particularly manifest and significant in a society whose leadership seeks a fundamental policy change in the face of certain major political and economic difficulties. The economic depression of the 1930s compelled Western states to "convert" to Keynesianism, which led to vital changes of economic policy in these nations (Hall 1989). Developmentalism, as a set of distinctive beliefs on economic development, responded to economic hardship in some Latin American countries in the 1930s and 1940s, caused by the crisis of Western capitalist economy. Developmentalism served to put in action strategies such as import substitution, rapid capital accumulation, and state involvement in countries like Brazil and Argentina (Sikkink 1991). China's economy was facing serious troubles in the late 1970s after more than two decades of Maoist socialism. The Chinese leadership desperately sought ways out of the predicament. At this juncture, the new vision of a workable economic system became critical for China's future development.

Fourth, constrained by dogmatic socialist economic thinking for a long period, Chinese leadership and policy makers had little knowledge about how to establish a viable economy when they started reforms. New ideas and knowledge were thus critical for policy innovations and, indeed, became the sources of policy initiatives. Not only did new ideas and knowledge open up a scope of policy options for the leadership and its policy advisors, they also served them well in their effort to reconceptualize economics and redefine the normative foundation of the economic system.

Finally, and perhaps most importantly, changes in ideas/ideology provide an important dimension for us to understand certain significant political conflict and policy controversies confronting

Chinese policy makers. What China's leadership had attempted to do in the past decade was to incorporate capitalist economic thinking into its official economic ideology. Irreconcilable tensions inevitably arose when they were trying to make capitalistic ideas work in a system that still needed to rely on the concept of socialism for its legitimacy. Thus, while technical difficulties might have been involved in policy innovations, self-contradictory elements of the new economic ideology were contributing factors to many policy dilemmas and, indeed, were a source of political conflict.

However, simply recognizing that ideas are important to China's economic transition is not enough. Ideas have no explanatory power in analyses of policy making if we do not know how a particular set of ideas penetrates into the policy thinking of decision makers, how ideas define and redefine the problems to be solved, and how ideas make differences in the policy process. New ideas do not exist in an ideological vacuum. Absorbing new ideas, especially those alien to the existing ideological system, can be a risky undertaking, which may cause damage to a regime needing ideology for its legitimacy. Thus, this book seeks to address two sets of questions: First, how have Chinese intellectual and policy elites managed to incorporate capitalist economic thinking into the official ideology to accommodate capitalist practices, and through what mechanisms are capitalist economic ideas filtered and reshaped to meet the policy needs of a party still claiming to be communist? Second, what are the policy outcomes and political consequences of China's attempt to reconcile the irreconcilable, and why would the Chinese economic transition to capitalism would deepen the legitimacy crisis of the Chinese Communist Party (CCP)?

Ideology versus Economic Development: The Goal Conflict

To address these questions, this book focuses on two aspects of the process by which new economic ideas entered into the policy agenda and helped form a new economic ideology: first, how intellectual and policy elites created the new economic ideology by first flexibly interpreting Marxism and then systematically borrowing capitalist ideas; and second, how the incorporation of capitalist economic thinking into the official economic ideology generated certain profound policy and political predicaments that put new pressures upon the leadership.

In the view of this book, the choices of China's policy makers were largely ideologically constrained during a long period of the economic reform. This constraint was reflected in a profound dilemma that confronted the reform-minded leaders: how to use all possible means (including capitalist ones) to improve economic performance, while avoiding undermining the ideologically based legitimacy of Chinese polity. In a sense, this was not an entirely new problem in communist systems nor was it unique to China. More than twenty years ago, Lowenthal (1970, 1976) pointed out that the fundamental goal-conflict confronting all communist states was "development versus utopia." According to him, with the advent of "mature industrialization," a communist state had to adapt itself to certain institutional changes (such as material incentives, managerial autonomy, specialization, and income differentials), all of which were incompatible with its fundamental ideological goals (such as equality and a classless society). Lowenthal believed that this type of goal conflict had been experienced by political leaders in the Soviet Union and Eastern Europe as these countries moved toward becoming industrialized societies. As China began its reforms, it was facing the same goal conflict; with the implementation of an all-out market-driven reform later on, this conflict was in fact exacerbated to an extent that Lowenthal did not anticipate.

The attempt to balance these two needs determined at the outset that China's economic reform was oriented toward problem solving rather than systemic change. In other words, Chinese policy makers did not have a clear vision of where the reform should go; as this was reflected in an official slogan, "crossing the river by feeling the way from rock to rock" (mozhe shizi guo he). Yet, as traditional socialist economics had proved ineffective and irrelevant, practical problem solving tended to invite capitalist thinking, because there were no other alternatives to improve economic performance. To avoid damaging the ideologically based legitimacy, Chinese policy makers attempted to interpret all reform policies as compatible with the official ideology. This effort gave rise to what this book terms the "fundamental-instrumental discrepancy"—a process in which the linkage of the pursued policies with ideological tenets, though maintained in form, was gradually eroded. This process was both educational and manipulative. It was educational because, by marginalizing the function of ideological principles in the economic domain, policy makers began to get acquainted with new ideas that had been advanced by liberal academics and had proved workable in problem solving. It was manipulative in the sense that policy makers and academics dissected liberal economic ideas, "neutralizing" some of their elements (e.g., arguing that some economic mechanisms embraced by liberal economics, such as the market, could serve both capitalist and socialist systems), and selectively incorporated them into the official economic ideology. By doing this, they were able to create a "gray terrain" in which the distinction between socialism and capitalism blurred. As a result, capitalist measures came to be carried out in the name of "socialism with Chinese characteristics."

The "fundamental-instrumental discrepancy" thus defined a context in which policy innovations and the introduction of new ideas were able to interact and were mutually reinforcing and in which the official economic ideology underwent fundamental changes. This book focuses on this process and explains how the process contributes to China's economic transition, on the one hand, and may inevitably lead to a crisis of political legitimacy, on the other.

Alternative Explanations

This book regards China's economic transition as an outcome of the change in official economic ideology and explains the CCP's policy and political dilemmas in terms of the tension between the fundamental and instrumental principles of its ideology. The approach used in this book differs from those that have been frequently applied to the studies of Chinese politics in general and its economic reform in particular. Three theoretical perspectives have stood out as "dominant" approaches to the politics of China's economic reform: the rational choice approach, the power struggle approach, and the bureaucratic approach.

The rational choice approach focuses on the response of policy makers to changing policy environments (Allison 1971; Simon 1976). This approach proceeds from assumptions about human motives and behavior, and draws logical institutional and policy implications from those assumptions. Two aspects are central to this approach: One is that all social phenomena are derivable from, or can be factored into, the properties and behaviors of individuals; another is that political actors (including organizations) are assumed to be interest maximizers (Almond 1990, 123). Policy outcomes, according to this approach, result from a selection of decision-making alternatives that maximize a policy outcome.

The rational choice approach has often been used to explain the Chinese policy process (Barnett 1974; Harding 1981; Solinger 1984). The latest application of this approach to China's economic reform can be found in Shirk's work (1993), which combines the rational choice approach with an institutional one. According to Shirk, China's current institutional structure sets the context in which Chinese officials compete with one another to advance their careers and make economic policies. The political logic of China's institution, Shirk argues, determines that Chinese officials at every level of the system embrace particularistic economic reform policies that enable them to claim credit and enhance their careers. Thus, the economic reform as a whole can be regarded as the result of this logic.

From the perspective of the rational actor approach, China's economic transition could be regarded as stemming from the alternative that leadership and policy makers had chosen to maximize their chances of staying in power. True, it was commonly held in the late 1970s, even by many leaders and policy makers, that the leadership could lose popular support if the rigid economic system was continued. Improving economic performance was in the best interests of the leadership and thus became a top policy priority.

The power struggle approach has long been prevalent in the study of communist politics. This approach views policy outcomes in communist systems as a result of elite power struggle. Political elites, it assumes, are sensitive to the implications of alternative policy choices for their power and stature. The relative power of elites and their strategies for advancing their beliefs and political interests motivate policy processes and determine decision making outcomes. "Power struggle" is in fact the key conceptual tool used by prominent China scholars, such as MacFarquhar in his account for the Cultural Revolution (1981) and Pye in his analysis of the dynamics of Chinese politics (1981). Harding (1987) and Nathan (1990) apply this approach to the reform process. Harding believes that, to some extent, China's economic reform can be viewed as power contentions first between restorationists and reformers and then between moderate and radical reformers. Policy process reflects the efforts of contending groups to maximize their representation in the leading body of the party and state. In Nathan's works of Chinese politics, factionalism, which means power struggle among different factions, is a particularly important concept. His analyses of China's reform focus on power alignments at the top, whereas his assessment of China's future derives from factional power relations. Moreover, given the fact that the Chinese political system is still uninstitutionalized, the power struggle approach might continue to be useful in explaining the dynamics of Chinese politics. Indeed, it is not entirely improper to explain reform policies in terms of the strategy used by reform-minded leaders to advance their political interests and strengthen their power and stature.

The bureaucratic politics approach explains policy process and its outcomes as the result of competing activities among bureaucratic entities and actors constrained by their organizational roles and capacities (Allison 1971; Halperin 1974). Change in policy, in the view of this approach, results from the potential for variable outcomes in bargaining, negotiation, and conflict among the bureaucrats involved. Scholars applying this approach to Chinese politics believe that policy process in China can be understood by examining the competition among government bureaucrats over preferred solutions to particular policy problems. Bureaucrats' views on which policy or policies should prevail are shaped by their position within the government (Lampton 1987; Shirk 1985; Bachman 1991; McCormick 1990; Lieberthal and Oksenberg 1988). Along the line of this approach, China's economic transition can be seen as a process promoted by those bureaucratic actors who have attempted to strengthen their own interests and positions. Liberal economic reforms are beneficial to certain bureaucratic actors while being harmful to others; the implementation of economic transition is therefore a consequence of bureaucratic competition in which those who favor reform policy triumph over those who oppose it.

The goal of this book is not to reject any of these alternative approaches, but to point out their weaknesses in addressing the specific questions raised by this volume. Undoubtedly, all these approaches have furnished important insights into Chinese politics, but none of them takes ideas seriously. Even though it is capable of explaining what will motivate policy choices, the rational choice approach seems to pay less attention than it should to the role of ideas in formulating and reformulating human perceptions of "rationality." Policy makers' perceptions of "rationality" about economics, as this book shows, are changing and often being redefined. Environmental constraints are not the only variable to explain changes in perceptions of "rationality." Ideas and knowledge are crucial for helping leaders and policy makers recognize and clarify what is "rational" and worth pursuing.

Because it focuses merely on the power relations at the top, the power struggle approach is apparently irrelevant to understanding the process of the perceptional change of policy makers. It is hard to explain the policy changes generated by the interaction between problem solving and the formulation of ideas. Furthermore, this approach is unable to explain why certain leaders change the content of their ideas when their relative power interests remain the same.

Given the state's extensive role in China, the bureaucratic politics approach provides important insight into the Chinese policy process. The problem with this approach, however, is that it assumes that bureaucracies remain constant in their purposes and tasks. It therefore has difficulty explaining why bureaucrats would sometimes change policy orientations, while their bureaucratic position remained unchanged. This book contends that a bureaucracy's position is not the only explanation for the process of bureaucratic policy making; with the same position, bureaucracies can redefine their purposes and tasks as they perceive newly emerging interests informed by new ideas and knowledge. Moreover, new ideas can play a role in forming a new consensus within bureaucracies in dealing with particular problems.

One may argue that these approaches do not necessarily exclude an analysis of ideas in policy process. At least, they might provide a reason for why ideas change: for example, because it is the rational thing to do, or because certain elites want more power over other elites, or because the bureaucracy wants to pursue certain interests. Nevertheless, none of them is well-suited for the purpose of this book. Although it discusses the origins of change in China's economic ideology in general terms, this book will mainly center on the process of this change. A different approach, therefore, is needed to reveal how ideas change—in which ways, with what outcomes and consequences, and toward what direction.

Analytical Framework

Ideas do not operate unfettered by material constraints. Change in ideas is always rooted in the emergence of new social conditions. By the late 1970s, China's central-planning economy was in such a shambles that reform became necessary. However, the economic reform at the outset was ideologically constrained. Even though the reform needed ideological justifications, the existing communist ideology was unable to play such a role for two reasons. First, revolutionary in nature, the ideology lacked a set of relevant precepts that could address complex problem solving in a market economy. Essentially anticapitalist, China's official ideology could not furnish a justifiable theoretical and moral underpinning for market-driven reforms. Second, to continue its function of legitimation, this ideology needed to preserve its identity by retaining some of its fundamental principles, which were at best irrelevant to, and at worst conflicting, with market-driven reforms. Chinese reformist leadership, then, was confronted from the very beginning with a significant dilemma: To cope with intractable economic problems, it needed to liberalize its official ideology, and even had to borrow ideas and concepts from the alternative ideology—capitalism—which undoubtedly would substantially contradict the official ideology; but to avoid undermining the ideology and weakening its political legitimacy, the leadership must continue to claim absolute ideological authority to define truth and reality. This dilemma thus led to an unprecedented effort by the leadership, namely, ideological reformulation: defining all reform policies, including those that were explicitly capitalistic ones, in terms of the existing ideology.

This book applies a "fundamental-instrumental discrepancy" approach to investigate the process of China's ideological reformulation. It argues that, to justify market-drive reforms, the leadership manages to realign two components of its ideology: fundamental principles and instrumental principles. The former are the core of the ideology, which sets the tone and parameters of political life in society. Fundamental principles tend to resist any significant change, for such a change might inevitably alter the nature of the regime. In this sense, fundamental principles become equivalent to the regime itself. Characteristically, fundamental principles epitomize "fixed" elements, which are rigid, dogmatic, and impermeable to argument and evidence (Sartori 1969). Instrumental principles function to interpret the nature of current tasks that confront the leadership and to justify current policies, thus indicating how political actors perceive, diagnose, prescribe, and make choices in specific problem areas. Both fundamental and instrumental principles have their own functions. The former justify the ultimate goals by which the regime claims legitimacy, while the latter deal with immediate goals and serves to legitimate the leadership by stressing "performance."

In the pre-reform period, the CCP leadership was largely able to sustain the compatibility between fundamental and instrumental principles in policy processes because its entire practice of remodeling social and economic life closely followed ideological fundamentals. During the market-driven reform, however, the need to experiment with capitalistic policies generated instrumental principles, which, though defined in "fundamental" terms, in fact deviated from, and even contradicted, the core values of the existing ideology. The fundamental-instrumental discrepancy, to some extent, provided the leadership with flexibility to maneuver policies, and created room for new ideas to be practiced in a variety of policy areas.

This two-dimensional approach to ideology has often been applied to the study of communist states. Major conceptual constructs reflecting this effort include Moore's theory of official (or formal) ideology versus operative (informal) ideology (Moore 1965), Schurmann's theory of pure ideology versus practical ideology (1968), Seliger's theory of fundamental ideology versus operative ideology (1976), and Shlapentokh's theory of mythological postulate versus pragmatic command (1986). Though their terms vary, all these authors share the notion that communist ideology is not monolithic and can be distinguished between two dimensions, one referring to the core values of ideology and the other to its practical application. This two-dimensional approach has been used mainly to study the gap between ideology officially promulgated and policies actually implemented in communist states, and political consequences from efforts made by these states to mediate between the official doctrine and actual policy needs.[4] In this dichotomous formula, the practical dimension of ideology is supposed to translate the core values of ideology into action directives, and in the process ideology itself may gradually be modified to adapt to practical needs. The early studies of this type seemed to assume the adaptability of communist ideology to changing reality and to believe that this ideology could be modified to accommodate socioeconomic modernization. The major problem with the previous applications of the two dimensional approach is that they fail to take into consideration the potential conflict between the two dimensions of ideology. They interpret the function of flexible application of ideology as if it would always strengthen ideology and, therefore, do not allow for a crisis of ideology that may arise when the conflict between the two dimensions of ideology becomes irreconcilable.

In this book, the fundamental-instrumental discrepancy is used to explain not only the CCP's ideological self-adjustment but also its ideological decay and transformation. The key to understanding the transformation of China's economic ideology, as this book suggests, is the process in which the leadership formulates its instrumental principles on the basis of capitalist economic thinking. Although China's decision makers have persistently interpreted these instrumental principles as compatible with fundamental ones, they cannot prevent the official economic ideology from becoming indistinguishable from its antithesis—capitalism. The hard fact is that, with the penetration of rival ideas, the discrepancy between fundamental and instrumental principles is no longer one of degree, as previous scholars believed, but one of kind.

The two-dimensional approach, or the fundamental-instrumental discrepancy, of this book is thus more than just a perspective from which to understand self-adjustments made by China's leadership to balance ideology and reality; it provides explanations for the process of fundamental changes in China's economic ideology, a process that contributed to the economic transition in four related and progressive ways. First, by first defining pragmatic problem solving and, later, capitalist measures, as instrumental principles that were compatible with the fundamental principles of official ideology, China's policy makers obtained necessary room to maneuver policy processes and widened the latitude for policy choices. At the same time, they warded off some inflammatory ideological controversies. Second, piecemeal experiments with capitalism, made possible under the fundamental-instrumental discrepancy, produced new and more policy "issue areas" that in turn stimulated, and sometimes compelled, policy makers and advisors to borrow more from capitalist economic thinking. The logic here was quite simple: Capitalism would not work well if it was allowed to function only in some areas (e.g., pricing) while it was barred in others (e.g., ownership). Thus, the practice of capitalist ideas actually had a spiral effect that led to more similar practices. Third, the cumulative incorporation of capitalist economic thinking, in the form of instrumental principles, allowed a new economic discourse to emerge, helped alter the conceptual apparatus of economic theory, and reshaped the perceptions of policy makers about cause-and-effect linkages in economics. Fourth, as the gap widened between them, fundamental and instrumental principles eventually became irreconcilable. Strictly speaking, a certain degree of compatibility between fundamental and instrumental principles is important for any functioning ideology.[5] Conceptual disarray and incompatibility would deprive an ideology of its power to reason, persuade, and hence govern. Chinese leadership had attempted to maintain the internal consistency of its official economic ideology under the "umbrella" concept of "socialism with Chinese characteristics," but systematic borrowing of capitalist ideas eroded the foundation of the official economic ideology and led to its fundamental change.

Fundamental Principles versus Instrumental Principles

The fundamental principles of the CCP's ideology involve a small number of belief elements, which define the "identity" of the ideology and play a key role in unifying it. The fundamental ideology of the CCP has several interrelated functions: They (1) determine the party's final goal, (2) legitimate the CCP's leading role in society, (3) define the social and political order the CCP wants to maintain, and (4) provide an ontological framework (namely, a worldview) to evaluate everything from policies to social behavior. Fundamental principles tend to resist any significant change, for such change inevitably changes the identity of the ideology per se and therefore the nature of the party. In this sense, fundamental principles become equivalent to the party itself. The party needs them for its self-claimed legitimacy, and to preserve the continuity of the polity, to define its unique status in society, to maintain a socialist image, and to prevent potential political groups from demanding power sharing.

The concept "fundamental principles" in this study differs somewhat from what Schurmann calls "pure ideology," and also from what Lowenthal calls "utopia." Schurmann's "pure ideology" refers to some abstract philosophical beliefs derived from Marxist theory, which gives individuals a unified and conscious worldview (Schurmann 1966, 22). According to his definition, some important principles, for example, party leadership, are logically excluded from "pure ideology," since they are created as an instrument for action rather than to give individuals a world view. In this study, "fundamental principles" are a sort of "political formula," which is more than some abstract ideas that define the future society. They include some concrete political doctrines by which the CCP claims legitimation and excludes other social groups from sharing power. They are politically unchallengeable, and their official position must be maintained in spite of great stress. For example, the notions of party leadership, socialist road, dictatorship of the proletariat, and Marxism-Leninism–Mao Zedong Thought—the so-called "four cardinal principles"—stand as the most fundamental elements of the CCP's ideology.

Lowenthal (1970) uses the term utopia to refer to the vision of an ideal future society envisioned by communist ideology. In this study, however, fundamental principles are regarded as a mixture of utopian ideas and political "realism." Undoubtedly, the CCP's ideology, at least officially, still retains some utopian elements, as typically reflected in the Party's constitution. By incorporating utopian elements into its legitimating doctrines, the CCP accepts a standard of perfection against which the present performance of party and other social groups can be judged (Gilison 1975). However, postrevolutionary social conditions have attenuated the utopian elements of the CCP ideology in two ways: First, the party has institutionalized utopia and turned it into a number of principles to defend the status quo. Utopia has thus lost its original role as a critique of existing society; second, the party becomes less receptive to utopian visions of society as it is engaged in intractable problem solving. Thus, while some of the fundamental principles remain utopian in character regarding ultimate goals, others are "realistic" in the sense that they function as the key for the party to control society and maintain political order. Fundamental principles as such inevitably confront the challenges from two fronts. Against the "ideal" vision of socialism, for instance, some think that socialism is distorted in China's political system. For others, socialism is never a realistic or rational way to administer the society.

As mentioned above, capitalist economic ideas permeated China's policy process during the reform, mainly in the form of instrumental principles. Instrumental principles are regarded in this book as (re)interpretations of ideological fundamentals and as a set of ideas derived from these interpretations to justify immediate policy goals. Instrumental principles differ from specific policies, though they are intimately related. As a theoretical construct and rationale behind policy making, an instrumental principle might be used to justify a series of policies. For example, the practice of justifying the "open door" policy to the outside world since the 1980s can sanction many specific open-door policies, from joint ventures and special economic zones, to sending students abroad.

Analytically, instrumental principles can be grouped into three types, in terms of their construction or more specifically, their relationship to fundamental principles: (1) Dogmatic: these principles are directly derived from, and serve to actualize, fundamental principles. (2) Pragmatic: These are simply grounded on practical needs but can be loosely linked to fundamental principles; therefore they represent new interpretations of fundamental principles and serve to fill the gap between ideology and reality. (3) divergent: These actually come from another ideological source but are defined in the terms of the existing ideology.

Although all instrumental principles serve to identify problems (e.g., cause-and-effect linkage in a policy area) and prescribe recommendations for problem solving, the different types of instrumental principles identify the problems to be solved differently and, consequently, offer different policy recommendations. In the context of communist politics, the dogmatic type is related to revolutionary orientations and policies that stick to ideological orthodoxy, whereas the pragmatic type portrays moderate and less ideologically inspired problem-solving orientations. Finally, the divergent type indicates the decline of the existing ideology and its failure to address the problems to be solved.

In China, the operation of the three types of instrumental principles basically corresponds to the phases of political development. The dogmatic principles mainly reflect the orientation of the pre-reform years, when ideology penetrated every aspect of life in society. In this period, major economic policies were ideologically inspired; in other words, they were derived from, and evaluated against, ideological fundamentals. The Great Leap Forward, the People's Commune, the pursuit of the higher degree of public ownership, self-reliance, and "politics in command" in economic activities in the Cultural Revolution best characterized this orientation. The pragmatic type had been extensively used by Chinese leadership in most of the reform period. Concepts such as "separation between ownership and management," "responsibility system," and "socialist commodity economy" could be put in this category. The divergent type emerged in the late 1980s, when the reform was demanding bold policies beyond the existing economic ideological framework.

Exemplifying this type were concepts such as "property rights," "stock market," "shareholding system," and "income differentials," all of which stemmed from capitalist economic thinking.

Until the late 1980s, Chinese policy makers and intellectuals had largely relied upon the pragmatic type of instrumental principles for policy innovations. They employed two methods to adjust the relationship between fundamental and instrumental principles. One was to reinterpret fundamental principles to make them more flexible and more inclusive. The CCP's "Resolution on Party History" in 1981 (*ZYWX*, 1983; 738–792) typified such an ideological reinterpretation. It recast the thought of Mao Zedong as being about, not class struggle, but "seeking truth from facts" and defined the latter as the core of Marxism. This new postulate gave Mao Zedong Thought a new function in Chinese politics without jeopardizing its formal legitimacy. In addition, the party leadership stressed "four modernizations" as its fundamental goal, which could encompass whatever methods were necessary to increase productivity. In short, a flexible and inclusive interpretation of fundamental principles broadened the CCP's ideological framework within which instrumental principles had great room to expand. The other method was to establish new "intellectual" linkages between fundamental and pragmatic-oriented instrumental principles. This would allow any new instrumental principles to be interpreted in terms of their consistency with the fundamental ones. For instance, the CCP argued that market mechanisms were not connected only with capitalism. They were also indispensable under socialism. Concepts such as "contracting," "leasing," and "shareholding" were also interpreted as applicable to socialist economy. Another example was the CCP's formulation of the "preliminary stage of socialism." This formula implicitly justified capitalist measures as necessary for China, for the reason that China's socialism had been built in a historical context of undeveloped capitalism, and hence legitimated capitalistic practices under China's socialism.

These distinctions are for analytical purposes only. In reality, these methods are inseparable from and intertwined with each other. Obviously, a flexible and inclusive interpretation of fundamental principles would make it easier to relate pragmatism to the existing ideology, while the need to integrate pragmatic ideas into the ideology would inevitably lead to flexible and inclusive interpretations of fundamental principles.

One important argument of this book is that in China's economic transition, the pragmatic and divergent types of instrumental principles were logically related. Application of the pragmatic principles, despite serving to fill the gap between official ideology and policy needs, could open up ways for the divergent principles to emerge. In other words, pragmatic thinking, when carried forward, tended to lead to the acceptance of whatever was workable. Moreover, certain pragmatic principles per se had implicit or explicit linkages to capitalist economic thinking; as they were pushed to their logical extremes, they became indistinguishable from the divergent type of instrumental principles. Thus, pragmatic instrumental principles, if carried out persistently, would generate divergent ones. This was apparently exemplified, as this book will show, by China's experience with allowing a limited "individual economy" in order to ease urban youth unemployment, and then with the justification of "private economy" as a legitimate part of the national economy.

The Fundamental-Instrumental Discrepancy and the Legitimacy Crisis

It is self-evident that the fundamental-instrumental discrepancy results from the CCP's unwillingness to repudiate its fundamental principles. Essentially, the CCP remains a Leninist party that still needs to rely on Marxist-Leninist ideology for its self-claimed legitimation. The major function of fundamental principles is to provide the theoretical basis upon which the CCP can claim the monopoly of political power. Socialism, for example, is the rationale for party leadership, for only the party leadership is said to be able to guarantee the socialist direction of Chinese society. In other words, the CCP defines socialism as a goal that can be achieved only under the leadership of a Leninist party like itself, since, as it always claims, only the Communist Party represents the tradition of scientific socialism and is able to command the course of history. A formal abandonment of socialism, or a demotion of socialism from being the ruling ideology to being an alternative one, may challenge the necessity of the party's leading status in society. For example, the party has to interpret the presence or absence of the state economy as related to, indeed as identified with, the vision of society to be built—a society that only the party knows how to establish. This orientation makes it difficult for the party to apply a practical perspective to some issues, for instance, the party could simply treat the state's role in the economy as a way to solve certain specific economic problems (such as providing public goods and allocating strategic resources and), rather than maintain it as imperative for ideological fulfillment. In this sense, the "ontological block" confronting the CCP is interest determined—it cannot be removed so long as the party continues to take ideological fundamentals as the ultimate source of its legitimacy.

On the other hand, while still relying on ideology for its self-claimed legitimacy, the post-Mao leadership has no longer been sure that this ideology can generate "legitimacy as believed," given its colossal failure in the past decades' practice. In fact, CCP's ideologically based legitimacy was in a serious crisis by the end of the Cultural Revolution. A strenuous task facing the post-Mao leadership was, therefore, to brace the fractured foundation of the regime's legitimacy. It chose economic reform as a means, which, in the eyes of Deng Xiaoping and his supporters, was perhaps the only alternative to win back "legitimacy as believed." As economic performance was thus employed to redeem what ideology had failed to establish, the fundamental-instrumental discrepancy ensued.

Nevertheless, economic performance-based legitimation and ideological legitimation involve two different sets of norms that can be highly incompatible. The former encourages the policy style of "instrumental consciousness" that strives to render all problems as strictly rational or technical ones and to justify whatever means capable of improving performance. Ideological legitimation, on the other hand, emphasizes certain high moral and normative principles that tend to link policy choices to ideology and consequently excludes certain means as incompatible with ideological tenets. As such, economic performance-based legitimation and ideological legitimation may clash, because the means to improve performance may violate the core values of ideology. This is a profound dilemma for the post-Mao leadership.

Undoubtedly, the redefinition of socialism in terms of economic productivity provided the post-Mao leadership with strong theoretical support for its modernization efforts. With this new conceptualization, socialism was reduced to certain ideas of modernization and the CCP could legitimately implement "whatever" means and methods necessary to pursue economic growth and efficiency.

However, the fundamental-instrumental discrepancy inescapably leads to what Habermas calls a "rationality crisis" (Habermas 1975)—a crisis caused by the disparity between current practices and original ideological tenets upon which the regime has been founded. Indeed, by justifying whatever means workable to improve economic performance, the leadership is increasingly incapable of preventing its economic thinking from becoming indistinguishable from its antitheses—capitalism—and thereby from losing the identity of its own ideology. If the aim of socialism is to develop productive forces, then, as Mmeisner correctly asks, "Wherein lies the difference between socialism and capitalism?" (Meisner 1982, 235) Moreover, to develop productivity is not something for which the party "can claim a privileged understanding" (Womack 1989). The CCP regime's growing commitment to economic development makes it increasingly harder to justify to society why only this part, with this particular composition, and its ideology should permanently maintain the right to rule.

Thus, the logic of the fundamental-instrumental discrepancy is paradoxical for the post-Mao leadership: It is both problem-solving and crisis-generating. It improved economic efficiency by allowing the regime to choose whatever means it felt was suitable. On the other hand, the primacy of production deprived the CCP of the persuasive power of its ideology and significantly undermined its self-legitimacy claim based on the ideology.

In terms of the basis of its legitimacy, the CCP as a Leninist party contrasts with what is called the "developmental state" (Wade 1990; Amsden 1989; Deyo 1987; Johnson 1982). Despite being as authoritarian and repressive in character as the CCP, a developmental state will not encounter the legitimacy crisis caused by the fundamental-instrumental discrepancy in pursuing modernization. The difference, as Johnson (1987, 143) finds in his analysis of East Asian authoritarian states, is that these states are "ultimately legitimated not by their ideological pretensions" but "by their results." In other words, these states are freer than Leninist states to take whatever means to boost economies without having to wrestle with the ideological implications. Similarly, Onis (1991) believes that the goal conflict is diluted in developmental states mainly due to the fact that these states do not have a strong ideological commitment to equality and social welfare; they simply define growth, productivity, and competitiveness as "the foremost and single-minded priority of the state."

Surely, developmental states are by no means conflict-free. Their conflict between capital and labor, for example, could be intense. Economic modernization could also challenge authoritarian rule. These states could fail due to their poor economic performance and results. However, they would not contradict themselves in choosing "whatever means" to promote economic growth, as long as they perceived these means as economically favorable and workable. In this sense, they would not encounter the legitimacy crisis of the kind that the Leninist state has to face, for two reasons: First, unlike that of Leninist states, developmental states' ideology lacks what Chalmers Johnson (1970) has called a "goal culture," that is, a pronounced commitment to an explicit program of social transformation with which to attain the sacrosanct goal of a communist society. Thus, developmental states are able to evaluate policy measures (such as private versus state ownership) in accordance with practical needs and possibilities rather than with a certain ultimate and transcendental goal that society should pursue. In fact, developmental states do not have clearly defined or exclusive fundamental principles that will restrict their choices for the means of modernization;[6] they are rarely confronted with the risk that particular methods and their outcomes would contradict the moral foundations of their regimes. Second, developmental states do not have to base their legitimacy upon ideological commitments. Therefore they are exempt from the kind of legitimacy crisis, caused by ideological ambiguity and fragmentation, that can undermine Leninist states.

A Leninist state faces a twofold legitimacy crisis: (1) like the developmental state, the Leninist state can be challenged as noncredible if it fails to maintain sustained economic growth and raise people's increased living standards. But (2) a legitimacy crisis can also occur in the Leninist state if it achieves economic successes in ways that deviate from fundamental ideological principles and therefore undermine the foundation of the system. Thus, compared with the developmental state, the Leninist state might, on the one hand, have a narrower range of alternative means to select from, and, on the other hand it will encounter more serious systemic difficulties if it bases its legitimacy on its economic performance. The fundamental-instrumental discrepancy, therefore, might compel the CCP to undergo a more thorough transformation or face eventual disintegration.

The Organization of This Book

This book focuses on China's reform of the ownership system, as a case study. The change in the ownership system, after all, is fundamental to China's economic transition. Moreover, it is in this most important domain of China's reform that fundamental-instrumental discrepancy becomes considerably manifest. The reform of the ownership system is necessary, indeed crucial, for restructuring the entire economy. Nevertheless, China's leadership must assert that public ownership is ideologically superior.[7] To improve economic performance, since 1978 China's leadership has adopted a series of liberal policies to reform the ownership system, such as contracting and leasing state enterprises to individuals, establishing the stock market, disbanding rural collectives, and encouraging private economy and income differentials. All of these policies are consistent with the post-Mao leadership's intention to use whatever means possible to promote economic modernization. These policies have decisively broken China's traditional unitary public ownership system and caused the dispersion of the means of production in its society. To justify these policies, policy makers and intellectuals have significantly reformulated the official economic ideology by enlarging the gap between fundamental and instrumental principles. They have used various practical interpretations to demonstrate that the liberal policies toward the ownership system are compatible with, or at least could coexist with, socialism. The fundamental-instrumental discrepancy serves to redefine the official discourse regarding the ownership system and makes policy innovations possible. But on the other hand, the discrepancy considerably dilutes the leadership's ideological fundamentals, which are still important for the maintenance of the system's legitimacy.

Given the nature of the study, this book basically uses textual analysis. It focuses on two types of texts: one involves official views, mainly from party documents, policy statements, resolutions, official party publications, and leaders' speeches; the other deals with academic views in various publications.[8] These two types of views are interrelated, the former serving to define and form the prevailing intellectual discourse, and the latter influencing and helping to change official conceptualization of the ownership system. Policy changes regarding the ownership system are then examined against the backdrop of the alternation in ideas. Chapter 2 discusses major problems with China's pre-reform ownership system and thereby demonstrates the necessity of reform. Chapter 3 delineates some conceptual changes in the post-Mao leadership that have affected the CCP's policy choices and reoriented China's intellectual thinking. It focuses on two theoretical debates in the early 1970s and the 1980s—one on the "practice criterion" and the other on the "productive forces criterion"—which have had a significant impact on China's economic thinking. An examination of these two debates defines an intellectual context in which to comprehend China's new conceptualization and policies of the ownership system. The rest of this study presents an investigation of four dimensions of the China's ownership reforms. Chapter 4 examines rural decollectivization; chapter 5, state enterprises; chapter 6, private economy; and chapter 7, the problem of income distribution, an issue closely related to the ownership system. Finally, chapter 8 summarizes the findings of this research and discusses their theoretical implications.

2
The Ownership System before the Reform: Its Rationale and Problems

The Domanance of Public Ownership: Its Rationale

China's traditional Marxists defined the rationale for public ownership in both fundamental and instrumental terms, in a compatible manner. From the perspective of fundamental principles, public ownership is considered a morally desirable end in itself as part and parcel of the preferred model of economic organization. It removes the distinction between owners and nonowners in a classless social arrangement. From an instrumental perspective, on the other hand, public ownership makes comprehensive planning possible, and thereby leads to a rational and efficient management of economies. Although Marx did not fully elaborate his vision of a communist society, public ownership is believed to be the centerpiece of his theory about future society, where humankind would be free from exploitation and alienation (Marx and Engels 1948). Public ownership, for Marx, would generate productive forces more efficiently than capitalist private ownership would. The communist system would adopt public ownership, along with central planning, as the heart of socialist economic policy.

However, the predominance of public ownership in communist systems in the twentieth century contradicts Marx's assumption that this type of ownership could be built only on mature capitalism. In fact, this century witnessed socialist revolutions that "turned Marx on his head" by succeeding in relatively backward and agrarian areas rather than in advanced, capitalist ones. Consequently, instead of being a historical successor to capitalism, socialism has become a historical substitute (White 1985, 3). But, due to a tremendous impoverishment of material conditions, communist leaders considered public owner-ship a solution to rapid industrialization. Thus, these countries adopted public ownership for both ideological and practical purposes: It served to create an important material foundation for an equal and just soci-ety, while providing an effective economic institution by which less-developed countries could catch up with Western capitalist ones.

If Marxism only vaguely depicted what public ownership would look like, Leninism offered its tangible form—state ownership—and also made its hegemony a fact of life in socialist societies. State own-ership has been defined as the basic form of public ownership since the Russian Revolution. According to Lenin, this type of ownership system was characterized by the fact that controlled planning was to become a major tool of state control over the economy. Under state ownership, "all citizens are transformed into hired employees of the state . . . All citizens become employees and workers of a single coun-try-wide state 'syndicate'" (Lenin, quoted from Kaminski 1991, 21). The assumption underlying Lenin's vision was twofold, or having both fundamental and instrumental aspects: On the one hand, the proletarian state could establish a just economy by representing the interests of the whole people; on the other hand, it would be respon-sible for solving all problems related to the coordination of activities throughout the whole economy.

A claim for the superiority of an order based on public (or state) ownership is the core of communist ideology. Not only is public own-ership viewed by ruling Leninist parties as embodying basic commu-nist principles and furnishing an institutional design for rapid economic development, but it also legitimates one-party rule. The Communist Party claimed that only its leadership could guarantee public ownership. Indeed, the dominance of state ownership and one-party control are doctrinally and institutionally compatible (Lindblom 1977; Kaminski 1991).

The state's overall control over the economy is the foundation of its control over other aspects of social life in a socialist society. The monopoly of state ownership makes the state a supplier, buyer, and rule generator, which leaves little room for any autonomous social forces. By owning most capital assets, the state became, as Lenin suggested, the main employer, thus controlling who would be employed and promoted. This creates a "patrimonialist" network, which constitutes the basis of the urban social order in a Leninist party-run society (Walder 1986).

Public ownership in practice, however, was not as desirable in economic terms as the political leaders of socialist countries had anticipated. The poor performance of public ownership (particularly state ownership) in sustaining economic development had engendered recurrent economic reform since the 1970s in Eastern European countries and was, indeed, a primary cause of the collapse of communism there. China's case also shows that although state ownership brought economic growth, it could not sustain the growth, nor could it bring economic affluence as expected. As a major economic institution, public ownership was not totally discredited in China, as it was in Eastern Europe and the former Soviet Union. But its significant restructuring had been under way several years before the radical transformation of the former socialist states. Chinese policy makers had begun to adjust the ownership system in the late 1970s in efforts to cure the ailing economy. The initial focus was thus on the instrumental dimension of ownership, that is, its effectiveness and efficiency. A view commonly held by policy makers and academics in the early days of the reform was that public ownership was an inherently viable institution; China's problem lay in its mismanagement. But as the reform went deeper, new ideas and policy innovation that aimed to address practical problems gradually turned out to be a challenge to the fundamental rationale of public ownership. A dilemma emerged then for China's policy makers: To improve economic performance, they had to continue policy innovations that could hurt the existing ownership system; but to maintain ideological legitimacy with which the party could claim a leading role in the society, they had to prevent public ownership from being discredited. In this predicament we see the discrepancy between fundamental and instrumental principles of China's economic ideology.

The Ownership System in Pre-Reform China

When the CCP took power in 1949, China's economy was composed of four sectors representing four forms of ownership. According to the "Common Programme" adopted in September 1949 (Spence 1990), which served as a national constitution until 1954, they were the following:

1. The state-owned sector: "All enterprises vital to the economic life of the country and to the people's livelihood shall come under unified operation by the State" (Article 28). These enterprises were once owned by the Kuomintang government or its officials and known as "bureaucrat-capital." They were put directly under the control of the new state after the success of the revolution and were regarded as socialist in nature, and indeed, the backbone of newly emerging socialist economy.

2. The cooperative economy: It mainly included supply and marketing co-ops organized by the government to supply industrial goods to the peasants and to purchase their farm produce. They were regarded as semisocialist in nature and to be accorded preferential treatment (Article 29).

3. The private sector: This sector was composed of two parts. (1) national capitalist enterprises continuing from the preliberation period, and (2) small producers, including peasants, handicraftspeople, and small businesspeople. They were regarded as a necessary part of the national economy. According to the Common Programme, the private sector was to be "encouraged and fostered" where beneficial to the national welfare (Article 30).

4. The state-capitalist sector: This comprised enterprises operated jointly by the state and national capitalists, and also included various forms through which private production was subject to state priorities: "For example, producing for state-owned enterprises and exploiting the state-owned resources through the form of concessions" (Article 31).

Although the coexistence of all four types of ownership were suited to the economic status quo, Chinese leadership did not allow them to last. For the leadership, the coexistence of different types of ownership in the early years of the People's Republic of China (PRC) was only a temporary expedient for rehabilitating an economy paralyzed by wars. The party never seemed prepared for the perpetuation of a mixed economy. If Mao Zedong and other CCP leaders perceived universal public ownership as a basic goal of socialist revolution, the coexistence of different types of ownership only meant to them that this revolution had not been completed yet. Indeed, to the CCP, the fact that in 1949 the state sector accounted for only 34.7 percent, and the joint state-private sector for only 2 percent, of the total industrial output value, while the private sector for 63.3 percent, meant that the struggle for leadership between the socialist sector and capitalist sector had just begun (Xue 1981, 19).

After a three-year "rehabilitation" of the national economy from 1949 to 1952, in 1953 the CCP started a drive to socialize the means of production—a task known as the "socialist transformation of the private sector," which finally established the dominance of public ownership in Chinese society.

In the countryside, the "socialist transformation" took the form of the Agricultural Producer Cooperative (APC). The first surge of cooperative formation came in 1954, in the course of which some 11 percent of peasant householders were organized into APCs (Riskin 1987, 85). The figure shot up to 96 percent by the end of 1956 (Xue 1981, 35). In 1958, APCs were transformed into People's Communes, which virtually eliminated private ownership of the means of production in agriculture.

From 1953 to 1956, China's industry and trade were also undergoing rapid reorganization. The principal method the CCP used to dismantle capitalist ownership in industry was to "buy off" the bourgeoisie and transform the capitalist economy into state capitalism (Mao 1960, 38). By "state capitalism" the CCP meant the enforcement of "joint state-private enterprises," in which former owners and managers were forced to accept status as state employees while receiving interest payments on the value—estimated by the state—of their shares in the enterprises (Riskin 1987, 95).

The practice of state capitalism reinforced the state's control over industry. In fact, by 1952, the end of the Rehabilitation period, state enterprises already produced over half of the gross industrial output value (56 percent), while state capitalism produced another 27 percent (5 percent by state enterprises and 22 percent by private enterprises executing state orders). This meant that in the three years after the establishment of the People's Republic, the state basically took the reins of industrial production. The first spurt in the formation of joint enterprises came in 1954. Relatively large private establishments were forced to transform into joint state-enterprises and by the end of the year the proportion of industrial output produced in jointly owned enterprises (12 percent) had more than doubled.

The final stage of transformation arrived in January 1956. Remaining capitalists rushed to sign petitions for joining joint state private enterprises with the realization that the revolution had befallen them and that any delay in joining would only gain them the reputation of being die-hard capitalists and cause them more harm. By the end of 1956, private enterprise in China's industry was virtually wiped out (see table 2.1).

Table 2.1 The Socialist Transformation of Industry: Percentage Distribution of Gross Value of Industrial Output (Excluding Handicrafts)

| | State-Capitalist Industry | | | | | |
	(1) State enterprise	(2) Total	(3) Joint enterprise	(4) Private enterprise executing state order	(5) "Pure private enterprise"	(6) Private enterprise (4) + (5)
1949	34.7	9.5	2.0	7.5	55.8	63.3
1950	45.3	17.8	2.9	14.9	36.7	51.6
1951	45.9	25.4	4.0	21.4	28.7	50.5
1952	56.0	26.9	5.0	21.9	17.1	39.0
1953	57.5	28.5	5.7	22.8	14.0	36.8
1954	62.8	31.9	12.3	19.6	5.3	24.9
1955	67.7	29.3	16.1	13.2	3.0	16.2
1956	67.5	32.5	32.5	—	—	—

Source: Ten Great Years, cited from Riskin, 1987:96.

Handicrafts were another sphere the socialist transformation swept over. At the time when the People's Republic was founded, handicraft workshops and household handicrafts accounted for about 20 percent of the country's gross industrial output value, while handicraft products accounted for 60 to 70 percent of manufactured goods consumed by the peasants (Xue 1981, 39). The socialist transformation of handicrafts also took the form of cooperation. Whereas in 1955, about 27 percent of artisans were organized in groups of cooperatives of some kind, by the end of 1956 more than 90 percent of them were absorbed into producers' cooperatives (see table 2.2).

Table 2.2. The Formation of Handicraft Cooperatives

	No. of Handicraft Persons (in Thousands)			Percentage Distribution	
	Total	In Co-ops	In Individual Handicrafts	In Co-ops	Individual Handicrafts
1952	7,364	228	7,136	3.1	96.9
1953	7,789	301	7,488	3.9	96.1
1954	8,910	1,213	7,697	13.6	86.4
1955	8,202	2,206	5,996	26.9	73.1
1956	6,583	6,039	554	91.7	8.3

Source: Ten Great Years (1960, 36).

With the completion of the socialist transformation in 1956, the means of production were basically placed under public ownership. More specifically, the coexistence of four types of ownership in the early years of the PRC was replaced by public ownership, which nevertheless took two forms, state ownership and collective ownership. The difference between the two forms of public ownership lay in the degree of socialization of the means of production. State ownership was referred to as "ownership by the whole people" (quanmin suoyouzhi), under which "the means of production belong to all working people as represented by the state" (Xue 1981, 45). Collective ownership characterized a form of property relation under which "the means of production are not yet the public property of society as a whole but belong to the working people in one economic collective or another" (Xue 1981, 45). However, collective ownership in 1957 still retained certain features of the private economy. For example, peasants owned their personal means of production, such as farm cattle, ploughs, and carts, even after joining cooperatives. They were also given plots of land for private use. Artisans organized into handicraft cooperatives could receive dividends according to the amount of shares they contributed to collectives (Yu 1985, 32).

Nevertheless, the CCP leadership's view on ownership became more radical after 1958. It began to seek a larger scale of collectivization and a higher level of public ownership. Collectively owned means of production were the target for further socialization. In 1958, on the upsurge of the People's Commune movement, 740,000 advanced agricultural cooperatives, largely based on natural villages, were merged into 26,000 communes within several months. In other words, 99 percent of the Chinese peasants lived in the communes that year (Yu 1985, 33). In principle, communes still were owned collectively. But they exceeded in size, and cut cross the boundaries, of the traditional geographical units of local economies, and put the means of production in rural areas under a larger public management. Communization affected the private property of the peasant, as well as property that had already been collectivized. Peasants were called on by the party to turn over to the communes plots of land reserved for private use under the previous collectives, as well as private house sites, livestock, and large farm tools (Riskin 1987, 125). Only means of consumption, such as houses, clothing, and bedding, were allowed to remain private property, along with small farm tools and small domestic animals. In August 1959, the government issued an order to shut down the traditional markets at which peasants sold or bartered some of the products of their private labor. The rationale for this move was that commodity exchange of this sort was incompatible, in its corrosive effects on individual ideology, with the surge toward communism and would breed spontaneous capitalism.

Regarding the handicraft cooperatives, the CCP also pushed hard to convert "small collectives" into "large collectives," and "large collectives" into "ownership by the whole people," namely, state ownership. Specifically, large and efficient handicraft cooperatives, with more advanced technology and bigger profits, were transformed into locally administered state enterprises; small cooperatives were upgraded to collective enterprises in which profits were turned over to the higher authorities and the workers earned fixed wages instead of drawing dividends according to their labor (He and Zhang 1982, 186). In fact, these collective enterprises did not differ in many ways from state enterprises, since in both cases the state determined what and how much to produce and appointed their leaders. Moreover, their wages, welfare benefits, and profits were also uniformly controlled by the state. Although some adjustment was made after 1961, the general tendency to submit collective enterprises to a higher level of public ownership persisted until 1977.

During the period of the Cultural Revolution, radical party leaders further advanced a policy aimed at both installing the absolute dominance of state ownership, and annihilating any trace of capitalism. By the end of 1977, the total number of employees of state enterprises reached 71,960,000, while that of collective enterprises reached only 19,160,000 (Yu 1985, 36), apparently as a result of deliberate restrictions on the latter. The individual economy, which had already been nearly extinguished since 1958 was further stormed, under the slogan of "cutting the tail of capitalism" (ge zibenzhuyi weiba). According to statistics compiled in Shanghai (see table 2.3), a city where the individual economy used to be very prosperous, the number of self-employed dropped from 200,000 to 8,000 in the period from 1956 to 1976 (He and Zhang 1982, 194).[1]

Table 2.3 Individual Workers in Shanghai, 1956–76

Year	Total Number of Workers
1956	2,000,000
1960	14,000
1961–62	40,000
1964	34,000
1966–76	8,000

Source: He and Zhang 1982.

As for China's cities in general, there were 9 million self-employed who paid taxes to the state in 1953, accounting for 16.6 percent of the national revenue. By 1978, however, their numbers had dwindled to 150,000 (see table 2.4), their taxes making up only 0.45 percent of the national revenue. Although pure private ownership was not entirely extinguished, its role in China's economy was limited by state policy to an absolute minimum.

Table 2.4 Individual Workers in Cities and Towns, 1953–78

Year	Total Number of Workers
1953	9,000,000
1955	6,400,000
1956	160,000
1957	1,040,000
1961	1,650,000
1962	2,160,000
1964	2,270,000
1965	1,710,000
1976	190,000
1978	150,000

Source: Riskin 1987:275; He and Zhang 1982, 194.

The CCP's policy toward ownership was closely related to its vision of the society to be built. In party economics, the ownership system was interpreted as a determinant of the relations of production,[2] which in turn defined the nature of a society. In other words, party leaders saw public ownership as a fundamental of socialism and a decisive step in wiping out capitalism. Mao's main worry in the fall of 1955 was the growing class polarization in rural areas.[3] As he said,

> What exists in the countryside today is capitalist ownership by the rich peasants and a vast sea of ownership by individual peasants. As is clear to everyone, the spontaneous forces of capitalism have been steadily growing in the countryside in recent years, with new rich peasants springing up everywhere and many well-to-do middle peasants striving to become rich peasants. On the other hand, many poor peasants are still living in poverty for shortage of the means of production, with some getting debt and other selling or renting out their land. If this tendency goes unchecked, it is inevitable that polarization in the countryside will get worse day by day." (Mao 1977, 201–2).

So Mao's decision to step up the pace of transformation of rural productive relations reflected his belief that a larger scale of collectivization was the decisive measure to contain capitalism and consolidate socialism.

In this way, Mao and his comrades were convinced that the higher the degree of public ownership reached, the more socialist China became, and the closer it came to communism. This mentality was clearly reflected in the People's Commune movement. Having established the dominance of state ownership in industry, the party firmly believed that a larger scale of socialization of the means of production in the countryside was the next and also the last step in the transition to communism. Chen Boda, one of the party's most authoritative theoreticians from the Yanan period to the late 1960s, asserted that commune experiments would "open a road on which our country can smoothly pass over from socialism to communism" (HQ, June 1958).

The party's Beidaihe Resolution on Communes on 29 August 1958, also directly linked the formation of communes to the speedy realization of a communist society. The party even proclaimed in the resolution that "The attainment of communism in China is no longer a remote future event. We can actively use the form of the people's

commune to explore the practical road of transition to socialism"
(*RMRB*, 6 September 1958). The immediate result of the Beidaihe
Resolution was that local cadres began to collectivize the small portion of land that had previously been set aside for use by individual
households and to ban the raising of pigs and other barnyard animals
for consumption or sale by families. This was believed by the party
leadership to be a big step toward a more completely communitarian
society (Joseph 1984, 118). The approach of "larger size and higher
degree of public ownership" (*yida ergong*), formulated in the People's
Commune movement, had in fact dominated the CCP's policy toward
ownership since then.

The party's feverish pursuit of a higher degree of public ownership led to a move to restrict collective ownership, though the latter
was formally recognized as an elementary form of public ownership.
According to the Shanghai school, a group of radical economists led
by Zhang Chunqiao and Yao Wenyuan, members of the Gang of Four,
the collectively owned economy was an incompletely transformed
structure within the public ownership system. The means of production, as well as the output of production, were private property
owned by individual collective units rather than by the whole society; in that sense production was private production. The economy
under collective ownership, party radicals argued, was still characterized by small units of production, which, according to Lenin,
would continuously generate the petty bourgeoisie. Thus, the deliberate restraint on collective economy during the Cultural Revolultion
decade became part of the task to consolidate the dictatorship of the
proletariat and prevent capitalist restoration (Tang 1980).

The CCP's drive toward a larger scale of public ownership was
not only inspired by the pursuit of an ideal society but also motivated
by practical economic needs. After taking over a crumbling economy
in 1949, CCP leaders believed that a universal collectivization was
necessary for laying the foundations for an advanced socialist economy (Selden 1988, 11). This faith partially arose from leaders' admi-
ration of the Soviet experience of industrialization. In fact, Mao
considered collectivization an essential prerequisite for fulfilling one
of the regime's primary goals—industrialization. He contended that
"if the CCP did not have the confidence in itself and the relations of
production to reconstruct, it would be impossible to achieve socialism in three Five Year Plans; and if it did not achieve socialism in that
time it would be impossible to complete socialist industrialization"

(MacFarquhar 1974, 17). Public ownership, party leaders believed, made comprehensive planning possible, which could create higher productivity than under capitalism. Xue Muqiao, a leading party economist, explained the relevance of collectivization to agricultural mechanization: "It would be very difficult to achieve mechanization on the basis of a small peasant economy which could accumulate little by operating on per household average of ten-odd *mu* of land" (Xue 1981, 35). Clearly, public ownership was treated not only as morally desirable but also as practically effective in terms of achieving the goals of national power and welfare.

In the 1980s, however, the CCP increasingly conceded that there were serious problems with the Chinese economic system, which had functioned for more than two decades. The effectiveness of public ownership was questioned and reevaluated by decision makers and intellectuals. This resulted in discord between those who wanted to maintain public ownership as a fundamental principle of socialism and those who sought to diversify the forms of ownership to facilitate economic efficiency.

3
Theoretical Adjustments: The "Practice Criterion" and the "Criterion of Productive Forces"

The change in China's economic ideology began with two important theoretical debates in the late 1970s and the early 1980s: One was on the "practice criterion," another was on the "criterion of productive forces." These two debates represented the CCP's initial effort to modify its ideology, which had proven destructive to Chinese society from the Great Leap Forward of 1958 to the Cultural Revolution of 1966–1976. The immediate motivation behind the debate on the practice criterion, launched by the reformist leaders, was to discredit the "whatever" faction, which emphasized the unchangeability of Maoist doctrine. But its implications went beyond that. From the perspective of this study, the practice criterion debate suggested that reformist leaders within the CCP had begun to recognize the necessity of adjusting the relationship between fundamental and instrumental principles of the party's ideology. It therefore marked the beginning of a transition from a dogmatic mode of ideological construction to a pragmatic one. The official emphasis on the political primacy of the criterion of productive forces redefined the basic goal of socialism and changed the socialist agenda. It therefore legitimated "whatever" means was necessary for the CCP to pursue its new modernization program. Both debates opened up a window to new ideas and contributed to changes in economic thinking and policies regarding the ownership system. Thus, an understanding of these two debates is crucial for comprehending the reformulation of China's economic ideology.

This chapter begins with an examination of the "whatever" faction's failure to reconstruct the CCP's ideology by remodeling Mao Zedong Thought. It then discusses the debates on the practice criterion and the productivity criterion—their significance in terms of ideological reformulation, their policy implications, their limitations, and the political tensions involved.

Remodeling Mao Zedong Thought: Hua Guofeng's Failure

In 1978, then party Chairman Hua Guofeng, Mao's handpicked successor, confronted a dilemma after the radical Maoists (i.e., the Gang of Four) were purged and the "new period" (xin shiqi) began. On the one hand, he had to keep his loyalty to Mao and Maoist doctrines, since the legitimacy of his personal power was derived from Mao's undated statement before his death—"With you in charge, I am at ease!" On the other hand, as the party redefined the Four Modernizations as the "general task of the new period" (xin shiqi de zongrenwu), Hua had to remodel the image of Mao Zedong Thought in order to accommodate it to the new situation. Hua's personal dilemma, together with Mao's deep-seated personality cult among party officials, led to an interesting attempt at remodeling of Mao's thought in 1978: Hua portrayed Mao as one who had long been concerned with economic problems.

To legitimate the Four Modernizations as the party's new focus, the Hua leadership used Mao's words to turn the nation's attention from "class struggle" to economic problems. One of its important strategies was to publish in newspapers a series of Mao's texts (most of them officially published for the first time) that dealt more or less with economic problems. The message the Hua leadership sent to the public was thus clear: economic development was one of Chairman Mao's major concerns; therefore, the new modernization program cohered with ideological fundamentals.

On 26 December 1976, the first of Mao's texts appeared in newspapers. It was On the Ten Great Relationships, written in 1956.[1] This speech marked a break with the Soviet model of economic development. It proposed a "dialectical" approach to problems of China's socialist construction, with the deliberate cultivation of tensions among economic sectors and the achievement of goals by roundabout means (Martin 1980, 56–61). Even though the book was written at a time of radical upsurge, Mao seemed willing to pay attenton to economic issues, such as the balance between sectors (e.g., heavy and light industry, coastal and inland development, growth and defense, center and locality, and production and consumption). The tune of this speech was quite distant from the "class-struggle-centered" Maoism that evolved in the 1960s and gave the Hua leadership sanction to focus more attention on economic problems.

The publication of Mao's commentary on the Anshan Steelworks Factory Charter (*Angang Xianfa*), written in 1960, was to justify the importance of workers' participation in factory management. Although it was essentially a radical document, its focus was on the management of production rather than on political campaigns. During the Cultural Revolution period, factory management was disturbed by endless political campaigns, which were responsible for low industrial efficiency. It might have been the Hua leadership's intention that this document provide a guide for the restoration of factory management. It was not a coincidence that this text came out right before the National Industrial Conference, scheduled to meet in April 1977 to discuss the long-term planning of industrial development.

"China Will Make a Great Leap Forward" was a short paragraph Mao added to Zhou Enlai's Government Report in the Third National People's Congress in 1963. It was officially published for the first time on 26 December 1977 under Mao's name. Setting aside mass mobilization, which characterized the Great Leap Forward in 1958, Mao seemed to redefine the meaning of the GLF in this short statement. He referred to it as a plan "to use advanced technologies to establish a strong socialist modern country in a not too long historical period" (*HQ* 1978, 1–2). With strong nationalistic sentiment, Mao predicted, by quoting Sun Yat-sen's words, that China would make a great leap forward in several decades to surpass "the Western bourgeoisie" in terms of economic development.

"A Letter on the Mechanization of Agriculture," written in 1966, showed Mao's concern with some concrete issues in economic development. Mao instructed that more power over the manufacture of agricultural machines be granted to localities. He also suggested lowering the rates of state accumulation and giving more money to localities to stimulate their enthusiasm for agricultural mechanization. The rejection of the Soviet solution to agricultural development was an important subtheme of this text. Mao asked concerned comrades to think about why Soviet agriculture was still in bad shape, even though it had achieved agricultural mechanization. The publication of Mao's letter was linked to the second National Agricultural Conference held in December 1976. Hua dominated this conference, in which agricultural mechanization was the top agenda.

Hua's most important effort to reiterate the guiding role of Mao Zedong Though was to sponsor the publication of *Volume V of the Selected Works of Mao Zedong,* which included Mao's sixty-nine articles and speeches of 1949–957.[2] As a sort of "political editing" (Martin 1982, 62), it signaled the leadership's deliberate resumption of the Mao cult so as to consolidate its own positions after 1976. On the other hand, compilation of *Volume V* also implied that Hua and his supporters had turned their attention to Mao's more moderate statements before the CR and neglected his more inflammatory subsequent remarks. *Volume V* in fact served to "project the image of a Mao still uncorrupted by the GLF and the CR" (Dittmer 1984, 351). By its publication, the Hua leadership sent its own political messages to the public in the post-Mao era.

First, *Volume V* included Mao's major articles devoted to analyses of class struggle in the first eight years of the PRC. The proletarian seizure of state power, for Mao, did not put an end to class struggle. The struggle between proletariat and bourgeoisie remained the major social contradiction after the transformation of ownership of the means of production. Thus, revolution should continue. According to Hua's own interpretation (*HQ* May 1977, 4), the "fundamental thought" (*genben sixiang*) throughout *Volume V* was "to continue revolution under the dictatorship of the proletariat." Hua asserted a firm commitment to this line.

Second, *Volume V* included Mao's speeches and articles dealing with economic development. To revitalize the Chinese economy in the early years of the PRC, Mao emphasized the importance of the development of productive forces. He claimed that a higher productivity constituted the material basis of socialist systems and the necessary condition for triumph over capitalism. The Hua leadership highlighted Mao's idea in this regard and defined the rapid development of the socialist economy as one of the basic tasks of the revolution under dictatorship of the proletariat (*HQ* May 1978 40).

Third, *Volume V* contained Mao's articles demanding cadres to be "red and expert." According to Mao at that time, socialist construction required party cadres to have professional knowledge as well as mastery over Marxist theory. Mao's call, in 1958, for the members of the Communist Party and the Youth League, and the public as well to "learn theory, learn technology, and learn professional skills" legitimated the Hua leadership's attention on works of science and technology as part of the modernization program.

By publishing Mao's texts one after another in a relatively short period of time, in addition to *Volume V of Selected Works of Mao Zedong*, the Hua leadership revealed a strong belief that even in the "new period" there were no alternatives to Mao's ideas as the ideological guideline for economic modernization. This stand was made clearer by a joint editorial of *People's Daily, Liberation Army's Daily*, and *Hongqi*: the Chinese should "resolutely defend whatever policies Chairman Mao formulated, and unswervingly adhere to whatever Chairman Mao has issued." The name of the "whatever faction" originated from this famous statement. Thus, Hua Guofeng and his followers were clearly locked into the dogmatic mode of ideological construction, which allowed only actions consistent with the party's fundamental principles—Mao's writings.

However, the Hua faction was also vulnerable to criticisms for its adherence to the leftist line. Although Hua attempted to dilute the doctrine of class struggle by limiting the scope of its application, he continued to recognize it as one of Mao's greatest contributions to the development of Marxism (*HQ* May 1977, 7). For party reformers, however, that doctrine mistakenly identified class struggle as the major problem in socialist China. The CCP needed a new theory to reidentify the "major contradiction" (*zhuyao maodun*) in socialism. A total break with Mao's theory of class struggle was thus an inevitable step toward redefining the party's basic task of solving the major contradiction.

Certainly, Mao was not always antagonistic to economic development, nor did he object to the concept of modernization. He was not hesitant to use the term from the 1940s to the late 1950s. During his last two decades, however, while he continued to stress the importance of economic progress, his increasing anxiety about the corrupting effects of prosperity and of inequality led him to adopt a series of radical policies, which in the end proved self-defeating. Actually, since the early 1960s, Mao no longer regarded the economy as a sphere independent of class struggle and continuing revolution. For him, economic development under socialism could be achieved only through continuous transformation of the relations of production and the superstructure. Thus, the Hua leadership's effort to highlight Mao's ideas about the economy was futile. Mao's "class-struggle-centered" development strategy offered no solutions to China's economic problems, which were partially caused by too many stormy political campaigns. Moreover, Mao's talks on economic problems were closely related to one of his core notions—mass mobilization. The Anshan Charter, for example, was in fact a model of the Maoist mass line and favored mass participation in factory management. However, from the GLF to the CR, the hard facts showed that mass mobilization presented a problem rather than a solution to China's economy.

In short, the "whatever" stand demanded unthinking adherence to anything associated with Mao, and therefore excluded any major policy adjustments. The deep implication of the "whatever" stand was that it left no room for ideological reformulation, which was badly needed to address various problems that afflicted Chinese society.

The Debate on the Criterion for Truth

The debate on the criterion for truth in the spring of 1978 was a public manifestation of the offensive against the "two whatevers." However, the dissatisfaction with this line within the party became apparent much earlier. Deng Xiaoping, who was ousted from office by Mao's decision in April 1976, and who was about to be formally rehabilitated at that time, explicitly criticized the "two whatevers" in a talk on 24 May 1977. He said that this slogan could rule out his rehabilitation and make it impossible to reverse of verdicts on the Tiananmen Incident of 5 April 1976 since Mao had made decisions on these two matters.[3] However, Deng also said that Mao himself said that Marx, Engels, Lenin, and Stalin all made mistakes, and so did he himself. Mao never claimed the "whatever" stand. Deng also emphasized the importance of an "accurate and comprehensive understanding of Mao Zedong Thought."

But the criticism of the "two whatevers" was not publicized until the publication of the article "Practice Is the Only Criterion for Testing Truth," in *Guangming Ribao* on 11 May 1978. The article was published under the name of the paper's "special commentator" and was reprinted the following day in *People's Daily*. The original author of this article was Hu Fuming, a lecturer in the philosophy department at Nanjing University. Deeply discontented with the "whatever" editorial of 7 February 1977, he drafted this article in the summer of 1977 and sent it to the *Guangming Ribao* editorial department in October of that year. Endorsed by Hu Yaobang, then president of the Central Party School, the article came out after being edited ten times by several well-known liberal party theorists.

The points of this article were nothing new to Marxists: Every theory or line has to be tested by practice to determine whether it is correct or corresponds to objective reality; neither boasting nor power can prove truth; practice, and it alone, can prove truth; Marxism-Leninism–Mao Zedong Thought is not the yardstick of truth, because it must still be subject to trial by practice (*FBIS*, 11 August 1978, N1). Although these points seemed quite simple and easy to understand, they aroused an ideological debate that would reorient the course of China's development in the 1980s.

The fact that the article became a focus of contention was due as much to the opposition it provoked as to its content. The key issue raised in this article was whether the Chinese should continue to deduce action from fundamental principles, or Mao's writings.

Not surprisingly, the response of the "whatever faction" to this article was vehement. The chief editor of *Hongqi*, Wang Shu, said of the article, "In theory it is absurd; in ideology, it is reactionary; in politics it cuts down [Mao's] banner." For some other "whateverists," the "intellectual fetter" that the article wanted to remove was Mao Zedong Though itself. For instance, as Wang Dongxing expressed in a conversation with the new chief editor of *Hongqi*, Xiong Fu, "the spearhead of this article is directed at Chairman Mao" (*HQRB*, 29 January, 5). Wang even explicitly ordered that *Hongqi* not reprint the article. Thus, *Hongqi*, the CCP's theoretical organ, deliberately kept silent on the discussion of the criterion of truth for several months, while other national and local newspapers made it one of the hottest topics. Even when Xiong Fu was under pressure to participate in the discussion, he still set a rule for articles to be published in *Hongqi*: They "should not emphasize the development and innovation of Marxism-Leninism–Mao Zedong Thought," rather, they "should emphasize adherence to and defense of the fundamental principles of Marxism-Leninism–Mao Zedong Thought"(*HQRB*, 29 January, 5).

Deng Xiaoping's speech at an All-Army Conference on Political Work in early June was a blow to the objection raised against the practice criterion and, indeed, marked the beginning of a broad attempt to reformulate the CCP's ideology. The first issue addressed in this four-part speech was "seeking truth from facts "(*shishi qiushi*). Deng criticized those people who "talk about Mao Zedong Thought every day, but often forget Comrade Mao Zedong's fundamental Marxist viewpoint and abandon or even oppose his method of seeking truth from facts, and of proceeding from reality and integrating theory with practice" (Deng 1984, 128). Deng's speech was to demonstrate that Mao himself always emphasized the primacy of practice, and that therefore, as Deng argued, it was those who parroted what was said by Mao Zedong, and not those who emphasized practice, that deviated from Mao Zedong Thought. Deng's emphasis on practice reflected his determination to wean the party leadership away from Mao's directives as a test of ideological reformulation. He also sought to ground his ideological principles in practice to launch a new modernization program that Mao would have definitely condemned as "capitalist." Since the CCP could only rely on practice to find out China's correct course of development, the debate about the "truth criterion" was "really a debate about ideological line, about politics, about the future and the destiny of the party and nation" (Deng 1984, 65).

Political implications of this debate soon became even more visible. Provincial leaders and regional military commanders vied with each other to show their support for Deng. For example, each of them contributed an article to *People's Daily* on the importance of the practice criterion.[4] At the same time, many national and local organizations held large workshops for cadres, using the *Guangming Ribao*'s article and Deng's speech as texts. Support from provincial officials and intellectuals for Deng's line signified that the "whatever faction" had finally lost its influence within the party, though its leaders, Hua Guofeng and Wang Dongxing, were not dismissed from the leading posts until 1981.

The Practice Criterion and the Guiding Role of Marxism

This debate inevitably led to a dilemma: What was the relationship between the practice criterion and the guiding role of Marxism? If Marxism were universally true, as the CCP claimed, why should it be tested by practice? If practice were the sole criterion for evaluating truth, why should the Chinese people use Marxism as a guide?

The advocates of the practice criterion addressed this question from two perspectives: (1) Regard Marxism-Leninism–Mao Zedong Thought as a method of analysis; and (2) treat Marxism-Leninism–Mao Zedong Thought as a system of thought open to practice.

In 1978, Deng Xiaoping and his supporters sought to reconcile the practice criterion with the guiding role of Marxism by positing a new fundamental principle in Marxism-Leninism and Mao Zedong Thought: "seeking truth from fact." Deng himself, on several occasions, emphatically referred to "seeking truth from facts" as "a fundamental viewpoint of Mao Zedong Thought" (2 June), as "the quintessence of Mao Zedong Thought" (16 November); and as "the basis of the proletarian world view and Marxism" (13 December). Deng also portrayed Mao as a revolutionary leader who derived his ideas and strategies from practice rather than from books. In his 2 June speech, for example, Deng demonstrated Mao's emphasis on practice by extensively referring to his revolutionary experience (Deng 1984, 129–32). In Deng's view, Mao always fought resolutely against the erroneous tendency to divorce theory from practice and to act unrealistically (according to wishful thinking), or mechanically (according to books and instructions from above). The Chinese revolution, Deng argued, would have never succeeded if Mao had understood Marxism-Leninism dogmatically, as those "returned students" from Moscow did.[5] Deng extolled Mao's *On Practice* (1937) which summed up the party's struggle with the dogmatism of "returned students." According to Deng this document laid down the ideological and theoretical foundation for the party. Deng's argument soon reverberated in many articles. Among them, one was seen by many commentaries as being important as the 11 May *Guangming Ribao* article. It was an editorial published on 24 June in *Liberation Army Daily*. Its eye-catching title was "One of the Most Fundamental Principles of Marxism." It explicitly elevated "seeking truth from facts" to the level of a fundamental principle.

The "whatever faction" strongly opposed this position. They protested that while it acknowledged Mao's thought as an analytical tool, it virtually rendered Mao's ideas obsolete when addressing any particular issue area. This position, they said, amounted to "an abstract affirmation but a concrete rejection" of Mao Zedong Thought (*RMRB,* 22 September 1978, 1). For Deng and his supporters, however, Marxism-Leninism–Mao Zedong Thought was composed of universal and concrete truth. Universal truth, such as dialectical materialism and historical materialism, was universally applicable for it was a scientific worldview. Concrete truth, however, was an application of universal truth in concrete circumstances and thereby true only under certain historical conditions. If we took every concrete assertion and conclusion made by Marx, Lenin, and Mao as universally true, they argued, we would not be able to handle current problems. Hence, they seemed to imply that it was necessary and inevitable to make some "concrete rejection."

The fundamentalization of "seeking truth from facts" united the practice criterion with the guiding role of Marxism. As long as a theory, view, or policy was produced from and tested by practice, then, according to Deng's logic, it should agree with Marxism. Indeed, this kind of interpretation of Marxism maximized the flexibility of the ideology Deng and his supporters needed to innovate for a new modernization program.

Some advocates of the practice criterion suggested that all theory should be subject to the testing of practice. According to a *Guangming Ribao* article on 11 May 1978, the power of Marxism-Leninism–Mao Zedong Thought lay in its objective truth, which had been tested by practice. However, Marxism-Leninism–Mao Zedong Thought must continue to develop, because practice was changing. For example, Lenin's theory that in the age of imperialism socialism could succeed in one or a few countries was drawn from new social conditions and thereby seen as an innovation of Marxism. Whether or not it was correct could not be tested by Marx's general theory of capitalism. In other words, a theory could not be tested by another theory; it had to be tested by practice. Lenin's theory was not proved correct until the practice of the Russian October Revolution. Thus, the question of whether a theory could guide practice must be answered by practice itself.

In another article, Wan Qing (*ZXYJ*, September 1978) argued that the practice criterion and the guiding role of Marxism were not mutually exclusive, for a number of reasons: First, the fundamental principles of Marxism were not derived from idle dreams. They were summaries of the experience of proletarian revolutionary movements and had been shown to be true by revolutionary practices. Second, Marxism was a science about general laws of social and natural development, and its stand (*lichang*) and methodology (*fangfa*) were universally applicable. Third, correct theory could reflect back on practice. Marxism, as a powerful and scientific weapon for epistemology, could help people understand reality, forecast the future, and develop correct lines and policies. However, argued Wan, Marxism was not the end of truth. It needed to be tested by new practices and to develop and enrich itself through assimilating new experience and knowledge. It seemed to Wan that the practice criterion and the recognition of the universal truth of Marxism could be reconciled by treating Marxism as an open theory.

Nevertheless, the advocates of practice never felt comfortable with reconciling the practice criterion and the guiding role of Marxism. Given that practice served as the sole criterion, how did one know that a certain mode of practice was revolutionary or correct without a prior set of theories and explanations of where they came from? Why did the CCP still affirm Lenin's famous statement that "without revolutionary theory, there would be no revolutionary movement"? Hu Sheng, an orthodox Marxist theoretician, argued at that time that if practice were the sole criterion for gauging the truth, the October Revolution would have never taken place and the People's Republic would not have been proclaimed (Martin 1982). Moreover, the practice advocates pointed out that the affirmation of the guiding role of Marxism led, in effect, to the marginalization of the practice criterion. The party's commitment to the guiding role of Marxism, however, ironically suggested a "truth" that was neglected by many advocates of practice: that any social practice was guided by human perceptions of reality, which was, to some extent, shaped by ideas.

The Practice Criterion versus The Political Criterion

Advocates of the practice criterion grappled with another difficulty at the same time, that is, the relationship between the practice criterion and the political criterion. The latter referred to a set of political norms designated to regulate social and political behavior in China under the CCP. Imposing ideological and political conformity over the society, the political criterion was an important device for the CCP to contain political and ideological deviation.

In 1957, Mao put forward six political criteria (*liutiao biaozhun*) to determine right and wrong in Chinese political life. According to

Mao (1960: 55-56), words and actions would be considered right if they

1. helped to unite people of various nationalities and did not divide them;
2. were beneficial, not harmful, to socialist transformation and socialist construction;
3. helped to consolidate, not undermine or weaken, the people's democratic dictatorship;
4. helped to consolidate, not undermine or weaken, democratic centralism;
5. tended to strengthen, not to cast off or weaken, the leadership of the party;
6. were beneficial, not harmful, to international solidarity and solidarity of the peaceful peoples of the world.

Of these six criteria, Mao emphasized, the most important were the socialist path and the party's leadership.

Nevertheless, these political criteria were purely subjective, since, for example, different people might have entirely different views on what actions were beneficial to socialism. The arbitrary application of these criteria during the CR further demonstrated that they were no more than political tools used by the radical Maoists to persecute their opponents within the party and intelligentsia. But reformists were not about to repudiate the six criteria (as we will see, the socialist path and the leadership of the party were later integrated into the "four cardinal principles"), though they condemned the abusive use of them by the Gang of Four.

The reformers' commitment to the six criteria, however, apparently contradicted their new emphasis on the practice criterion: If political criteria could be used to judge right and wrong, then the practice criterion was meaningless. On the other hand, if practice was the only criterion for truth, then political criteria were unnecessary.

An article by Xia Yang (*JFRB*, 13 November 1978) attempted to reconcile the "double criteria." Xia's article began with the importance of political criteria. According to him, political criteria were set by each social class in light of its interests and political position. It could help the members of the class define their own interests and thereby make political choices in accordance with these interests. With orthodox rhetoric, he claimed, proletarian political criteria reflected the demands of revolutionary practice, and therefore proletarian political criteria and the practice criterion were consistent in terms of determining right and wrong. On the other hand, Xia put much weight on the practice criterion. How could one know, he asked, if an action or a theory accorded with the six political criteria or not? The answer, he said, should be found in practice. That is, only those actions or theories that were tested by practice as "correct" could be regarded as in accordance with the six criteria.

Another writer, Lin Jingyao (*XSYJ* 1978, no. 4), further extended Xia's claim that political criteria alone could not judge right and wrong. Lin argued that whether a view or a theory was right or wrong (i.e., consistent or not consistent with the six criteria) was not a problem that could be solved in the domain of thought. It could be solved only in practice. For Lin, therefore, the six criteria per se were of no use for determining truth.

Although Xia, Lin, and many others attempted to highlight the practice criterion, they all were very ambiguous about whether the six criteria themselves also needed to be further "tested" by practice. They tried to be monistic by emphasizing the primacy of practice, but never made clear why, if practice was the sole criterion for truth, political criteria still needed to exist.

The Primacy of Practice: Significance and Limitations

By emphasizing the primacy of practice, Deng and his "practice faction" decisively recast Mao Zedong Thought and hence paved a way for the CCP's ideological reformulation. The rationale of interpreting "seeking truth from facts" as the core of Mao Zedong Thought implied a shift "from its previous emphasis on substantive conclusions to a stress on its use as a method of analysis" (Tsou 1986). Drawing from such an interpretation of Mao Zedong Thought, Deng and his supporters argued that Mao's ideas addressing any particular issue area might fit only a specific phase of history and therefore might be irrelevant to current problems. At least, they must be tested again.

The primacy of practice naturally justified the innovation of instrumental principles that aimed to address concrete policy problems. It also allowed for a very flexible interpretation of the relationship between fundamental and instrumental principles and, in fact, granted instrumental principles autonomy from fundamental ones. Deng and his supporters seemed to believe that practical principles did not have to rely on fundamental ones for their own justification. They were justified so long as they could solve practical problems.

For Deng Xiaoping, the utility or effectiveness of an ideology was in addressing and solving practical problems. As he made clear in his speech on 2 June 1978,

> If we hold meetings, make reports, adopt resolutions and so on, it is all for the purpose of solving problems. Whether or not what we say and do actually solve problems correctly depends on our ability to integrate theory with practice, to sum up experience well and to base our actions on objective reality by seeking truth from facts and proceeding from actual conditions. Only when we do all this will it be possible for us to solve problems more or less correctly. The correctness of the solutions is something which needs to be tested in practice. But if we fail to act in the way I have described, then it will surely be impossible for us to solve any problems correctly (Deng 1983, 108-9).

Thus, pragmatic problem solving was Deng's driving motive to emphasize the primacy of practice, and indeed it was the driving force behind the CCP's making innovations in practical principles. Mao Zedong Thought, for Deng and his supporters, was not very relevant to current issues in terms of problem solving, for two reasons: First, Mao's early thought presented solutions to the problems of the revolutionary period and was of little use in addressing issues of modernization. Second, Mao's late thinking mistakenly identified the problems of postrevolutionary China and lost touch with the actual conditions of Chinese society. Hence, the party must return to the principle of "seeking truth from facts" and base its policies on new practice rather than on Mao's writings.

To reorient the CCP's ideology to the problem solving of "the new period," Deng asserted a relativism: there was no absolute truth, because situations were always changing and knowledge was constantly developing. This was also a theme of Mao's in *On Practice*. However, Deng's relativism was different from Mao's. Mao's relativism served to underpin a revolutionary voluntarism critical of classical Marxism. According to it, human beings, especially those armed with "correct" ideology, were able to overcome material restraints to create an ideal society. Deng, however, tended toward the deterministic aspect of Marxism. He stressed the limitations on human will imposed by objective constraints. This relativism justified building instrumental principles on an empirical basis rather than on abstract and transcendent fundamentals. From this perspective, the Deng leadership legitimated the retreat from those socialist programs that were considered divorced from current social conditions.

Deng's emphasis on practice highlighted the instrumental dimension of ideology. In Mao's time, especially during the CR, ideology mainly addressed the ultimate ends of communism, which colored every concrete practical principle and policy choice. This had proved counterproductive and even destructive. Deng believed that ideology did not have to address problems that were related to ultimate goals of communism. Rather, it should be more concerned with problems directly relevant to the reality. This postulate justified the autonomy of instrumental principles from fundamental ones and to a large extent, freed policy from dogmatic criticisms.

The "practice theme" seemingly reflected the reformers' effort to emphasize "performance" as a basis of the party's legitimacy. This new orientation had two implications. First, it was a tactic against the "whatever faction." Hua Guofeng's own leadership rested exclusively on his selection by Chairman Mao. He had a vested interest in reaffirming Mao's reputation for infallibility, precisely because his own selection could be justified only by that criterion (Dittmer 1984, 349). The emphasis on practice challenged Hua's position by stressing actual performance rather than Mao's charisma as the base of the leadership's legitimacy. It was not surprising that the predominance of the practice theme was followed by the removal of Hua from the chairmanship of the Central Committee.

Second, the primacy of practice was a powerful lever for the reformers to restore the party's legitimacy by emphasizing the improvement of performance. In 1978, when the CR ended, discontent with current political and economic conditions prevailed. Intellectuals resented the persecution they had suffered; students felt betrayed by the suppression of the Red Guard movement and by being sent to the countryside; workers were upset with stagnant consumption levels and crowded living conditions; peasants were angry about persistent poverty; and the whole population was tired of continuous mass campaigns and ideological indoctrination. The Chinese people were dismayed by the intense factionalism that plagued the leadership of the party (Harding 1987, 26–37). In short, the CR produced a strong skepticism among the population and a crisis of confidence in the party (Liu 1982; Falkenheim 1982). Political unrest and bad socioeconomic performance seriously hurt the party's legitimacy.[6] All these conditions underscored the necessity of actual performance for rebuilding the party's legitimacy.

From the very beginning, however, the "practice" theme had met with some conceptual difficulties, which reflected the political dilemma the China's reform leaders confronted. First of all, facts did not speak for themselves. What constituted a "fact" was necessarily conditioned by a certain world view. One could not start from perception, because without a theory-informed concept one could not have a percept (Brugger and Kelly 1990, 121). Therefore, identifying a "fact" was very likely to involve some ideological predisposition. Individuals with different worldviews would thus interpret "facts" differently. They would give "facts" different meanings and derive different "truths" from them. Often the same fact could generate different "truths." Thus, in advocating the practice criterion, the party actually fell into a dilemma: If it claimed an exclusive power of knowing the facts, it violated its own formula of "seeking truth from fact," since the implied assumption was that other people or social groups were not capable of knowing the facts. However, if the party allowed free interpretations of facts and admitted that everybody could seek truths from facts, then, whose truth should direct policy making and guide the society?

Second, there was no abstract practice. Practice had concrete meaning and was always directed toward a certain end, and to serve one end might mean to neglect another. Practice would never be value-free. Hence, the question arose as to whose or what practice would serve as the criterion for truth. This was certainly a political rather than an epistemological issue. Again, here was a dilemma for the party: If people could test the truth with their own practice, the party could no longer claim a privileged understanding of the truth. However, if the party prohibited some particular mode of practice, the practice criterion turned out to be ideologically predisposed and "essentially meaningless" (Burton 1990, 12). Some advocates of the practice criterion claimed that not all practices, but only successful ones served as criteria of truth. But the question remained, What was the criterion of the success? Mao and his supporters certainly would not consider the practice of Deng's reform as successful, even though it was economically efficient. Deng's reform worked to justify, among other things, the role of the market and increased income differentials, whereas Mao's practice had stressed a high degree of public ownership and egalitarianism. Here, what was "correct," obviously, was a matter of political choice and power, "not some mechanical measurement of truth by the criterion of an abstract practice" (Moody 1983, 68).

The limitation of the practice criterion became clearer when, in the spring of 1979, the ideological relaxation of 1978 stimulated criticisms from the society against the party and the government, and finally led to the Democracy Wall movement in Beijing in November 1978. Fearing challenges to its leadership, the CCP promulgated the "four cardinal principles" (namely, upholding socialism, the dictatorship of the proletariat, the CCP leadership and Marxism-Leninism–Mao Zedong Thought) as the guideline for all political, economic, social, and cultural work. The party leaders had never explicitly addressed the relationship between the four principles and the practice criterion. The four cardinal principles and the practice criterion evidently represented two opposite types of criteria, and the emphasis on the one meant the dilution of the other. But the CCP needed both: It needed the four principles to maintain its legitimacy and combat ideological deviations; it also needed the practice criterion to justify "whatever means" were necessary for modernization. Reconciling both proved to be a tough job, however. From the perspective of the practice criterion, the emphasis on the four cardinal principles inescapably raised such a question (see Brugger and Kelly 1990, 120), because one was not sure how the socialist road could be rerouted, how the people's concept could be redefined, what the role of the Communist Party was to be under new social conditions, and which writings of Mao qualified as Mao Zedong Thought. How could one tell what kind of practice was legitimate and "correct"? The question might further be turned into this: What did the four cardinal principles have to do with truth? Were they not subject to testing, and were they valid forever?

On the other hand, the primacy of practice prevented party leaders from setting overall criteria for evaluation and regulation of social and political life, since "practice" meant different things to dif-

ferent people. Without such overall criteria, the party found it difficult to exercise social control by determining which practice was ideologically undesirable. The promulgation of the four principles thus
meant that practice itself was not the "only criterion for evaluating
truth." Rather, truth must be evaluated by ideological criteria. This
also indicated that the CCP virtually did not believe in the existence
of any abstract practice that could function to measure truth.

However, in the years to follow, the policy implications of the
practice criterion and the four cardinal principles were complicated.
The emphasis on the four principles did not mean that the party
returned to the pre-reform time sand really strictly used fundamental principles as the point of departure for major policy making (i.e.,
following the "dogmatic model"). It only signified that they were
indispensable for the party to claim legitimacy and to undo ideological deviations. Thus, their impact might be more visible in some issue
areas than in others, depending on how much a particular issue was
involved with the "legitimacy problem."

Nevertheless, for some party reformers the proclamation of the
four principles was necessary because it prevented conservatives
from taking the opportunity to attack the reform line of the Third
Plenum. As one of the most eloquent party reformtheorists, Liao
Gailong, explained, conservative charge of the reform program led
the Party Central Committee to consider that, "in order to continue
to implement thoroughly the correct line of the Third Plenum call-
ing for liberating thought and to continue to liquidate the influence
of the erroneous line of the `two whatevers,' it was necessary to reaf-
firm the four principles." (cited from Schram 1984, 10). In other
words, the proclamation of the four principles was a tactical necessity to preserve the possibility for carrying out reforms in a systematic way, from above.

Despite official affirmation of the four cardinal principles, the
practice criterion continued to function as a powerful lever for
reform. The four principles, after all, did not provide any solutions
to knotty problems in economic modernization. In fact, the party
itself never clearly defined the content of those principles. For example, in his speech of 30 March 1979 that formally proclaimed the four
principles, Deng Xiaoping only abstractly defined socialism, whereas
he firmly emphasized the importance of the four principles in no
uncertain terms. He pointed out that socialism was based on public
ownership and that production under socialism was designed to meet

the material and cultural needs of the people to the maximum extent possible—not to exploit the people. Moreover, according to Deng, socialism was a system that made it possible for the people of China to share common political, economic, and social ideals and moral standards (Deng 1984, 174). But Deng Xiaoping did not explicitly designate what means should be used to meet the people's needs or what policies might be appropriate for achieving the goal. The vagueness of his "socialism," therefore, left room for the practice criterion to continue to work. By the mid-1980s, China's policy makers actually considered any measure that could improve economic performance as socialist.

Revolution versus Production

With the shift from "class struggle" to "modernization" in 1978, the CCP began to emphasize the political primacy of economic development. This led to some profound ideological changes regarding the relationship between revolution and production.

During the past decades, Mao Zedong emphasized the importance of revolution over production, due to two assumptions: First, only incessant revolutionary changes could prevent Chinese society from degrading into capitalism; and second, revolutionary movements could liberate and adjust the relations of production and therefore promote production. The second assumption accounted for Mao's initiatives for the Great Leap Forward and the People's Commune movement, while the first accounted for the Socialist Education Campaign and the Cultural Revolution. There is no dispute that it was Mao's suspicion of Liu Shaoqi's line, which stressed production over revolution and therefore was leading to revisionism, that drove Mao to launch the CR and to demolish Liu's political career. One of the major charges against Liu when he was formally removed from power in 1969, was his "advocacy" of the "theory of productive forces" (wei shengchanli lun).[7]

The CR radicalized official thinking on the relationship between revolution and production. Radical Maoists in power followed the logic that production was best promoted by "grasping revolution" and that "when the revolution is handled well, production will automatically go up" (FBIS, 24 February 1978, E13). In daily practice, however, the Maoist leadership believed that revolutionary goals should be pursued even at the expense of production. One slogan that exemplified Maoists' relegation of production to an insignificant role was to "take count of gains and losses in political-ideological terms instead of economic terms!" For example, during the CR it was routine that workers stopped working to engage in political studies. As machines lay idle, the economy suffered badly from underproduction. When this manner of economic management was questioned, the official reaction usually was "Don't use purely economic yardsticks to measure things! Underproduction represents merely economic losses. How can these losses be compared to the great gains obtained from political studies?" (Ding 1988, 1118). Radical Maoists repeatedly argued that emphasis on productive forces over the relations of production would lead to revisionism and capitalism, which they called "satellites [symbolizing productive progress] go up and red flag [representing revolution and socialism] falls down" (*weixing shangtian, hongqi luodi*), and which they believed had happened in the Soviet Union.

The cost the Chinese economy paid for this radical Maoist ideology was tremendous. Not only did radical policies hinder the development of production, they in fact destroyed many productive forces. Although there are no official statistics to show how seriously the economy suffered from the Great Leap Forward, the People's Commune movement, the Socialist Education Campaign, and various other political campaigns, it is widely agreed in China and abroad that heavy economic losses were involved.[8] The Chinese government acknowledged that the economy was virtually on the brink of collapse.

The Criterion of Productive Forces

The Third Plenary Session of the Eleventh Central Committee in 1978 formally ended the Maoist line that emphasized the primacy of revolution. For the first time since the CCP took power, economic construction replaced class struggle as the central task of the party. The new task needed to be ideologically justified, and therefore it was necessary to make an ideological adjustment regarding the relationship between production and revolution, or the relationship between the relations of production and the productive forces. The criterion of productive forces, along with the practice criterion, served as an important concept upon which certain important policy changes were based.

Deng Xiaoping was the first of the top CCP leaders to emphasize the political primacy of production in the post-Mao period. At
the Central Conference for Theoretical Work held in 1979, Deng
(1983, 168) explicitly pointed out that the major contradiction in
contemporary China lay in the gap between low productivity and
people's increased demands for consumer goods, thus overturning
Mao's long-standing belief that the struggle between socialism and
capitalism constituted the major contradiction in socialist China.
By redefining the major contradiction, Deng in fact rehabilitated
Liu Shaoqi's line, advanced at the Eighth National Party Congress
in 1956, that highlighted the development of productive forces as
the party's major task. This so-called "line of the Eighth Congress"
(bada luxian) was formally praised by Deng Xiaoping in his open-
ing address to the Twelfth National Party Congress in 1982. The
party's mistake, Deng said, was to thwart this line. In 1984, Deng
(1987, 52–53) further related the development of the productive
forces to ideological fundamentals: "Marxism pays the greatest
attention to the development of the productive forces." His logic
worked like this: Marxism was a theory of communism; communism must be built upon advanced productive forces and material
wealth; therefore, Marxism was a theory of production. With this
logic, Deng defined the development of productive forces as the
fundamental task for socialism. If, he contended, socialism could
not create more advanced productivity than capitalism could, the
party would not be able to convince people of the superiority of
socialism. For Deng, the superiority of socialism over capitalism
must present itself in terms of the speed and efficiency of economic
development.

It was clear that, with consistent emphases on the primacy of
the productive forces, Deng virtually set a new criterion—the productivity criterion—to measure the party's, the system's, and, indeed,
socialism's performance, a criterion that would even test genuine versus phony Marxism. Ironically, a complete expression of the productive forces criterion was found in Mao's (1972) work and widely cited
by official publications to buttress the political primacy of production:

> Whether policies and practices of all Chinese political parties are
> good or bad to Chinese people, in the final analysis, depends on
> whether they facilitate the development of the productive forces

for Chinese people, and whether they restrict or liberate the productive forces. (Yuan et al. 1989, 87)

Mao's speech, made just before the CCP took power, was directed
against the Kuomintang regime. Mao believed that this regime had
forfeited its right to rule because it had allowed relations of production to decay, to the detriment of China's productive forces. Mao certainly never expected his words to be used to reverse his
revolutionary vision of socialism.

As the political primacy of production became manifest in official rhetoric regarding economic reform, it became necessary to provide a theoretical justification for it. Indeed, it was considerably
important for the leadership to establish a "relationship" between the
productive forces criterion and Marxism. Reformers experienced no
difficulty in interpreting the productive forces criterion in Marxist
terms because, after all, production was a central concept of Marxist
historical materialism. They even believed that the emphasis on the
primacy of production was a return to genuine Marxism, which they
believed had been distorted by the radical voluntarism of past
decades. Undeniably, the concept of the productive forces criterion
was critical to China's post-Mao modernization program. It fundamentally reoriented China's social development and ultimately challenged the premise of socialism.

The Revival of Historical Materialism

To most reformers, the strongest argument for the productive forces
criterion was its compatibility with Marxist historical materialism.
Productive forces, they argued, were the only criterion by which
Marxism should measure historical progress. In a pamphlet published by the General Political Department of the People's Liberation
Army (Yuan et. al. 1989), the primacy of production was justified in
a framework of historical materialism. According to the pamphlet's
authors, production was the most basic human practice, one that
determined and sustained the whole social structure. The relations
of production and the superstructure reflected corresponding productive forces and would change sooner or later with the advancement of the latter. This, as the most active and revolutionary
element in human history, the productive forces played the deter-

mining role in propelling history forward; it was the nature of the productive forces that made them the only fundamental objective criterion for judging social and historical progress. Thus, seeking criteria beyond the productive forces, the authors argued, was doomed to failure. Western utopian socialists, for example, attempted to use criteria such as rationality, morality, justice, and human nature to measure historical progress. But they established nothing in practice because their criteria were illusive. The critique of utopian socialism's ignorance of the productive forces in fact served as a criticism of China's reality. A big mistake made by the past leadership, the authors argued, was to pursue "advanced relations of production" without taking into account the state of the productive forces. Mao and his followers took the relations of production as the sole criterion by which to measure social progress. This made them believe that the larger the scale of the public economy, the more complete and perfect socialism became. As a result, their effort to progressively upgrade the ownership system did serious damage to production. By criticizing Mao's mistake, the authors implied that in terms of seeking a nonproductive forces criterion to measure social progress, Mao's socialism was utopian.

The productive forces criterion for social progress logically led to the view that the development of productive forces was the prerequisite for all other social and human developments. As Zhang Xianyang (1988), a well-known liberal Marxist theorist, argued, the full development of human beings (a goal of Marxist communism) must rely on a high degree of productive advancement. Without progression of production, he went on, we could not eliminate poverty and fulfill the socialist premise of common prosperity, let alone realize the full development of human beings.

The productive forces criterion was an abstraction, however. Some concrete indices were required to measure it. According to the pamphlet mentioned above, these indices might include the quantity of major products, total social output, GNP, industrial structures, applications of scientific and technological know-how in production, management, and the like. In short, the authors believed that the productive forces criterion could be translated into a set of measurements independent of any ideology and social system. They were universal and applicable to all societies pursuing economic modernization.

The Criterion of Productive Forces and
the Preliminary Stage of Socialism

The concept "preliminary stage of socialism" was the most important theoretical construct the CCP developed in order to justify the primacy of production. The defining characteristics of preliminary socialism, according to Zhao Ziyang (1987), were low productive forces and an underdeveloped commodity economy. Such a vision of socialism seemed to logically justify the political primacy of production. The reasons, for many reformers, appeared self-evident. Zhao Ziyang argued in his political report delivered to the Thirteenth National Party Congress (1987, 10), that the major contradiction then confronting China was between the continuous growth of people's material and cultural demands, and backward social production. And, he argued, development of productive forces was the only solution to this contradiction. For some theorists (for example, Jiang et. al 1983), development of productive forces was crucial for diminishing the "three differences"—namely, differences between working class and peasantry, between urban and rural areas, and between mental versus physical labor. Mao's solutions to these three differences (such as setting up people's communes, and sending intellectuals and young students to the countryside) were criticized as misplaced.

To many reformers, if preliminary socialism was still characterized by the prevalence of poverty, then the priority of socialism must be to increase productivity in order to eliminate poverty. Although poverty could not be avoided and, indeed, was a starting point of China's socialism, its persistence had hurt the image of socialism, reformist leaders and intellectuals believed. It was clear to them that popular discontent and a "crisis of faith" or "confidence crisis" in the early 1980s were partially related to the perceived poverty. Popular resentment was reinforced by international comparisons, which were made possible by the open door policy that allowed people to know more about the outside world through the mass media and foreign exchanges. Thus, the political significance of developing productivity was apparent to the post-Mao leadership; slow productivity might undermine socialism as a viable system. Indeed, if socialism could not surpass capitalism in productivity, it could lose much of its legitimacy.

Deng Xiaoping (1983, 215) made it clear that what China needed was a socialism that exceeded capitalism both in the speed of growth and in economic efficiency. Without high productivity, Deng pointed out, socialism was nothing but a boast. China's socialism could assert its superiority over capitalism only when China reached the living standard of middle-range developed countries in the middle of the next century. Thus, for Deng Xiaoping and other reformers, to developing productivity was virtually a struggle to maintain the system's credibility and legitimacy. A quote from Lenin frequently cited in official publications reflected the post-Mao leadership's view on the crucial importance of productivity: "Labor productivity, in the final analysis, is the most important and most principal thing that guarantees the success of the new social system" (cited from Yuan et al. 1989, 56).

As we have seen, the 1980s witnessed an intellectual trend that identified high productivity, rather than equality, with socialism. Not only was high productivity necessary for China's preliminary socialism; for many reformers, it was also a fundamental characteristic of socialism in general. Socialism as an alternative to capitalism was based on the assumption that it provided a socioeconomic arrangement that would allow much speedier productive development than capitalism did. As Deng Xiaoping said, "The fundamental manifestation of the superiority of socialism lies in its permission for unprecedentedly rapid development of the social productive forces, which was impossible in the old society" (1983, 123). Deng knew that this was a proposition about what "ought to be" and that was far from the reality. But this "ought to be" vigorously justified the political primacy of production under socialism. If, Deng asked once, the development of the socialist economy was permanently slower than that of the capitalist economy, where was the manifestation of the superiority of socialism? The identification of productive development with socialism was more explicitly emphasized by Wu Jiaxiang (1987), a member of Zhao Ziyang's think tanks. According to him, "qualified" socialism was a form of socialism that was able to generate high productivity. China's current socialism, from his point of view, was less qualified in terms of the productive forces criterion. Certainly, Wu argued, high productivity did not amount to socialism, but its absence would disqualify a country for socialism. Thus, to Wu and many reformers, the adherence to socialism needed to be substantialized through the development of the productive forces.

China's Marxist justification for political primacy of production also reflected reformist leaders' and intellectuals' anxiety that China had lagged behind the remarkable development of the world economy in recent decades. The sentimental debate in the early and late 1980s on whether China would be deprived of its "global membership" due to its low productive forces aroused a "crisis consciousness" (*weiji yishi*), which reinforced the notion of the primacy of production. Low productivity, as many reformers argued, tremendously weakened China's national strength and ranked China among the poorest countries in the world. This intellectual ferment was pointedly reflected in an edited work titled *China's Crises and Reflections* (Li 1989). Various statistics were cited by the authors to demonstrate that China was falling far behind advanced nations. For example, as Li Ming contended, China's GNP accounted for 4.7 percent of the total world GNP in 1955 but dropped to 2.5 percent in 1980. In 1955, China's GNP equaled Japan's and was 460 billion yuan less than that of the United States; it was only one fourth of Japan's by 1980 and was 3.68 trillion yuan less than that of the United States by 1985. The primacy of production was thus considered critical for China's national competitiveness and status in the world. A growing realization among China's reformers was that the contemporary world was following the law of survival of the fittest. This sentiment was summed up in a catchword: "Backwardness invites attack" (*luohou jiuyao aida*).

The Criterion of Productive Forces and Capitalist Practices

Once the productive forces criterion was established, it was logical that all means conducive to production were justified. The productive forces criterion, indeed, was the core of post-Mao economic pragmatism, which legitimated "whatever means" could bring about growth and efficiency. Deng Xiaoping had long been famous for this type of "means pragmatism," as manifested in his saying that it hardly matters whether a cat is black or white, as long as it catches mice. Reformers linked the primacy of production to socialism and viewed all means favorable for production as being conducive to socialism. For Lu Yingling and Fang Li (1988, 78–79), for example, the criterion of production could be summed up as follows: Whatever is conducive to the development of the productive forces would fit with the basic interests of people, and thereby be required by, or permissible for and acceptable to, socialism. Such a new "whatever" view was endorsed by reformist leaders. Zhao Ziyang (1987, 11) declared in the Thirteenth National Party Congress, for example, that whatever is conducive to the development of production should become the starting point of all policy considerations and the criterion by which to judge the party's work.

One implication of the official endorsement for this "whatever" approach was self-evident: It in fact prepared the way for justifying capitalistic practices. But at first reformers attempted to define capitalist methods favorable for production as variables independent of social systems. In other words, they were not capitalist "patents" and could serve socialism as well. In his appeal for bolder reforms, Zhao Ziyang (1987) pointed out that in the past, many elements (such as the market, a commodity economy, and the stock exchange) favorable for the development of productive forces and commodification, socialization, and modernization were mistakenly labeled as "capitalist"; in fact, they were neutral in character and could benefit socialism.

Some authors (Yuan et al. 1989) distinguished between two types of practices that used to be alien to socialist China but now could serve productive development. One was the use of methods that were not exclusive to capitalism but had been treated as such under the previous ideology; these included the market, a commodity economy, the shareholding system, and the stock exchange. Another category, such as private ownership (including both domestic and foreign capital owned), was capitalist by nature but was "acceptable" to a "preliminary socialism" in order to promote productive development. Reformers further related this new "whatever" approach to institutional changes. In Deng Xiaoping's famous statement in the 1960s, which vividly reflected his pragmatism: "Black cats, white cats, what does it matter? So long as they can catch rats, they are good cats," Wu Jiaxiang[9] (*SJJJDB*, 19 December 1988) argued that Deng's "cat" could mean more than certain concrete means and methods; it could mean institutions. That is to say, whatever institutions were favorable for production were good institutions. Thus, Wu proposed to meet the productivity criterion at institutional levels. He seemed to believe that the socialist system should not restrict China's choices for means, methods, and institutions that could promote productive development. The idea that certain means, methods, or institutions were exclusive to certain social systems was, he said, "means fatalism."

Echoing Wu's argument, some commentators (Sun 1989) went further by saying that putting the label *socialism* or *capitalism* on policies was meaningless, since productive development was the only criterion by which to judge whether a policy was acceptable or unacceptable. An article in *GMRB* (12 September 1988, 3) argued that from the perspective of the productive forces criterion, socialist and capitalist systems would apply the same criterion to their socioeconomic performance, which could mean an eventual convergence of the two systems.

The Criterion of Productive Forces:
Its Significance and Implications

The emphasis on the primacy of production significantly changed the orientation of the post-Mao socialism, which, to a large extent, was reduced to certain ideas of modernization. Undoubtedly the redefinition of socialism in terms of economic productivity provided the post-Mao leadership with strong ideological support for its modernization efforts. With this new conceptualization of socialism, the CCP could legitimately implement "whatever" means and methods to pursue economic growth and efficiency. China's reform of the ownership system, as this study shows, demonstrates the considerable ideological flexibility that the productive forces criterion provided for the CCP in its effort to seek institutional changes.

To what extent this emphasis on the primacy of production was consistent with Marxism is subject to further dispute. But an economically deterministic interpretation of historical materialism, subordinating all to the overriding task of developing the productive forces is problematic. Productive development is, after all, not a universal panacea for all the ills and contradictions that afflict society. An overemphasis on economic growth can repeat the errors made by many developing nations, which defined economic growth as the single most important goal and neglected the multiple dimensions of social development.

But the problem for the CCP leadership was more than this; using productive forces to measure social progress raised some questions regarding how to evaluate China's current socialist system and contemporary capitalist systems. Judging in terms of the productive forces criterion, is socialism premature for Chinese society, given its low productivity? How far should China retreat, if necessary, from the current relations of production that are said to exceed the development of the productive forces? If the productive forces, rather than the relations of production, are the only criteria by which to judge social progress, does that mean that Western capitalist systems are more "progressive," "advanced," and "superior" than China's socialism? These questions, which may be academically uninteresting, have critical political implications for the CCP and Chinese society. They concern how the leadership, with its emphasis on the primacy of production, justifies to the public its current system and its criticism of capitalism. These are questions that, in the final analysis, concern the system's, and hence the party's, legitimacy.

The post-Mao leadership's emphasis on the primacy of production pointed to the dilemma that had confronted the CCP in steering postrevolutionary social development. As a Leninist party, the CCP needed to continue its revolutionary momentum in order to keep socialism vital and hence to maintain its own legitimacy. Tremendous scarcity of material conditions, on the other hand, compelled the CCP to focus on economic modernization. Mao Zedong, pursuing the first goal at the expense of the second, believed that incessant revolutionary change of the relations of production would bring about productive development in the long run. For him, the socialist transformation of social relationships and especially the consciousness of the masses were the precondition for modern economic development. From the Great Leap Forward to the Cultural Revolution, however, his ideas proved unworkable. The post-Mao leadership subordinated all other social goals to economic development. For those leaders, the development of material productive forces was the essential prerequisite for social and intellectual change; socialism could not continue without a solid material basis. The primacy of production was therefore necessary to build such a condition. The primacy of production, however, not only eroded revolutionary momentum, it also invited capitalism. Indeed, from the perspective purely of the productive forces criterion, capitalism was tempting and useful for China. As Meisner (1982) pointed out, if China avoided many evils of capitalism by its revolution's being rooted in a basically agrarian society, it suffered all the more because its avoidance of capitalism retarded productive development and facilitated the persistence of its pernicious feudal heritage. A socialist emphasis on the primacy of production thus could legitimate China's capitalist practice.

Nevertheless, the primacy of production could undermine the CCP's ideological foundation. It could generate various socioeconomic practices that met the productive forces criterion but conflicted with fundamental principles of socialism. Thus, the logic of the primacy of production was paradoxical for the post-Mao leadership in that it was both problem solving and crisis generating. It might improve economic efficiency by allowing the CCP to choose whatever means it thought suitable. At the same time, however, the primacy of production could deprive the CCP of its ideologically based claim to legitimacy. Productive development, after all, was not what a Leninist party was established for and not something that a Leninist party could claim privileged knowledge about. More importantly, capitalist practice encouraged by the productive forces criterion could dismantle all the Leninist political and economic institutions.

In short, the CCP's struggle with emphasizing practice and the productive forces criterion and maintaining its ideologically defined legitimation characteristically epitomized its dilemma of reconciling the functional conflict between fundamental and instrumental principles. Pragmatic reform, on the one hand, and the attempt to prevent ideological erosion, which might undermine the system's and the party's legitimacy, on the other, provided the backdrop for China's reform of the ownership system.

4
Agricultural Decollectivization[1]

China's ownership reform began in the countryside. This was largely because China's agriculture had been on the brink of drastic deterioration in the late 1970s. The existing agricultural economic organization—the people's commune—proved unable to sustain economic growth. Peasants were so intensely disillusioned with the status quo that they were compelled to seek changes by themselves. Their spontaneous action to try to create for themselves a better life touched off a sweeping reform that later restructured China's agricultural ownership system. The ideological reformulation regarding the agricultural reform focused on how to cope with the collective ownership system. From a fundamental perspective, collectivization was the core of China's socialist agricultural structure and should not be changed. From the instrumental perspective, on the other hand, the current collective ownership impeded agricultural production and needed radical reform. The conflict between these two perspectives raised a central question of how far the decollectivization of the agricultural ownership system should go. From the very beginning of the rural reform, the post-Mao leadership was forced to wrestle with a dilemma: improving rural productivity by releasing peasants from the "collective fetter," while keeping a collective structure to maintain an image of socialism. This dilemma proved unresolvable.

The Agricultural Ownership System: Performance and Problems

As the dominant agricultural economic institution since 1958, the People's Commune epitomized the CCP's ideologically defined vision of a rural socioeconomic structure. By collectivizing the basic means of production—land, implements, and draft animals—the commune system, to the CCP leaders, represented a transitional stage toward a full communism where the means of production were under total public control. Theoretically, communes were based on a three-level ownership of the means of production: ownership by the commune, by the production brigade, and by the production team. All three levels had the right to handle their own production. In practice, however, a prevailing tendency was to enlarge the scale of management of the means of production. In the early years of the commune movement, it was commonplace that commune cadres freely confiscated household and cooperative assets to put them under the management of the commune. And they also freely transferred collective assets from one brigade to another without compensation (Howard 1988). There was a temporary retreat from the larger-scale public ownership in the early 1960s when the country experienced economic hardship. But it soon gave way to a fanatic drive toward the large public ownership system of the CR period. The campaign to "Learn from Dazhai"[2] indicated Maoist leadership's intention to continue to enlarge accounting units until a final switch from collective to state ownership took place.

It would be unfair to deny certain remarkable achievements under the commune system in the pre-reform period. Communes provided the organizational basis for the mobilization of vast armies of labor. Peasants built, largely by hand, eighty thousand reservoirs, with a total capacity of 400 billion cubic meters and irrigation systems for 76.6 million acres of land (Lin and Chao 1982, 124). The people's communes also provided the network for rural health services and a cooperative medical care insurance system. Through communes, tens of thousands of primary schools were built and staffed. Countless roads were built, numerous small power stations were constructed, and electricity was supplied to many villages.

But these very real advances were bought at a high price. As Howard (1988, 44), noted

> Through the process of cooperativization, peasants had lost individual ownership rights over their means of production, includ-

ing land, animals, carts, and larger farm implements. As the collective grew and the communication links between the producers and their leaders became more and more tenuous, peasants increasingly lost their collective control over "their" means of production, the organization of "their" labor, and the distribution of "their" product. Peasants were being "proletarianized" not in the sense of becoming free wage labor, but in the sense of becoming a "community labor" paid more or less equal wages by the "community" as "universal capitalist" as conceived by Marx in the Economic and Philosophical Manuscripts.

The tremendous cost did not result in the spectacular productivity gains promised. As *Hongqi* (1 May 1983) reported, per capita output fell by 0.2 kilograms and oil-bearing crops by 1.2 kilograms between 1958 and 1979. But peasants were particularly discontented with the stagnation of their incomes. Between 1965 and 1976, peasants' per capita income from work points earned by working for the collective increased merely 10.50 yuan, or less than 1 yuan per year, enough to buy a single pack of quality-grade cigarettes. In 1978, per capita earnings from collective sources averaged only 74 yuan, and nearly one-quarter of peasant households had per capita incomes of less than 50 yuan. According to Chen Yizhi (1990), the former director of the China Economic System Reform Research Institute and an aide to Zhao Ziyang,[3] the living conditions of two thirds of Chinese peasants in 1978 were worse than in the early 1950s; those of one-third were worse than in the 1930s.[4] The annual per capita income of 200 million peasants was less than 50 yuan, plus about two hundred *jin*[5] of grain. This is to say, one fourth of Chinese peasants by 1978 toiled all the year around without enough to eat and wear.[6] The worst case was in Pinglu County of Shanxi Province, where peasants' annual per capita income was only 22 yuan. Peasants expressed their predicament with a common complaint that they were being "roped together to live in poverty." It was time to cut the rope.

The Emergence of the Contract System and Ideological Controversy

The initiative for an alteration to the status quo came from Anhui, one of the provinces where peasants suffered most from poverty and hunger.[7] In 1978, the year when peasants began to seek change, per capita grain production there had fallen below that of 1952 (Howard 1988, 49). Twenty years of collective agriculture failed to overcome seemingly intractable problems of poverty, underemployment, and apathy. In the summer of 1978, Anhui Province encountered one of the severest droughts in history, which further worsened the peasants' livelihood. No longer believing that collective farming was an effective way out of the plight, village leaders sought to reorganize the system of production management and income distribution. At a cadre meeting of the Huanghua Brigade, Shannan Commune, Feixi County, a historic decision was made that would later affect the fate of hundreds of millions of Chinese peasants and reshape Chinese agriculture. The decision was to institute a contract responsibility system (*chengbaozhi*), composed of "five fixings" (*wu ding*): fixing land (namely, contracting pieces of land to peasant households); fixing quotas; fixing costs; fixing rewards for surpassing quotas; and fixing methods of penalty.

The core of *chengbao* was to closely tie payment to the quantity and quality of labor and output. Some other villages in Anhui Province also practiced *chengbao* in different forms to reorganize production in order to alleviate the impact of the natural disaster. Although *chengbao* by no means privatized collective property, its designers bore a great political risk in implementing it. In the Xiaogang Brigade, a village in Fengyang County, Anhui Province, three brigade cadres called the village's eighteen households together and signed a joint pledge, which included the following: that they would strictly keep *chengbao* secret, and that if cadres were put in jail for initiating this pact, other households would take care of their families and bring their children up until they were eighteen years old. The heads of the eighteen households made fingerprints on this "top-secret" pledge.[8] Indeed, Chinese peasants in 1978 would rather risk political danger than continue to suffer from the rigid agricultural economic system.

Highly encouraged by the prospect that they could get more by working hard, the peasants showed enormous enthusiasm for the *chengbao* system. Within only two days after the Huanghua Brigade made their bold decision, Huanghua's 1,700 *mou* of land was contracted out to peasant households. Meanwhile, the method spread like wildfire from village to village. By the end of October 1978, seven communes of Feixi County had adopted the contract system, and, as a result, 160,000 *mou* of land were quickly contracted out. Later on, more and more villages tried this forbidden fruit. It has been estimated that thirty thousand brigades in Anhui Province had implemented the contract system by the end of 1978. The outcome was dramatic: The total output of summer grain crops in 1979 shot up to 7.8 billion *jin*—a historic miracle for this province. A brigade in An County tripled its best record of output in history (Wang et al. April, 1989). Anhui peasants had pulled themselves through a calamitous year.

The spontaneous implementation of *chengbao* in Anhui, and later in other provinces, was done in three major ways. The first was to contract output quotas to work groups (*baochan daozu*). Under this system, the production team divided its labor force into several groups and contracted a certain amount of land to each. The team and the group agreed on the targeted output, the pay in terms of work points (*gongfen*),[9] the expenses required, and so on. After the crop was brought in, the group received the stipulated number of work points for the targeted output. Any extra output was given to the work group as bonuses, either in full or in part, according to the agreement. The production team would reduce the work points if the group failed to fulfill the agreed-upon output quota. In this system, the form of collective production was maintained, though it was reduced to a group level.

The second method was to contract output quotas to individual households, with the production team conducting unified accounting (*baochan daohu*). In this system, the production team contracted all its farmland to individual households for separate cultivation. The contracted part of the output went to the production team for unified distribution among the members, and the rest was either shared between the team and the contractor or granted to the latter as a bonus.

The third method was to contract output quota to individual household, without the production team's conducting unified distribution (*baogan daohu* or *dabaogan*). According to this system, the production team divided the land and the general run of farm tools among individual households. By contract, each household had to bring in specified crops in a specified amount as payment for the state agricultural tax and as a contribution to the team's public accumulation and welfare funds. Apart from this, the household could grow anything and handle the extra output in any way it wanted to. Unified accounting and income distribution by the production team ceased to exist under this system.

None of the three methods changed the basic property relations in agricultural production, however. The state still claimed the right to own the land and delegated collectives to manage it, while the collectives were the immediate owners of other means of production, such as implements and draft animals. Also, fundamental differences existed among these three forms. The first form, contracting to groups, still left the means of production for collective use, and therefore it at least retained a certain tangible form of collectivism. In the second form, production was individualized, though distribution was partially controlled by the collective. In the third form, the collective ceased to function in either production or distribution, and its role was reduced to that of a contractor or "rent collector." The second and third forms virtually dismantled the collective economy by individualizing production. Because there was no unified official policy toward *chengbao*, different localities developed different forms according to their own needs.

If the practical benefit of *chengbao* for Chinese peasants as well as for Chinese agriculture, was obvious, its ideological implications for many party officials and ideologues appeared ambiguous or questionable, especially when more and more brigades were engaged in the practice of the individual households contract (IHC). Focusing on the experiment with the household contract by the Huanghua Brigade, in a complaint letter to the party committee of the province, someone raised the question of what direction peasants were being led in (Chen 1990, 26). Actually, after *chengbao* had already been implemented in more than 50 percent of the brigades in its jurisdiction, the party committee of Feixi County, uncertain of the ideological implications of the practice, issued a formal document prohibiting "contracting the land to individual households" (Yang et al. 1989). For some local leaders, contracting to groups at least still retained the collective nature of the economy, whereas contracting to individual households might mean a disintegration of collective ownership. Even Wan Li, the reform-minded Anhui party secretary who privately supported *chengbao*, had to order that it be kept low-key. The opposition of local party officials to the household contract was dramatized by a widely told story: After inspecting a number of brigades that had carried out the new system, some officials from the Shuxian prefectural party committee wept bitterly, saying that "[we] had worked hard [for socialism] for dozens of years and now ["they"—referring to these brigades] returned to preliberation time (that is, pre-1949) overnight" (*xinxin keke jishinian, yiye huidao jiefangqian*; Yang 1989). Thus, *chengbao* was accused of "capitalist restoration" by a large number of party officials at commune, county and prefectural levels. The party secretary of Liyuan Commune, the immediate superior of the Xiaogang Brigade, called on the three brigade cadres who initiated the secret pledge and bitterly denounced them for involving themselves in capitalist activities. The commune punished the Xiaogang Brigade for its capitalist practice by stopping the supply of seeds, fertilizers, and loans (Yang 1989). In many other areas, conservative party officials tried to prevent the spread of *chengbao* by various means, ranging from reduction of planned resources, such as electricity and water, disciplinary penalties, and exclusion from party membership (Wang et al. 1989, 54).

For some party officials, even the group contract also deviated from socialist practice. Wang Renzhong, director of the Agricultural Commission of the Central Committee, complained in a phone call to Wan Li that the group contract would undermine the principle of the three levels of ownership of the means of production (Chen 1990, 33).[10] At his suggestion, *The People's Daily* (15 March 1979, 1) published, on the front page in the name of a basic-level cadre, a letter opposing the group contract. The letter complained that the group contract, which allocated land, farm tools, and animals to a group for its use, would lead to the virtual breakup of the team and creation of smaller accounting units. A comment attached to the letter by the editor supported this stand. This letter and the editor's comment in *The People's Daily* panicked many peasants and grassroots cadres, who thought that the political climate had changed again.[11] Backed by Wan Li, an official in Anhui's provincial Agricultural Commission defended the group contract in a reply letter to *The People's Daily*. He pointed out that teams were still viable collectives inasmuch as they still drew up a unified plan for crop production and implemented unified distribution of crops and cash income at the end of the harvest. On 39 March 1979, again on the first page, the editor of *The People's Daily* revised his views and acknowledged the group contract as an acceptable form for linking remuneration to output. However, he maintained his objection to letting groups retain all surplus production beyond the target. Instead, he recommended retention of a small portion of the excess as a bonus. A worry underlying this objection was that the increase of surplus production on the groups' side might eventually dismantle production teams as owners of the means of production.

The central leadership's initial reaction to the rapid spontaneous changes in agricultural economic organization was ambivalent. The communiqué of the historic Third Plenum of the party's Central Committee, published at the end of 1978 when *chengbao* was like a raging fire in China's countryside, unexpectedly did not make any comment on *chengbao*. It is unlikely that this was an oversight. There are two possibilities for this unusual silence: the leadership as a whole was uncertain what to do with it, or reformers and conservatives were deadlocked over it. In either case, the ideological implications of *chengbao* were the central concern.

With regard to agricultural policies, the communiqué of the Third Plenum affirmed the following adjustments: (1) upholding the distribution principle according to the quality and quantity of labor; (2) emphasizing private plots[12] and the free market as necessary complemenst to the socialist collective economy; and (3) decreasing price scissors between industrial and agricultural products (*ZYWX*, 1982, 7). The first measure implied an endorsement of the ongoing practice of "fixing quotas." On the other hand, the communiqué reiterated that people's communes must firmly observe the principle of a three-level system of ownership of the means of production[13] and take the production team as a basic accounting unit (*sanji suoyou, duiwei jichu*). That is to say, the party at that time still considered it unacceptable to break the production team as the basic unit of China's agricultural collective economy. With the emphasis on the production team as an accounting unit, the party's intention might have been to contain the previous radical tendency toward a larger-scale public management of the means of production. But this also implied that the party was not going to allow a practice that might go beyond or undermine this principle.

The leadership's ambivalence about *chengbao* was clearly reflected in a draft document circulated at the Third Plenum, *Decision on Some Questions Concerning the Acceleration of Agricultural Development*.[14] According to it, "under the prerequisite of unified accounting and unified distribution by the production team, it was also permissible to assign responsibility for particular tasks to work groups, calculate rewards for work by linking them to yields, and award bonuses for surpassing output quotas" (*ZYWX* 1982, 172). Here, the party accepted the "contracted production" at a group scale (which was certainly smaller than production teams) as not deviating from socialism. This was an important retreat from the previous pursuit of large collective farming. On the other hand, the document restated that "individual farming" *(dangan)* was not allowed *(buxue)*, that land could not be divided among individuals, and that contracting land and other means of production to individual households was not recommended *(buyao)* (ZYWX 1982, 172). It is clear that in 1978 and 1979, the CCP, though becoming pragmatic, still considered "individual farming" capitalistic and ideologically unacceptable. The "group contract" was therefore set as a bottom line for reform of the agricultural production system.

Redefining the Contract System: Expedient Measure versus Alternative Organization

As *chengbao* spread in China's rural areas and increasingly demonstrated its merits in practice, the reform camp embarked on a campaign for formal legitimation of this innovation. From late 1979 to the summer of 1980, some research fellows from the Institute of Rural Economy of Chinese Academy of Social Science, along with officials from the Ministry of Agriculture, conducted investigations in areas where the household contract had been practiced illegally. They found that the production output of these areas was higher than that of areas implementing the group contract only, though the output of the latter areas was much higher than that of areas continuing collective farming. The findings and a policy recommendation for a comprehensive implementation of the household contract in the countryside were presented to the top leaders in the report *Countryside's Dawn, China's Hope*, prepared by Chen Yizhi. As Chen (1990) recalled, he got a chance to talk with Hu Yaobang about its basic ideas. Their conversation lasted 4 to 5 hours. Hu explicitly supported the policy recommendation proposed by the report. He told Chen later that the report had considerably influenced the Party Center's decision to sanction *chengbao*.

We do not know if Deng Xiaoping read this report. But he was surely interested in what was going on in the countryside. *Chengbao*, notwithstanding its vague and controversial ideological implications, was compatible with Deng's logic regarding the productive forces criterion. Thus his endorsement for it did not come as a surprise. On 31 May 1980, Deng had a talk with several "leading comrades" and explicitly applauded *chengbao* (Deng 1983, 275–76). He rebutted some officals' worry that such a practice would make the collective economy "unnecessary" and asserted that the growth of productive forces brought about by *chengbao* would eventually consolidate the collective economy. While affirming that "our general direction was to develop the collective economy," Deng admitted that the pace of the socialist transformation of agriculture was too fast. As a result, Deng believed, the current form of the collective economy had far overstepped the limitations of the agricultural productive forces and hence had become destructive to production. It was notable that such comments implied a criticism of the People's Commune.

The *chengbao* problem finally reached the table of the central decision makers. In August 1980, the CCP held the Central Work Conference, with agricultural development at the top of its agenda. Naturally, *chengbao* became a focus of debate. The opposition to it was purely ideologically based. Some central and provincial officials asserted that the commune was the "open road" (*yangguandao*), while the household contract was the "log bridge" (*dumuqiao*). They contended that to divide the land among individual peasants amounted to the restoration of capitalism. Some of them accepted *chengbao* only as a temporary expedient to improve production in poor areas. After practicing the household contract for a while, they argued, these areas still must go back to large-scale collective farming (Chen 1990, 35).

The intense debate ended with Central Document no.75, which sanctioned the group contract while restricting the individual household contract to the poor areas. Sustaining the collective economy was central to this document. The individual household contract was therefore treated as an expedient measure for the poor areas to solve "eating and wearing" (*wenbao*) problems. To distance the individual household contract from capitalism, the document vaguely defined it as an economic form subordinated to the socialist economy. According to the document, this practice would not lead to capitalism, since it was undertaken in the context of the "absolute dominance" of the socialist economy (*ZYWX*, 508). Finally, the document explicitly prohibited labor hiring and reiterated collectivization as the only right direction for China's agricultural development.

It was widely believed that this document represented a significant retreat by the party from its radical agricultural policies that had prevailed for most of the years since the socialist transformation. However, the document also indicated that what the CCP planned was to reduce the degree of collectivization rather than to start a total decollectivization. There were not too many practical difficulties in implementing decollectivization, as experience demonstrated. The difficulty at this point was ideological. In the leadership's view, with the development of *chengbao* the degree of the collective economy had been reduced to the minimum, and a further step would dismantle it.

However, the CCP's public affirmation of the collective economy did not dispel its own ambivalence with, and uncertainty about how to define the nature of, the IHC. A policy dilemma, and, indeed, a severely disputed ideological issue, that confronted the leadership from the very emergence of the IHC was the following: Was the IHC an expedient measure to alleviate the vicious poverty in some localities, or was it an organizational alternative to China's entire agricultural production? A *Hongqi* article (no. 12, 1980) reflected this unsolved problem. The author treated the IHC as a spontaneous reaction by peasants to the improperly large-scale management of the means of production, which had proved to be unable to sustain economic growth. The justification of the IHC, for the author, could have two practical bases:: First, it was appropriate given the extremely low level of productive forces in China's poor areas; second, it provided a strong working incentive for the peasants. But these two reasons were apparently incompatible. According to the former, the IHC was good only for the poor areas, while the latter implied a universal applicability to all areas. The ambiguity was also reflected in the author's assessment of the collective economy. He blamed the "collective operation" (*jiti jingying*) for the failure to improve the living condition of the countryside and praised the IHC for freeing the peasants from "blind commands," "heavy burdens," and "the appropriation of the fruits of peasants' work by cadres." But he was evasive about whether these situations were the cases only in poor areas or in the entire countryside. Despite his praise of the IHC, the author still related it to the lower level of productive forces and believed that there would be no need for the IHC in the areas where the level of productive forces was higher (whether or not the maladies he criticized existed in these areas was not mentioned). In fact, it had been an official position that the problems with the current collective economy were universal rather than isolated in the poor areas. But at the same time the official ideology could not face up to this question: Since the IHC as a cure had proven more effective than others, why should it be limited only to the poor areas?

An editorial commentary in the same issue of *HQ* presented a more pragmatic argument. According to it, the critical criterion for judging an organizational form of economy was whether it was conducive to production. The IHC, the commentator argued, obviously was positive in that it made peasants care about, and hence have the incentive to increase, production. The commentator seemed to suggest that it was unnecessary for the central government to stipulate which areas were appropriate for implementing the IHC, given the enormous variations in the rural areas in terms of natural, economic, managerial, educational, cultural, and habitual factors. Thus, this commentary suggested that the choice for the correct organizational form of the economy be left to the peasants. This argument implied a break with the prevailing view that the IHC should be related to the state of the productive forces. The IHC therefore could be carried out anywhere, as long as the peasants perceived it to be good for them. This commentary therefore closely paralleled the pragmatic productive forces criterion and represented an attempt to universalize the IHC.

Both articles, however, claimed that the IHC was compatible with the maintenance of the collective economy. They distinguished the IHC in the context of the collective economy from the small-farmer economy based on private ownership. The IHC, they believed, did not privatize the ownership of land and other major means of production but only contracted them to the peasants for their individual management and use. This certainly had nothing to do with the restoration of capitalism, they argued. Interestingly enough, both articles also regarded the IHC as a method of improving and restoring peasants' confidence in the collective economy. Yet the question of where the meaning of the collective economy lay, if the whole production and distribution processes were individualized, was left unaddressed. For the first article we have reviewed, the IHC would not become the main body of China's agricultural sector, and therefore the nature of the existing collective economy would remain unchanged. This was virtually the party position that could be found in various official publications. Nevertheless, the party soon found that the IHC, though it arose in poor areas, was attractive to peasants everywhere. It spread like an epidemic that eroded the collective economy so rapidly that in many places collectives existed in name only. Ironically, this process of decollectivization was called by peasants the "second liberation."[15]

The Legitimation of the Individual Household Contract

Document no. 75 of 1980 did not formally legitimate the IHC, though it approved its limited practice in poor areas. It was reasonable to believe that this document was a result of a compromise between reformists and conservatives, given the fact that Deng Xiaoping was ascending, while the "whatever" faction was still in power. But reformist ideas were gaining influence because they kept in touch with the changing rural reality. Also, the political alignment tended to be favorable to reform as more reform-minded leaders entered the central leadership.[16]

The ideological justification for the agricultural reform in general, and the IHC in particular, was initially undertaken by one of the most influential think tanks of the reform camp—the Rural Policy Research Office of the Secretariat of the CCP, which reported directly to Hu Yaobang. Its director, Du Runsheng, was regarded as a chief designer and promoter of the liberal agricultural reform.[17] His ten-year career, as a top aide first to Hu Yaobang and then to Zhao Zhiyang, represented a vigorous effort within the party to seek a more liberal and flexible interpretation of Marxism in order to justify the retreat from orthodox socialism. Du's central idea was that China's agricultural collectivization had overstepped the limits of productive forces and thus had become detrimental to the rural economy (Du 1985). By making such an argument, he raised a more basic question of how Marxists should treat the peasantry in backward and agrarian countries after a socialist revolution. According to him, although collectivization was necessary for socialist modernization, it could not be coercively enforced regardless of objective conditions. It must be based on a certain level of productive forces. Moreover, the peasant, as a private owner, would not unconditionally accept socialist collectivization. Thus the process of collectivization should be gradual, incremental, and long-lasting. The peasantry should be guided toward, rather than forced to live in, collectivization. A collectivization imposed from above amounted to a confiscation of the peasantry's property, which could seriously damage peasants' interests and party-peasantry relations. The collectivization based on a scattered and backward small-farmer economy, Du went on, simply did not work well. When someone commented that the peasants' enthusiasm for the IHC reflected their low levels of confidence in socialism, Du contended that this should be blamed not on peasants but on the fact that "our socialism did not improve their living standards and lacked any attraction for them" (Du 1985). For Du, the IHC should be more than just a temporary measure of placating peasants. Rather, it should be an organizational form of rural economy through which a meaningful collectivization could be gradually reached. Du granted the IHC a universal meaning for restructuring China's agriculture.

Of the various methods of *chengbao*, Du strongly favored the most radical one—the IHC without the production team conducting accounting (*baogan daohu*). In a speech to officials of Hubei Province on 22 May 1981, he advocated a further spread of this method to put both production and distribution under the control of peasants themselves. More specifically, as production had been largely individualized, Du saw a necessity of further freeing distribution from the control of the production team. In his view, the control of the production team over distribution provided no benefits for peasants; rather, it made distribution more arbitrary and unfair and also created an opportunity for cadre corruption, both of which peasants resented. Citing some data from the investigations he had led, he revealed that 25 percent of peasants' work points were used to subsidize cadres who virtually did not engage in production. As the production team ceased to function in distribution, a distribution based on contracts between peasants and the production team became simpler and tended to be more fair. In peasants' words, the distribution would "ensure payments to the state, set aside enough for the collective, and leave everything else to peasants." Du saw an IHC without much interference of the production team as not being an end of collectivism. He told the audience that the in provinces he toured as an inspector, he found quite a few individual households working together in a cooperative manner, from sharing money to buy some fixed assets, to joint ventures in constructing infrastructures. This kind of voluntary collectivism from the bottom, he pointed out, might be more viable than one imposed from the above.

Another institute actively involved in the ideological reformulation of rural policies was the Research Group of China's Rural Development, a quasi-official institute led by Chen Yizhi. Its aim, as Chen recalled later, was to formulate policy recommendations through empirical research and to seek theoretical innovations rather than to annotate orthodox theories. Beginning in 1980, this institute conducted both theoretical and empirical studies of the rural economy. Within less than a year, the group compiled various articles regarding the IHC into the two-volume *Readings of the Individual Household Contract*, which sold eighty thousand copies.

In April 1981, the Research Group presented its initial investigative report, based on the field studies in Yunnan, Guizhou, and Sichuan Provinces, to the Party Center, pushing for legitimation of the IHC. Later, another report, based on an investigation of Chu County of Anhui Province, was submitted to the top leaders. This report detailed the long-term impact of the IHC on rural development (including such issues as the land system, food, income differential, cooperation, and rural cadres) and outlined policy recommendations for the transformation of rural economic organization. Upon reading this report, Zhao Zhiyang commented: "This report has thoroughly straightened out rural problems. I suggest that party secretaries and governors of all provinces read it seriously" (Chen 1990, 37).

Some reform-minded governmental officials were also urging the central leadership to legitimate the IHC. A deputy director of the Central Agricultural Commission, after inspecting Hubei, Shanxi, and Shandong provinces, presented a report to the Central Committee and the Council of the State in February 1981 (Wang, et al., 1989). In the report, he appealed to the center to face the reality that the IHC became increasingly popular and had stirred the peasants' unprecedented enthusiasm for production. He pointed out in the report that for a long time the party had wrongly equated the superiority of the collective economy to a collectivized production and an egalitarian distribution, both of which had considerably stifled the peasants' enthusiasm and had hindered economic development. The fact that many peasants and village cadres dared to take risks to practice the IHC demonstrated that this was something that really was good for them and therefore was irresistible. He predicted that although production was individualized under the IHC, some small-scale cooperation would emerge, when peasants saw a need for it, and would lead to a new type of cooperative system that was more suitable for China's rural conditions.

The historic Document no.1 of 1982, ratified at the National Agricultural Conference held 5–21 October 1981, acknowledged the fait accompli that more than 90 percent of production teams had practiced various forms of *chengbao*. More importantly, it was also an official ideological affirmation of the IHC. Contrasting with previous ambiguity in terms of the nature of *chengbao*, especially in the form of the IHC, the document explicitly asserted the significance of *chengbao* for restructuring China's agricultural production relations. The sweeping spread of *chengbao* in the rural areas, the document explained, reflected billions of peasants' desire for a socialist agriculture that fit China's rural conditions better. According to the document, *chengbao* broke the rigid organization of production and overcame the deeply ingrained "eating rice in a big pot" problem, both of which meant a partial but substantial adjustment of the current production relations.

As far as the IHC was concerned, Document no. 1 abandoned the previous official position of viewing it as an expedient measure for poor areas and stated explicitly that no form of the contract, whether with groups, or with individual households, or even with individuals, was necessarily related to the level of the productive forces. This implied that the peasants in any area, whether poor or prosperous, could choose any form of *chengbao*, as long as they saw it as conducive to production and their welfare. The party, therefore, granted peasants adequate flexibility in determining ways of handling production and distribution. All of these, the document claimed, would not change the nature of the collective economy, for two reasons: (1) Land was still collectively owned, and the peasants enjoyed only the right to use it; and (2) peasants were bound by contract with collectives, namely, production teams, which represented the state to supervise the peasants to fulfill the state plan.

Document no.1 endorsed all forms of *chengbao*, including the IHC. But its actual effect was to stimulate the introduction of the IHC anywhere and everywhere. By early 1982, 94 percent of production teams in China had practiced the IHC (without the production team's conducting accounting), leaving other forms of *chengbao* behind. The party also seemed ready to accept the IHC as an alternative to the existing agricultural organization. There were two important meetings at the top level regarding agricultural reform that year. In October, the Central Committee sponsored a conference on rural ideological work. Wan Li (*XHS*, 24 December 1982), then the vice premier in charge of agricultural affairs, in his speech, openly and unequivocally identified the IHC as a road of socialist agricultural development with Chinese characteristics. The core of the IHC, he emphasized, could be summed up in a word, namely, *contracting (bao)*, which closely connected peasants' incomes with their work and therefore truly realized the socialist principle of distribution—from each according to his ability, to each according to his work. He believed that contracting had changed the status of the peasants in the collective economy—from simple producers to both producers and operators of production—and made them the real masters of the rural economy. Pointing out the embryo voluntary cooperations among individual households, he seemed optimistic about the emergence of a new model of socialist agriculture out of the IHC.

Du Runsheng also made a speech at this meeting (Du 1985). Recognizing the friction between the IHC and the CCP's ideology, he held that current policies were not necessarily derived from ideological commitment. For him, maintaining communist commitment was one thing, and making current policies was another. They did not have to be consistent. His logic, which was shared by a large number of reformers, was that current policies did not have to have any explicit moral implications for communism; as long as they could promote production, they could be seen as a step toward communism. Was not communism, after all, seen by Marx as a system with highly developed productive forces? Thus, while admitting that the IHC and other pragmatic rural policies were not communist in nature, Du portrayed them as "practices at the current stage of socialism" and as imperative for China's transition to communism. He advocated that China should adopt various policies with "the highest elasticity" to foster rural modernization.

Out of this meeting emerged a new perspective, which passed in a Politburo meeting in December 1982 and was spelled out in Document no. 3 of 1983. The document, entitled *Some Questions concerning Current Agricultural Economic Policies*, interpreted *chengbao* for the first time, especially in the form of the IHC, as a new development of Marxist agricultural cooperative theory in China's practice. The document defined *chengbao* as a form of agricultural cooperation, which could "overcome the disadvantages of over-centralized management, the inefficiency of large work groups, and egalitarianism" and "best suited the present situation in which manual labor predominated." It particularly emphasized the difference between *chengbao* and the former small-scale individual economy based on private ownership (*ZYWX* 1987, 172–73). In short, the document finally legitimated *chengbao* ideologically.

The single most important institutional change brought about by the IHC was the dismantlement of the commune system. The

People's Commune, to a large extent, was an ideological artifact. It epitomized the CCP's attempt to impose a unitary public ownership as a step toward communism. Its failure indicated a wide gap between ideological fundamentals and social reality. The IHC effectively eroded the commune system. Indeed, as key decisions as to what to produce, and to whom to sell products and for what price shifted to peasant households, communes existed in name only. It seemed that in 1983 the party leadership reached a consensus that the commune system did not fit China's agricultural productive forces and should be changed. Document no. 3 of 1983 officially proposed to remove the economic functions of communes and convert them into township governments (*xiangzhengfu*), which would handle only administrative affairs. Given that economic management had dispersed to households, the document stipulated that whether to retain or abolish the commune as an economic organization should be left to peasants to decide. We do not know whether the Chinese peasants werereally involved in any serious discussions of this matter. The fact is that by 1985 communes vanished from China's countryside.

The Long-Term Contract: Its Implications

Document no. 3 of 1983 marked a significant conceptual change in the CCP regarding agricultural ownership. As we have noticed, the IHC initially was treated by the leadership as an expedient measure for some poor areas. There were strong feelings among the top leaders that this was a method of last resort (*meiyou banfa de banfa*) that was ideologically questionable though practically acceptable for a time. As the IHC increasingly showed its strength, and more and more areas tended to take to it, the leadership considered it as a form of economic organization complementary to the existing collective economy. In other words, the top leadership did not legitimate the IHC by identifying it with socialism until it became a *fait accompli* in most of China's countryside. In document no. 3, the IHC was no longer perceived as peripheral to the collective economy. Rather, it was defined explicitly as a new type of collective economy, characterized by combining public ownership of the land with totally individualized operations of production. To the leadership, such an arrangement retained public ownership while providing strong working incentives and productive freedom for peasants. The document indicated that control over the most essential means of production, namely, land, was still fundamental to the CCP's claim for socialism. However, such an arrangement assumed that ownership of the land was not a factor that would affect production. However, as later experience demonstrated, individual producers without ownership rights of the land had little interest in long-term investment in the land. This was manifested in a tendency toward predatory land use by its new occupiers, who, in fear that it would be taken away again, treated it as a short-run asset and failed to replace soil nutrients or invest in improvements (Riskin 1987).

The structural weakness of the IHC challenged the rationality of individualized production based on collectively owned land. This strained the ideology, which had established public land ownership as a fundamental principle.

It did not take too long for the policy makers to realize that the peasants' shortsighted behavior was caused by the separation of land use rights from land ownership rights. The Central Rural Work Conference in 1984 presented a solution, another Document No. 1, in which the three- to five-year land contracts were extended to more than fifteen years. It allowed to prolong the land contract from 3-5 years to above 15 years (*XHS*, 1987). This new decision was intended to enhance peasants' confidence in the IHC and encourage their long-term concern with the land. Legally, according to the document, the land was still collectively owned. But the land contracts were believed to be long enough to arouse peasant interest in improving and investing in the land. Such an arrangement, policy makers believed, could make the IHC more rational and efficient, while preserving an image of socialist ownership.

Even though this arrangement of long-term land contracts excluded private property in title, it already had some features of private property, such as exclusive use rights and ownership of surplus product over a longer period of time. In other words, the long-term contractual arrangement amounted to the creation of a quasi-private ownership. Nominally, the contract was not in perpetuity. The length of the responsibility contract varied considerably across different regions or for different types of crops. But there was a clear tendency for contracts to have longer terms. In some regions, local authorities stipulated no time limitation at all in order to assure peasant confidence in the IHC. With the passage of time, contract holders gradually assumed that they had an implicit perpetual right. This policy, as Wan Li explained, was "necessary to encourage the peasants to make investments in the land and increase soil fertility" (*BJZB*, 27 February 1984, 21). Given that their apparent merits were compatible with the logic of the IHC, long-term land contracts in effect further diluted the collective ownership of the land. The state remained the collector of a "property tax," but its control over the land was largely nominal and had only tenuous impact on the peasants' long-term use of the land.

Extending the land contracts suggested the CCP's recognition of the role of private property rights in the new agricultural organization. This was a logical outcome of the IHC. Although the IHC initially was not intended to change property relations, it was the starting point of the change. By capturing incomes from the land under their exclusive use, peasants were able to accumulate their own private property. According to a report by the Development Institute (1988), by 1985 the average value of the fixed productive assets, housing, cash, savings, and excessive grain owned per household had amounted to 3,812.77 yuan. It was estimated that entire amount of rural household assets in the country reached over 700 billion yuan. What underlay the IHC was apparently the logic of private ownership, but this logic could not work well in the long run within a framework that was essentially incompatible with it. The problem that lay with the IHC was that it was characterized by individualized farming on the basis of state-owned land. Document no. 1 of 1984 aimed at solving this problem by granting the peasants the collective-owned land for long-term private use. It sanctioned quasi-private ownership of the land, thereby pushing decollectivization of the rural economy further ahead.

The IHC and the Land System: Search for New Alternatives

The IHC was one of the major factors that generated the first sustained growth spurt in Chinese agriculture since collectivization and significantly increased the peasants' income level as well (see tables 4.1 and 4.2).[18]

Table 4.1 Agricultural Performance, 1957–78 and 1978–84
Per capita output kilograms

Year	Grains	Cotton	Edible oil	Meat (pork, beef, mutton)	Aquatic Products (fish, seafood)
1957	306	2.5	6.6	6.3	4.9
1978	319	2.3	5.5	9.0	4.9
1984	397	5.9	11.6	14.9	5.9

Average growth rates in percentages
(Per capita annual growth rate in parentheses)

1957–78	2.1 (0.2)	1.3 (–0.6)	1.0 (–0.9)	3.7 (1.7)	1.9 (0.0)
1978–84	4.9 (3.8)	18.7 (17.5)	14.6 (14.0)	10.1 (9.0)	4.6 (3.3)

Source: Selden 1988, 170.

Table 4.2 Rural Per Capita Net Income, 1978-1985
(Percentage Distribution)

Income Group	1978	1980	1981	1982	1983	1984	1985
Over 500 yuan		1.6	3.2	6.7	11.9	18.2	22.3
400-500	2.4	2.9	5.0	8.7	11.6	14.1	15.8
300-400		8.6	14.4	20.8	22.9	24.5	24.0
200-300	15.0	25.3	34.8	37.0	32.9	25.6	25.6
100-200	49.2	51.8	37.9	24.1	19.3	11.3	11.3
Below 100	33.3	9.8	4.7	2.7	1.4	0.8	1.0
Average Income	133.6	191.3	223.4	270.1	309.8	355.3	397.6

Source: State Statistical Bureau (cited from Selden 1988). Data for 1979 are not recorded.
Note: Net income is based on a calculation of the value of income in kind plus cash income.

After several years of spectacular success, however, the IHC began to display its weaknesses (see Development Institute 1988; Wen 1989; Zhou and Du, SJJJDB, 25 April 1988; Li 1989). First, the IHC reduced the scale of agricultural operation. As some social scientists commented, under the IHC China's peasant household became the smallest in the world, with per household arable land of less than 0.51 hectares. Besides working on the land, most households were more or less involved in other operations, such as transportation, sideline production, commerce, and industry. All these operations further decreased the scale of production. The small scale of production made peasant households vulnerable to price fluctuations and tended to pull them back to "self-sufficiency" in order to minimize the negative effect of markets. Thus, according to many policy specialists and social scientists, the current IHC had turned out to hinder the further commodification of the rural economy, as intended by the reform.

Second, as opposed to the original design of contracting out pieces of land according to the labor force, in most places land was distributed according to family size. That meant, for instance, that a seven-member household with five laborers was granted the same amount of land as a household with two laborers. This met the egalitarian distributive principle but led to a less efficient use of land. Policy makers noticed this phenomenon. A commentary in *Hongqi* (May 1987) reflected the official concern that under the current IHC arrangement the scale of land operation was constantly diminishing. The negative effects of this on agricultural producltion were twofold: Small scale operation (1) caused the waste of both land and labor, since the household with fewer laborers could not make sufficient use of land while the household with more laborers did not have enough land to work, and (2) made agricultural mechanization and the maintenance and construction of rural infrastructures difficult.[19]

Third, for some policy researchers, even the long-term land contract could not assure peasants' confidence in the IHC. The prolonged duration of the land contract, after all, was only a policy rather than a law. Peasants' confidence varied with the political climate. In addition, the long-term contract still could not eliminate land abuse. Many peasants demonstrated little interest in long-term investment in the land, and conducted "predatory production," resulting in soil degeneration.

Fourth, the IHC failed to specify property relations. In theory, the collectives owned land on behalf of the state. But as Li Yining (1989, 28), a well-known economist, asked, Who represented the collective? The commune? It had already ceased to exist. The township government (*xiang zhengfu*)? It was an administrative agency that only nominally represented the collective. As Li pointed out, village cadres became the real owners of the land. There was strong evidence, Li went on, that cadres from the village bureaucracy or state agencies tended to force the peasants to share with them their net profit. This was done through ad hoc taxes or arbitrarily increased fees for all purposes, like "voluntary" contributions for building new roads or other public facilities. Cadres also tended to act on personal interests by abusing the power to make contracts with peasants and engaging in racketeering in the name of the collective, against the peasants. Another researcher (Zhou 1988) showed that the assets turned over to the collective by the peasants under the contract were terribly mismanaged in many places. Bookkeeping and account squaring just did not exist in some villages. A national account inspection conducted by the Ministry of Agriculture, Animal Husbandry, and Fishery, from the first half of 1985 to the middle of 1986, revealed that the collective assets appropriated by village cadres, by various means, reached 60 billion yuan. All these phenomena were related to obscure property relations in which peasants were still denied one essential property right—the right to claim residual profit (Krug 1991).

It was normal that any social practice, while aiming to solve certain problems, was likely to generate some others. This was just the case with the IHC. People began to seek new solutions, which could address two silent and overlapping issues: dispersion of land and ambiguity of property relations. New instrumental principles emerged, motivated by new needs for problem solving.

Transfer of Contractual Rights

China's reform attempted to solve the problems without losing its the image of being socialist. For example, to prevent dispersion of land, Du Runsheng (1985) suggested a concentration of land in the hands of 30 to 40 percent of skillful peasants by transferring contractual rights. The transfer of contractual rights could be achieved through negotiations among involved parties and should be ratified by collectives. Land ownership rights, he emphasized, still belonged to collectives and were forbidden from free sale. What about those peasants who yielded their land? Du expected that the expanding rural and township industries would gradually absorb them. To encourage the concentration of land in the hands of fewer skillful peasants was actually an official policy from 1984 on. But in practice this proved difficult. One reason was that, for most peasants, land operation had a function of "social insurance."[20] They perceived land as a stable source of income. Unless nonagricultural income exceeded that from land and became enduringly stable, the peasants would not easily give up their land. Consequently, as a survey showed,[21] in two years only 0.7 percent of arable land was transferred among households.

Party decision makers set the state's legal ownership of the land as a bottom line for agricultural reform. As a result, the selling of land in the market was forbidden, and all party documents regarding agricultural reform banned the buying and selling of land, seeing it as a development that would have meant the dismantling of socialism in the countryside. As Du (1985, 229) claimed, public ownership rights of land were a fruit of many years of revolutionary struggle and should not be given up. On the other hand, decision makers realized the importance of transferability of land as a production factor; without it the IHC could lose its momentum in sustaining agricultural growth. Permission to transfer contractual rights was an innovation to prevent the dispersion of the land. It virtually emulated the logic of private ownership. Transferability was believed in Western economics to be a basic feature of private property. As many Western economists assumed, it provided incentives for resources to move from less-productive to more-productive owners. Although the transfer of contractual rights in China was not tantamount to a capitalist-style transfer of ownership rights, it was a functional equivalent of the transferability of private ownership rights and could also hurt the weak in society.

Commoditizing the Land

While party decision makers believed that the problem of land transfer should be solved outside the market, some policy researchers suggested the contrary. The Development Institute, a branch of the Center of Rural Development of the State Council, completed a set of research projects in 1986 aiming to find the way out of the baffling IHC.[22] Based on firsthand findings from different localities, the authors of these reports expressed a consensus that the current land system no longer fit the IHC arrangement, and that without an "institutional innovation" (*zhidu chuangxin*) of the land system, the vitality of the IHC would be exhausted. They suggested, as a solution, that land be commoditized.

Commoditizing land, as Yang Jinglun pointed out (Development Institute, 1988, 195), meant to treat it as a commodity eligible for market exchange. The object in this transaction, Yang emphasized, was land ownership rights. According to him, when all land belonged to one owner (the state), it was not a commodity; but if commoditizing land had to rely on a system where private ownership of land prevailed, how, then, could it be applicable to China? Yang suggested a "quasi-commodification" (*zhun shangpinhua*) arrangement. Under this arrangement, what would enter the market for exchange was not land ownership rights but land use rights. That is, while the state's macro-control over land was to be retained, the right to use the land would be completely privatized and allowed to go to the market for trading and renting. Such an arrangement, Yang argued, had three main advantages. First, by a compensable transfer of rights of use, those peasants who yielded land could receive a market-determined payment that might help them to start a business. This would provide a new incentive mechanism by which the peasants might be encouraged to shift to nonagricultural operations. This would speed a benign separation of the peasants from the land, which was imperative for rural modernization. Second, as use rights were commoditized, land would move to the hands of those peasants who had more funds and a stronger interest in land operation. With this development, a more optimal allocation of land would grow and break the land distribution structure based on number of family members. Third, by the same token, land renting would transfer land to skillful peasants and therefore lead to the best use of the land. A renting practice might be good for both renters and tenants: It would make them feel more secure because they could take land back when the lease expired; and tenants needed only to pay a certain amount of rent, which was far below the price for a land transfer, to have more land to farm. In short, the "quasi-commodification of land," as Yang explained, could facilitate an optimal combination of land, capital, and human resources and could bring about efficient economies of scale.

Under the quasi-commodification arrangement, state ownership of land would become purely nominal, while the collective would be eliminated as the state's representative in land ownership. State ownership of land would manifest itself basically in the sphere of macroregulation of land, which might include prerogatives such as land planning, resource preservation, issuance of land-use licenses, supervision of land use, regulation of land price, requisition of land, protection of the legal rights of land users, arbitration of land disputes, and so on.

In contrast with the official policy of contractual rights transfer, which was usually administratively implemented, the recommendation of quasi commodification was intended to introduce the market mechanism to promote land transfer. In doing so, it proposed almost total independence of use rights from ownership rights, that is a substantial dilution of state ownership of land. In fact, except for retaining state ownership in title, the quasi commodification proposal basically followed capitalist methods of land operation, emphasizing efficiency over equality.

Land Bidding

For some economists, the worst defect of the existing land system was that it hindered an optimal combination of land, capital, and labor. They argued that equal distribution of land according to the number of family members restricted the movement of land to more-productive peasants. The transfer of land among peasants of the same village, let alone across villages, was very difficult. That meant that one of China's scarcest resources—land—was being wasted due to its improper combination with labor and capital. This land system was supposed to be egalitarian, but the egalitarianism it embodied was false. Villages varied in the land acreage and population size. Therefore, an equal distribution of land immediately became meaningless beyond the boundary of a given village, since peasants in different villages might be given different amounts of land. Some villages and township governments pushed the process of transferring more land to more capable peasants. But this was done through government selection and maneuver rather than market mechanisms. Moreover, the transfer was confined to the peasants in the same village and therefore excluded competitors from outside villages. Thus, under the current land system of the IHC, some capable peasants could "monopolize" partial-use land in a village against their more capable counterparts from the outside.

According to Wen (1989), a solution was to use land bidding to encourage the optimal combination of land and labor. To do so, he thought, it was necessary to divide the land into two parts. One part, which he called the "food field" (kouliangtian), would be given to peasant households permanently to guarantee their basic livelihood. The other part, the "responsibility field" (zeren tian), would be returned to a village committee of land management as contracts expired. The committee then would invite bids on the land, which, divided into pieces, could go to the highest bidders. The bidding process should be open to any potential bidders from different geographical areas. In this arrangement, the peasants who failed to bid for a responsibility field would not suffer too much because they could still live on food fields for a living. Their failure in bidding, Wen asserted, might force them to improve their farming methods or to look for other opportunities in nonagricultural sectors. Both would be good for China's rural modernization.

The land-bidding proposal made rural property ambiguous. Under this arrangement, the ownership rights to food fields belonged to the peasants in perpetuity. But it was not clearly specified who should own responsibility fields and where the rents would go. In a sense, this proposal advocated a mixed land system in which private ownership and a certain form of communal ownership (namely, village committees) would coexist. However, the trading of responsibility fields was basically capitalistic.

Private Ownership Based on the Nationalization of Land

In 1989, Li Yining proposed private land ownership based on nationalization. According to the proposal, reform of China's existing land system would take two steps. The first was to nationalize all land and abolish the collective ownership of land. Second, after the nationalization, each piece of land should have an owner. That is to say, each peasant would be granted a piece of land permanently. Peasants would enjoy full rights to keep, rent out, sell, or give away their land. Their offspring could inherit the land. Given that the state would be the ultimate owner, the state's ownership rights of land would be manifested in three respects: Only with the state's ratification could peasants (1) shift land from an agricultural to a nonagricultural use, (2) rent out or sell land to nonagricultural users, or (3) rent out or sell land to foreigners.

Li believed that this arrangement, if implemented properly, could solve problems brought on by the IHC and make it more effective. First, permanent rights to dispose of land would consolidate the peasant confidence in the IHC and also would create a precondition for the mobility of land resources. Li predicted that, with the implementation of this proposal, land trade and rental would flourish and thereby accelerate the concentration of land ownership and use in peasants who had funds and abilities. In this process, some types of household farms might emerge and become dynamic agencies of rural modernization. Second, the state's ultimate ownership of the land would effectively check land abuse, the tendency to use land for nonagricultural purposes, such as building private houses, factories, brick kilns, and so on. Nationalization of the land granted the state the legitimate power to regulate land and could arrest the rapid decrease of arable land caused by land abuse.[23] Third, given the fact that the collective ownership of land in many localities had been perverted into "cadre ownership," its termination would give peasants a real freedom in terms of productive operations.

Like the quasi commodification of the land, Li's proposal also based China's rural economy on the working of de facto private ownership. Although he argued that his proposal was not about privatization, the property relations he designed for China's rural economy virtually followed capitalistic logic. He seemed to think that an emphasis on the state's ultimate ownership rights of the land could distance his proposal from a capitalistic one. But his defiinition of regulation as the main function of state ownership rights, failed to distinguish his proposal from a capitalistic one, since almost all modern capitalist states also regulated economies for differing purposes.

It was evident that since 1985 China's reform leaders, policy researchers, and social scientists had begun to focus their attention on the land ownership system. This process was driven by the logic of the IHC, which, while bringing remarkable agricultural growth, intensified the contradiction between individualized farming and collective land ownership. The basic aim of the IHC was to stimulate productivity. The assumption underlying the IHC was the one undergirding Western liberal economics, that is, that individual wealth-maximizing behavior is a motor of economic growth. By giving the peasants relative discretionary power to dispose of land, the IHC was an institutional arrangement to accommodate and, indeed, to encourage the peasants' wealth-maximizing behavior. The IHC had been defined as socialist in nature because it was situated in a framework of a collective-ownership land system. But once the individual wealth-maximizing behavior was set in motion, it moved to contradict the concept behind collective ownership and to generate difficulties that were hard to overcome in the framework of existing property relations. Thus, the call for a thorough reform of the land system was in fact a logical progression from the IHC.

The policy recommendations described above reflected the view that the IHC had brought the current land system into question. They also shared in common the idea that the reform of the land system should aim at promoting productivity, even at the expense of egalitarian distribution principles. The official sanction for the transfer of contractual rights, though it excluded land trading in markets, already shook property relations by allowing a redistribution of land among the peasants according to funds and abilities. Collective ownership of land existed only in title, as a symbol of socialism. But a land transfer based on nonmarket mechanisms proved inefficient. Thus, the other three proposals mentioned above, though designed differently, all attempted to introduce market mechanisms to foster an optimal combination of land resources, capital, and labor. But the optimal combination of productive factors was possible only when peasants could treat land as their property. Hence, the three proposals, while not asking for a repudiation of public ownership of the land, advocated the transfer to the peasants of substantial power of land disposal, which amounted to de facto ownership rights. Formally, in their suggestions, the state would remain the owner of the land. But the function of state ownership wold be reduced to regulation. The state would be disengaged from all disposal powers of land, leaving production, distribution, and allocation to markets. However, state regulation was by no means unique to socialism, and it in fact could work well in systems where private ownership dominated. People therefore could legitimately ask where the difference lay between their proposals and private ownership of the land. Apparently these liberal proposals wanted to push the IHC to its logical extent and rely on a de facto private property rights arrangement to facilitate rural modernization.

Predicament and Limitations: An Uncertain Future

The agricultural reform significantly altered property relations in the countryside of China. From the beginning, as shown in this chapter, the CCP confronted the dilemma of how to reconstruct agricultural organization without abandoning socialist fundamentals. The dire economic situation in the countryside and peasants' strong desire for change pushed the CCP to emphasize practical needs over ideological principles and hence to sanction policy adjustments. However, this remarkable change took place under the banner of "socialism with Chinese characteristics." The CCP legitimated a sharp retreat from public ownership in agricultural production and permitted a substantial penetration of capitalistic property relations into the countrysid, as a practical adjustment between the relations of production and the productive forces. This policy orientation created a host of problems that further stimulated capitalistic solutions.

However, a difficulty for the CCP was that it was not able to bear the social and political consequences brought about by ideological fragmentation. As an editorial in *The People's Daily* (13 July 1991) complained, the rural reforms led to confusions among cadres and the masses about socialism; the sense of responsibility to the state and to the collective disappeared among some peasants; quite a few rural basic-level party organizations were paralyzed; a large number of party cadres and party members could not play a vanguard role; capitalist ideas gained ground; and feudalist vestiges began to flourish. All of these shook up the party's authority in the rural areas. It was self-evident that they were related to the pragmatic policies that sought economic growth by relaxing state control and to the ideological reformulation undertaken to justify policy flexibility.

The leadership apparently could not undo these maladies by reversing the reform, which would damage peasant interests and cause a decline of production. Yet the leadership was also deeply concerned that, as capitalistic methods were exercised extensively, the party would eventually lose control over the rural areas. As a result of this predicament, the CCP decided in early 1991 to conduct socialist education in the rural areas. The main purposes of this activity, as stated by a central party official in charge of it, were to "take over the rural areas with socialist ideas," "strengthen the vanguard role of party branches," and "enhance peasants' concern with the state and collectives" (*RMRB*, 12 July 1991). By sending six hundred thousand county cadres to rural areas to undertake propaganda work, the central leadership wished to help peasants realize that "only socialism can save China" and "only socialism can develop China" (RMRB, 13 July 1991).

In a talk with provincial participants in a workshop held in Beijing, Jiang Zemin, the Party General Secretary, affirmed as a long-term task the education of peasants with socialist ideas (RMRB, 15 November 1991). It was ironic to talk about socialist ideas when socialist fundamentals, through its pragmatic and divergent interpretations, were virtually collapsing and capitalist practices were officially sanctioned in the rural areas. This self-contradiction was unavoidable, and in fact the leadership needed a fundamental-instrumental discrepancy to maintain its two imperative but conflicting goals in the rural areas: preserving a socialist image of the rural economy and improving economic performance through market-driven reforms. But it was questionable whether this discrepancy could be sustained in the long run. Compared with industries, the fundamental-instrumental discrepancy in the rural economy had reached its maximum, in the sense that agricultural production and distribution had been totally privatized. The next logical step—the formal privatization of land—could formally extinguish the last fundamental principle of the rural collective economy. Nobody knows whether and when China's current leadership will take this step. But the IHC, implemented by this leadership, has created many new problems, in response to which privatization of land seems to be a logical development.

5
Reforming State Ownership

In a talk in 1989 with Milton Friedman, Zhao Ziyang, the CCP's general secretary at that time and a reformist leader, outlined China's plan for the reform of state ownership. Zhao described this plan, already under way since 1979, as comprising five steps that had been, or would be, taken by the CCP: (1) to expand the autonomy of state-owned enterprises (SOEs) (*kuoda qiye zizhuquan*); (2) to decrease the tax rate from enterprises and concede profits to enterprises (*jiansui rangli*); (3) to carry out "tax for profit" (*li gai sui*); (4) to implement the contract system (*chengbao zhi*); and finally, to transform China's SOEs into shareholding enterprises (*gufeng jingji*) (Chen 1990, 30).

Basically this was the line China's reform of state ownership had followed. However, it was by no means a blueprint that the CCP had designed for state ownership reform at the very beginning. As a matter of fact, there was no discernible plan when the CCP started to reform SOEs; each of these steps was taken to solve the problems left by a previous one. Each step involved complex policy and technical difficulties that created contending approaches as to how the reform should be carried out. On the other hand, the reform of SOEs was far more than a concrete policy or technical problem. It involved some major ideological adjustments--each of these steps was generated by,

97

and also generated, new conceptualizations or reevaluations of state ownership. This chapter examines the interactions among the conceptual innovations and policy changes in each step of the state ownership reform. It also investigates the process and political implications of the fragmentation of doctrinal ideas about state ownership.

Problems of China's State Ownership before the Reform

State ownership was the backbone of China's socialist economy. Its rationale, according to Xue Muqiao (1981, 55), lay in the claim that it "represents the common interests of the people throughout the country," on the one hand, and "conforms to the needs arising from the development of modern industry," on the other. By enforcing state ownership, China had achieved a twofold goal: eliminating capitalist exploitation and establishing an industrial foundation. The most outstanding feature of China's state ownership system was its ability to mobilize resources, both physical and human, to generate a relatively high rate of economic growth. Indeed, from 1949 to 1979, total industrial output value went up 42.5 times, and the portion from heavy industry rose 98.6 times (Zhou 1985, 44–45). Under state ownership, 84,000 industrial enterprises had been built since 1949, with a gross output of 372 billion yuan (World Bank 1983, 121).

However, the massive buildup of productive forces during the pre-reform decades did not yield sufficient "economic results" in terms of raising living standards, technological modernization, and productive efficiency. The most troublesome problem under China's state ownership system was the gap between the government's rising investment in state enterprises and sluggish growth. According to Harding (1987, 31), "The rate of investment, already high during the First Five-Year Plan, had been rising rather steadily even since, from about one-quarter of national output in the mid-1950s to one-third in the early 1970s. But the rates of growth were declining, from 11% to about 8% over the same period." In other words, China's SOEs were requiring more and more investment to obtain smaller and smaller increases in output.[1] The inefficiency of state ownership could also be measured by productivity of SOEs. The increase in national output resulting from each additional 100 yuan in investment fell from 52 yuan to 34 yuan from the 1950s to the early 1970s. Labor productivity in industry, which had risen rapidly during the mid-1950s, increased very slowly thereafter (Harding 1987). CCP top leaders themselves conceded that the inefficiency of the state-run economy was a serious problem. According to Zhao Ziyang (1982, 18), for example, between 1952 and 1980 industrial fixed assets increased 27 times, gross value of industrial and agricultural product 9.1 times, but net domestic material product only 5.2 times. He acknowledged that many features of China's state-run economy were "far from rational."

State Ownership as an Issue of Management

The reform of state ownership was initially raised as an issue of management. In the early years of the reform, party leaders and intellectuals still regarded state ownership as morally desirable and practically workable. For them, China's economic problems lay not in state ownership per se, but in mismanagement of the ownership system. More specifically, the main problem with the present state ownership system lay in the "incorrect relationship between the state (including the central and local authorities) and enterprises" (HQ no. 4, 1982, 32). Under this system, the economy was run mainly by administrative rather than by economic means. This reduced every enterprise to being an appendage of administrative organs, deprived them of independent decision making power, and, therefore, hampered the growth of productive forces. According to this approach, the solution to the inefficiency of China's SOEs was to grant greater power, or more autonomy (zizhuquan) to them.

This approach dominated Sichuan Province's experiment with expanding enterprises' power in 1979, initiated by then provincial party secretary Zhao Ziyang and endorsed by Beijing. At the outset, about one hundred large- and medium-sized SOEs were selected as experimental units. Several measures were taken to readjust the relationship between the state and enterprises. First, by reducing the scope of command planning and increasing that of directive planning and market adjustment, enterprises were given greater autonomy in terms of what and how much to produce. Second, enterprises were allowed to retain profits after they met the state plan. Third, enterprises were granted power to award bonuses to individual workers with good performance. Fourth, enterprises took charge of their own personnel management. As a result, profound change took place in

these selected "spot-testing" enterprises. Of 100 enterprises that conducted the experiment, 84 achieved output growth of 15 percent and
profits growth of 33 percent, compared with their figures for 1978.
Their gross profit far exceeded that of other SOEs that had not yet
started the experiment (Lin 1986, 14). Sichuan's experience was soon
spread to some six thousand large state enterprises throughout the
country (World Bank 1983, 152).

However, the practice of enlarging the decision-making power
of enterprises was not meant to challenge the state ownership system in any sense. Rather, as the party leadership claimed, it aimed at
improving the management of the system. Even so, this practice still
led to a modification of the official theory with regard to the nature
of state ownership and the relationship between the state and enterprises. Would enlarging the decision-making power of enterprises
weaken the state's control over industry and undermine a socialist
economy? Would it violate the principles of socialist production if
enterprises were encouraged to pursue profit above quotas? Would
the autonomy of enterprises lead to the anarchy of production, as
existed in capitalist societies (Lin 1986, 19)? These questions had con-
spicuous ideological implications. Indeed, to make answers favorable
for the ongoing practice, an ideological reformulation was necessary.

Official conceptual readjustment of state ownership at the early
period of the reform centered on the managerial relationship
between the state and enterprises. However, the new conceptualization of this relationship was still based on some fundamentals in
terms of the nature of ownership and the superiority of socialist state
ownership. For example, in an article aiming at justifying the autonomy of enterprises, Yun Xiliang (HQ December 1980, 22–28) began
with an emphasis on the prevailing orthodox definition of the ownership system. According to him, the core of the ownership system
could be reduced to who controlled the means of production. Under
socialism the means of production was owned by working people as
a whole, who nevertheless regulated the means of production
through their representative, the state. State ownership was thus
defined as an economic form by which economic activities were organized according to people's interests.

Though Yun referred to China's ownership system more often
as "ownership by the whole people" than as "state ownership," he
seemed to never doubt the identity of the two in China's context. On
the other hand, the author rejected the view, which he called "one-

sided," that the state's regulation of the means of production on people's behalf meant its overall control of enterprises. Actually, he argued, the state weakened its own managing function by excessively interfering with enterprises' economic activities. Enterprises also lost efficiency while being subordinated to the state's commanding plans. Thus, the way out of the trouble was to give enterprises more autonomy in terms of production management. This would not change the socialist nature of China's state ownership, contended the author, because what enterprises were granted was not the right to own, but the right to manage, the means of production. In other words, the state was still the sole owner of the means of production, and enterprises were just given the right to use the means of production according to the will of people (more accurately, of the state).

However, the modification here of the previous doctrine was subtle but clear: It implied for the first time in the CCP's official publication a possible separation of ownership of the means of production from their actual use. That is, the state's ultimate control over the means of production did not necessarily mean that the state should meddle in the management of enterprises. By arguing that, the author further contended that enterprises could be seen as agencies of the state, and that therefore they could run production in accordance with people's needs. While this article denied that the interests of enterprises were independent from the interests of the state, and failed to specify how enterprises, once given autonomy, could be guaranteed to manage production in people's interests, its argument for a separation of ownership from actual use provided a starting point for further conceptual adjustments and practical innovations.

For some Chinese theorists, justifying the autonomy of enterprises required rejecting a dogma that had prevailed in Chinese economic thinking since 1949: that within the ownership by the whole people, there was no commodity-exchange relation among state-run enterprises. This dogma originated from Stalin's *Economic Problems of Socialism in the USSR.* According to Stalin, exchange value was fundamentally an alien element in the socialist economy but unavoidable due to the fact that there was not yet a single state ownership comprising all sectors of the economy. There still had to be commodity exchanges between the collective and the state enterprises. But within planning domains, "the law of value has no regulating function in our socialist production" (Stalin 1972, 19) or in relation to exchange within the state sector. Thus, commodity relations were seen by Stalin as an outer shell.

The logic was simple here: Commodity exchange could happen only between different owners of the means of production; it lost grounds for existence within the ownership by the whole people, since the state was the single owner of the means of production. Such a "single owner" or "noncommodity exchange" dogma ruled out the necessity of enterprises as independent economic entities in terms of calculating costs and benefits in production. It also legitimated the state's unified allocation of the means of production among enterprises without cost calculation. Worse, this dogma deprived enterprises of the right to retain profits, since they were not independent commodity producers. Thus, Jiang Xuemo (*HQ* June 1980), one of China's leading economists, suggested that recognizing commodity-exchange relations within state ownership should be the prerequisite of enterprise autonomy. According to him, only when enterprises were treated as commodity producers could they have an incentive to increase efficiency. But they were not commodity producers in the sense of being independent owners of the means of production. Rather, they were supposed to assume sole responsibility for the efficient use of the means of production and, thereby, for their own profit or loss related to management.

Obviously, Jiang favored a separation of ownership of the means of production from their actual use. But he differed from Yun in that he went farther to specify that this separation was a result of commodity-exchange relations among enterprises. But for Jiang, as for most Chinese economists at that time, enterprise autonomy was limited to the extent that it did not undermine state plans.

State Ownership as an Issue of State-Enterprise Financial Relationships

Before 1984, the objective of industrial reform, as China's policy makers defined it, was to "stir the enthusiasm" of enterprises and workers. Deprivation of the enterprises' right to retain profits was identified by them as a major obstacle to this objective. Hence enterprise autonomy, to the policy makers, could be realized through a readjustment of the profit distribution between the state and enterprises—that is, by permitting enterprises to retain incentive funds drawn from profits upon completion of planned tasks.

Following Sichuan's experience, China's reform of state ownership moved to nationwide experimentation with expanding enterprise autonomy in terms of profit redistribution. Three steps were taken, each giving greater power to enterprises.

1. *Profit retention (lirun liucheng)*. Profit retention was basically what Sichuan Province had practiced in its experiment. It allowed an enterprise to set up an "enterprise fund" by retaining 3 to 5 percent of its planned profits. Furthermore, to increase retained profits, the enterprise could produce and sell more after fulfilling the state-set target to meet market demands, or it could accept processing jobs through individual arrangements with materials supplied by clients; however, only 15 to 25 percent of the profit earned in excess of planned targets would go to the enterprise itself. Finally, the enterprise was given more depreciation allowances and could increase depreciation rates if production grew. Under the profit retention system, the profit an enterprise could earn was limited. However, a more serious problem was that because an across-the-board profit-sharing ratio was applied, the retained profits had no relation to enterprise management and performance.

2. *Profit contract (lirun chengbao)*. The profit contract was developed as a reform measure to avoid arbitrary imposition of profit shares upon SOEs. Under this system, an enterprise was allowed to negotiate with its administrative superior over the "basic figure" of profit it should deliver to the state. The enterprise could then retain a very high proportion of profits above this basic figure, ranging from 20 to 100 percent, with the retention rates frequently increasing with the degree of overfulfillment. This system aimed at giving SOEs more incentives to make profits; but the negotiation between the government and enterprises could hardly be a rational process, because all the decisions were ad hoc arrangements based on the particular conditions of an enterprise. As a result, "the plea of adverse conditions was almost always a convincing defense against high targets or penalties for non-fulfillment."[2] This led to what J. Kornai termed "soft budget constraint," where SOEs were not forced to be strictly responsible for their losses.[3] In some cases, the financial responsibility was negotiable, while in others the government would automatically cover the losses by subsidies or loans.

3. Tax for profit (li gai shui). Trying to solve the soft constraint problem, China's leadership implemented the "tax for profit" system. This new reform measure substituted a series of taxes paid directly to state treasuries for the previous system of profit deliveries channeled through an enterprise's administrative superior. Under the system, large- and medium-sized SOEs paid a 55 percent profit tax and small ones a progressive income tax, while the government levied an excess profits tax, using 1983 profits as a base. The tax-for-profit system was a big improvement, as it put more constraints on an enterprise's soft budget, increased its incentives, and simultaneously ensured that growing profits would be equitably shared by the state treasury and the enterprise. However, the substitution of tax for profit did not solve the budget constraint problem. In principle, SOEs faced a uniform tax system. But in practice, since tax payment was part of the contract responsibility system, it was still subject to negotiation.

All these measures were intended to invigorate enterprises by the state's yielding a proportion of profits (*rang li*) to the enterprises. Nevertheless, the profit redistribution between the state and enterprises was only part of the overall issue of enterprise autonomy, which required that enterprises have the authority to use their own resources on behalf of their own objectives (Wang et al. 1989, 350). Hence, the further need to expand enterprise autonomy generated a more developed form of the "separation of ownership rights from operating rights"— of the industrial contract system (ICS, *gongye chengbaozhi*).

State Ownership as an Issue of Separation of Ownership and Control

The "separation approach" became the CCP's most important conceptual adjustment undergirding China's policy innovations of the state ownership system since 1984. Decision makers as well as specialists reached the consensus that the management of the means of production was the business of enterprises, that should be relieved from state interference. However, how much autonomy enterprises should enjoy was disputed. Limited autonomy might not be able to redress the intractable problem of inefficiency facing China's industry. On the other hand, state ownership might cease to exist except in name if too much autonomy was granted to enterprises. With this dilemma, the CCP's policy orientation toward the reform of the ownership system was caught between ideological requirement and practical need.

The *Provisional Regulations on Further Extending the Decision-Making Power of the State Industrial Enterprises* issued by the State Council in 1984 (*RMRB*, 12 May 1984) signaled a significant step in SOE reform. According to these regulations, SOEs had the the following rights: to produce for the market after fulfilling their plan; to sell these products as well as overstocked items and goods rejected by state purchasing agencies; to vary the prices of marketed producer goods by up to 20 percent on either side of the state price or to negotiate them with purchasers; to choose their suppliers of state distributed materials, and to pass by the state distribution network and buy raw materials directly from producers. Other expanded powers involved the use of retained profits, leasing and sale of surplus equipment, personal and wage matters, and the formation of joint ventures that cut across official administrative divisions (*ZYWX*, 1987, 207–10). All of these paved the way for the ICS.

The success of the contract system in the countryside had stimulated the thought among Chinese policy makers, and especially intellectuals, in 1981, that this system might also be a solution to intractable problems of state enterprises. Yet the focus at the time on the adjustment of profit sharing between the state and enterprises obscured some other major institutional problems that made ICS difficult.[4] The State Council's new regulations (*RMRB, 12 May 1984*) legitimated enterprise authority over production and operations planning, sales, pricing, materials purchase, management of assets, funds, and personnel, wages, and relations with other establishments. With these discretionary powers, enterprises were situated as relatively independent managing units (*duli jingying danwei*) that could contract with the state.

The ICS indicated some significant changes in ownership rights. Normally, ownership gave the property owner a "bundle of rights," including the right to the income generated by the property, the right to transfer and dispose of the property, the right to control or manage the property, and the right to trade these rights. Under the ICS, these rights were divided between the state as property owner and the contractor as property manager. The state contracted enterprises out to collectives or individuals who took full responsibility for management, while the contractor could retain all the profits after turning over to the state a certain amount set by the contract. Now that the rate of profit handed in to the state was fixed, the possibility of enterprises getting more profits became open-ended. On the other hand, enterprises would be forced to use their own capital to complement the unfulfilled proportion of profit which they were supposed to turn over to the state. Such an arrangement, according to many Chinese commentators, could give enterprises a complete "operating right," and therefore provide them with internal incentives to take full responsibility for their profits or losses (e.g., Gu et al. 1989, 350; Zhou 1987, 94; H. M. Wang et al. 1989, 350–51).

Contracting became the prevailing form of the reform of SOEs after 1984. By December 1988, more than 90 percent of SOEs had implemented the ICS (*SJJJDB*, 19 December 1988, 15), which was a contributing factor to the growth of the gross value of industrial output from 1984 to 1987 (World Bank 1990, 136).

One of the remarkably successful enterprises carrying out the contract system was the Capital Steel and Iron Corporation (CSIC, *shoudu gangtie gongsi*), which in fact became a new official model for Chinese industry, as did Daqing Oil Field, a self-reliance model, in the 1960s and 1970s. A giant enterprise with hundreds of thousand of employees, the CSIC in 1982 experimented with a form of contracting that required it to turn over its profits to the state at a progressively increased annual rate of 7.2 percent, and permitted it to retain whatever was left (Yang 1987, 131). After the implementation of State Council's regulations of 1984, the CSIC enjoyed more autonomy in decisions with regard to production, planning, pricing, sales, and employees' welfare. The state ceased to invest in, or provide any loans, for it. "Self-accumulation, self-improvement and self-development" were claimed by the CSIC as the philosophy of its operation (Yang 1987, 131).

The practice of contracting yielded some economic results that the CSIC was never able to achieve under the previous system. From 1979 to 1986 the CSIC had progressively increased its annual profits by 20 percent. Per capita production of tax and profit increased from 4,717 yuan in 1978 to 12,355 yuan in 1985 and then to 14,396 *yuan* in 1986 (Zhou 1987, 92). The production cost was reduced. Whereas per capita monthly income (including wages and bonuses) in 1978 was 61.15 yuan, it increased to 161.5 yuan in 1986 (Yang 1987, 133). Housing and environmental conditions were also considerably improved. While the CSIC enormously bettered itself from the contracting system, the state was also a beneficiary. According to Zhou Guanwu (1987), the general manager of the CSIC, the CSIC turned over about 88.15 million yuan to the state treasury in 1986, a 139 percent increase over the 368 million yuan in 1978. During only eight years (1979–86), the state received 582 million yuan (including taxes, planned profits, and reinvestment in fixed assets) from the CSIC, a figure 1.6 times higher than the total amount the CSIC had contributed to the state in the previous thirty years.

While the CSIC was typical of collective contracting, some medium- and small-sized state enterprises were contracted out to individuals. In the latter case, which was at the outset tried only in ill-managed enterprises, the individual signed a contract with the government, voluntarily bearing responsibility for running an enterprise that was in deficit or in bad shape. As in collective contracting, the contracted enterprise could retain all profits after turning over taxes and target profits set by contract. The crucial difference from collective contracting, however, was that the individual contractor was given vast personal power, ranging from production management and hiring and firing to setting the level of wages and bonuses. Moreover, corresponding to his or her responsibilities, the individual contractor was also allowed a much higher income level than average workers (I shall discuss this issue in chapter 6).

Ma Shengli, portrayed as a heroic factory manager in China's official media and publications, represented a dramatic success of individual contracting. A former head of the sector in charge of sales, Ma contracted in 1984 to manage the Shijiazhuang Paper Mill, a medium-sized factory that had failed to turn over any profit to the state from 1981 to 1983 and that relied on the state's subsidy for survival. By a drastic reorganization of the factory's managerial system, from diversifying operating methods to tightening the system of rewards and penalties, Ma rescued the factory from the brink of bankruptcy. Whereas the factory still had to ask for 105 thousand yuan "loss subsidy" (kuisun butie) from the state in 1983, in 1985 it turned over to the state 2.2 million yuan in taxes and profits. By 1987, its contribution to the state had reached 3.4 million yuan.[5]

The contract system also took the form of leasing medium- and small-scale shops and factories to individuals (zulinzhi). Under this "state-as-renter" arrangement, potential managers bid on shops or factories, promising to deliver the state a set amount of money over a fixed period. The successful bidder and his or her guarantors were allowed to retain all earnings after paying the contracted amount. The rent could be turned over to the state in the form of profit. If the leased units failed to produce the required amount, the manager and his or her guarantors were responsible for making up the difference (W. Li 1988; Bachman 1990, 279–81). Leasing improved the performance of some shops and factories that had been in bad shape. In Shengyang, for example, 248 industrial, commercial, transportation and construction units were leased out by the government from 1984 to 1987. The leasing experiment multiplied the profits of these units, many of which had suffered losses for a long time and/or were virtually on the brink of bankruptcy. Guan Guangmei's story was a dramatic success. A former ordinary shop assistant in a store in Benxi City, Liaoning Province, Guan leased eight formerly state-owned shops that had suffered losses to form a large commercial group, the Dongming Commercial Group. In two years, five of the eight shops increased their profits by nearly 600 percent and the other three by more than 300 percent (*FBIS*, China, 16 February 1988, 39).

Generally speaking, China's theoretical justification for the ICS did not go beyond the proposition of separating ownership right from operating rights. However, the theoretical discourse since 1985, backed up by some successes in practice, tended toward more pragmatic and flexible explanations of socialist state ownership.

An ideologically, as well as practically, sound justification for the ICS was that this system could improve the public ownership system by increasing its efficiency. Socialist public ownership, especially its leading form—the state economy—had long been vulnerable to Western criticisms of its inability to allocate resources efficiently. For some influential Chinese economists, the ICS represented an alternative that could counter the criticism. This system, as Liu Guangdi (1987, 159) argued, stimulated an optimal use of resources by enterprises. Under such a system, enterprises, constrained by their own interests, were forced or encouraged to become profit maximizers. On the other hand, Liu explained, the contract system would not alter the current ownership system since it did not involve any change in the relations of property rights.

The ICS was also justified as a means of solving the problem of enterprise responsibility. Some Chinese critics had recognized that the basic defect of state ownership lay in the fact that under it nobody took serious responsibility for enterprise operations (see N. Li 1989, 8). In other words, "state-run" virtually became "nobody-run." Li

Zhongfan (1987, 152), an economist from the Commission of the State System Reform, believed that only when an enterprise was given corresponding power (*quan*) and benefits (*li*) could it bear certain responsibility (*ze*) for efficient operations. Li contended that contracting was just a method that could "organically combine power, benefits and responsibility in an enterprise."

Even though the ICS was mainly a pragmatic design for problem solving, it was interpreted as ideologically justifiable. Its practical advantages in remedying maladies with the state ownership system were ironically used to defend rather than to reproach it. For some Chinese theorists, the success of the ICS in China just demonstrated that the socialist state ownership system, contrary to those arguments against the system, could be efficient (Liu 1987, 161). At least, it gave evidence that public ownership could be made efficient (H. M. Wang 1989, 153). The previous defects, it seemed to some theorists, were by no means inherent in state ownership. Rather, they originated from "some artificial restrictions and irrational distribution" imposed on the state ownership system (Wang 1989, 144). This reasoning perfectly paralleled a prevailing official response to the popular suspicions and criticisms of the current system, namely, that the socialist system was superior in nature and that China's problems did not lie in this system but in the failure to bring the superiority of the system into full play, due to some policy mistakes. The increase of industrial efficiency under the contracting system, thus, from the official point of view, provided eloquent proof that socialist state ownership still had great vitality and, perhaps more importantly, it was superior.

However, beneath the ideological defense of state ownership was an intellectual undercurrent to dilute the ideological fundamental of state supremacy in a socialist economy. Some theorists considered a fallacious view that ownership by the whole people must present itself as a state-run economy. As Chang Xiuze (1986, 339) argued, the state virtually did not have the ability to run all of the public means of production because (1) this portion of the means of production was too huge to be directly managed by the state, (2) there was no way for the state to know varying consumer demands crucial for decisions on what and how much to produce, and (3) it was impossible for the state to run, in a single and unified way, numerous enterprises with very different conditions. Thus, it was unrealistic for the state to run, presumedly on the behalf of the whole people, the means of production at the societal level. However, according to Chang, the means of production could be practically run at a more basic level—that of the enterprise, which could be seen as representing a component of the "whole people." In fact, Chang argued, enterprise was the only feasible unit in which people could run the means of production. Chang seemed to justify the ICS by defining it as a form through which people could really, rather than nominally, enjoy the right to run the economy. In reality, however, to expand enterprise autonomy was one thing and to involve people to run the economy was another. Making them identical was only a way of legitimating the practical need to attenuate the state's control over enterprises.

Whereas Chang designated "economic power," an ambiguous term, as being inherent in an enterprise, Zhou Shulian (1987, 141–42), a very prestigious economist who was directly involved in many reform programs, made it explicit that the right to own the means of production was not something completely alien to enterprises. To be an owner of the means of production, he argued, was a prerequisite for an enterprise to become a commodity producer. It was preposterous to recognize an enterprise as a commodity producer but to deny its right to own the means of production. But did it mean that socialist state ownership could be reduced to "enterprise ownership"? Or, put another way, could socialist ownership exist in the form of "enterprise ownership"? Zhou apparently realized the difficulty with these questions. He thus suggested a dichotomous scheme in which the state held an "absolute right" to own the means of production, while enterprises had a "relative" one. Although intended to justify more autonomy for enterprises, this scheme was problematic, because a differentiation between "absolute" and "relative" rights of ownership was difficult in practice, if not impossible.

Leasing enterprises was more controversial. Guan Guangmei was once accused of "taking the capitalist road" (*FBIS*, 1 February 1988, 39). This led to the well-known debate on the "Guan Guangmei phenomenon," which attracted extensive attention in the mass media. The central question in the debate was whether a leased enterprise was a "socialist" or "capitalist" enterprise. A commentator's article in the authoritative *Economic Daily* (*JJRB*, 14 July 1987, 1) reflected the official endorsement of the "Guan Guangmei phenomenon." According to it, to lease enterprises was an effective form of operation under the system of public ownership that conformed with the level of development of the productive forces at the preliminary stage of socialism. Guan Guangmei and a lot of other "Guan Guangmeis" did not change the nature of public ownership of enterprises, since the state still owned the means of production.

The contract system inspired conceptual confusion as well as innovations. This was partly because the CCP wanted to restructure the state ownership system so that it could bring more private as well as social returns, while maintaining the current relations of the ownership system understood as socialist. The separation of ownership and control per se was a dilemma. As Brus and Laski argued (1989), when "control" became more specific and located within the right to manage (the right to determine how to use assets), it covered part of the ownership rights themselves. Thus a real divorce between ownership and control was infeasible. Any degree of even managerial independence from the owner (i.e., the state) was tantamount to attenuation of the substance of ownership. As some Chinese economists observed (e.g., Ji et al. May 1987), even though the purpose of the ICS was not to alter the relations of ownership, it had led to an actual, though partial, partition of ownership rights between the state and enterprises by transferring to the latter the right to dispose of some components of the means of production. However enterprises were to remain state owned. This implied that "the state retained the status of principal, keeping the ultimate power of control over enterprises, whose management remained in the position of an agent acting on the principal's behalf and hence in a dependent position" (Brus and Laski 1989, 124). Thus, managerial rights detached from ownership rights could not liberate enterprises from the subordination of the state.

It was apparent that the ICS was still locked up in the ideological fundamental of emphasizing the superiority of state ownership, which prevented enterprises from having full independence. However, the ambiguous status of enterprises under the ICS created a series of problems for it. First, the ICS reshaped enterprises' behavior by diverting their focus to short-term gains. A contractor was supposed to be responsible for, and therefore only cared about, the enterprise operations for three or five years—a common contractual term. In order to maximize returns in their terms, collective and individual contractors tended to overuse enterprise resources at the expense of long-term development, which some Chinese commentators (e.g., Zheng and Shu 1987, 8) called "plundering production."

Enterprises' eagerness for quick success and instant profit generated their pursuit for the increase of output value, which in turn enlarged the gap between demand and supply that had already existed in China's "scarce economy." In addition, enterprises also tended to increase profits by boosting prices. All of these, to a large extent, were responsible for China's runaway inflation in 1988.[6]

Second, the ICS obscured the relations of ownership rights in the state-run economy and generated the irresponsibilities of enterprises for fund allocation. In the previous system, relations of ownership rights were quite straightforward, because the state owned everything and enterprises were entirely excluded from resource allocations. Under the ICS, however, enterprises were granted the power to allocate funds that they had accumulated for their own use, which meant they had a de facto right to partially own the means of production. On the other hand, enterprises were required to put part of their own retained funds into investment. In other words, enterprises had to lose rights over part of their own resources, which were transformed into the fixed assets that were subject only to the state's disposition (see Su and Jiang August 1988, 29–30). This forced enterprises to deliberately conceal their own property in money terms, or to channel it into consumption funds. In addition, under the ICS, collectives and individuals theoretically should be responsible for both profits and losses of enterprises for which they had signed a contract. But in practice, they benefited from profits while the state had to provide necessary funds to keep enterprises running if they were in the red. That is, the ICS left the "soft budget" problem unsolved.

Third, a general practice among contracted enterprises to spur production was to increase employees' wages, bonuses, and other forms of material rewards, which were responsible for the expansion of the consumption funds.[7] The predicament here was that if the government limited the amount of wages and bonuses issued annually by an enterprise, it would run directly against the primary purpose of the ICS, namely, to increase incomes of both enterprises and individuals while ensuring adequate state revenues. But if there was no certain macrocontrol, the increase in consumption funds would get out of control, disrupting the stability of the national economy in general and the price system in particular.

Undoubtedly, the ICS considerably improved the performance of China's state-owned enterprises. But its limitations were so apparent in 1987 and 1988 that a search for a remedy was under way. Indeed, the greatest significance of the practice of the ICS, as one Chinese economist commented (Chen, *SJJJDB*, 24 October 1988), lay in the fact that the serious problems resulting from it were making more people realize that China must make some thorough structural changes in the state economy. As China's state ownership started to be identified by the reformers as an irrational property rights structure, the doctrinal conception of state ownership further crumbled.

State Ownership: The Property Rights Problem

The property rights problem was raised in 1987 in response to the demand for more enterprise autonomy. The ICS was not intended to change the relations of property rights in SOEs, though it conceded partial de facto property rights to enterprises. In fact, it was only a readjustment of the domain of activities between the state and enterprises. The defects of the ICS generated some new conceptual adjustments, which made property rights as a central issue in the reform of SOEs. This began with a criticism of the "separation approach."

From 1986 to 1988, the separation approach continued to be the CCP's dominating theoretical approach to state ownership. In his report delivered to the Thirteenth National Party Congress of the CCP, Zhao Ziyang highlighted "the separation of ownership right from operating right" as the first important measure for economic reform. He stressed that "this would never change the nature of the ownership by the whole people," rather, "it would only put the superiority of public ownership in full play" (Zhao 1987, 27). In fact, however, due to the problems of the ICS, the separation approach had been under serious challenge since 1987, which led to further fragmentation of the official economic ideology regarding state ownership.

Some Chinese theorists found that the main defect of the ICS was enterprises' deprivation of the ownership rights. For them, an enterprise without the right to own the means of production was not really autonomous from the state. The state's continuing right to dispose of the means of production, specifically fixed assets, hampered enterprises' options in terms of optimal allocation of resources. In fact, a "managing right" detached from an ownership right could only result in its arbitrary use and therefore negatively affect the macroeconomy (Lu 1988, 5). Indeed, this was what happened with the ICS.

Reflection on the ICS led China's economic thinking to under-score property rights as a key to restructuring the state ownership system. The concept of property rights entered Chinese intellectual discourse mainly from the introduction of Western property rights economics, which focused on the impact of alternative institutions (such as property rights) on the allocation of sesources and the flow of innovation. The relatively liberal atmosphere from mid 1987 to early 1989 made property rights a popular analytical and conceptual tool for reevaluating China's state ownership.[8] There appeared to be an emerging consensus among party reformers and liberal intellectu-als that Western property rights economics could throw light on China's reform of socialist public ownership.

With the property rights perspective, problems of the state own-ership system were reidentified in the reformers' circle. The previ-ous criticisms largely centered on the state's having too much centralized power over enterprises, and a diffusion of managerial power was presented as a solution. In general, the relations of prop-erty rights were barely raised as a problem. Rather, most critics claimed in their writings that state ownership reform was by no means intended to touch the prevailing property relations. For those who took the new perspective, however, locating the problems of the current ownership system in a managerial dimension was quite mis-leading. They saw the state's monopoly of property rights in the state-run economy as a fundamental obstacle to economic modernization. By arguing this, they questioned the long-presumed superiority of state ownership as an institution to effectively promote productivity. Here, as Tian Yuan and Zhu Yong (December 1988, 5) argued, a basic misconception must be pointed out: The ownership system was not merely about who owned the means of production, as China's ortho-dox theory interpreted it; it was also about an institutional arrange-ment related to resource allocation. The previous theory, while addressing the political and moral issue of who controlled property, basically ignored the question of the optimal allocation of resources; it simply assumed that state property rights were inherently more rational in terms of planned production than other types of property rights were. Wu Jiaxiang (1988, 33) criticized as "illusory" the doctrine that state property belonged to the people. No single citizen or enter-prise of the PRC, he argued, had true ownership relations with the property of the state-run economy. In short, it was not an exaggera-tion to say that from 1988 to early 1989 China's reformers' circle embraced Western property rights economics, whose conceptual framework was soon widely used in the reassessment of China's state ownership.

The Exclusivity of Ownership

In property rights economics the exclusivity of ownership means that the owner decides what to do with his or her assets and bears sole responsibility for the results of those decisions, be they benefits or costs. Property rights theory thus assumes a strong link between one's rights and one's responsibilities as a property owner. The exclusivity of ownership generates strong incentives for the owner to seek the highest-valued use for his or her resources. Clearly this concept was constructed to justify private ownership. But to many Chinese theorists it became relevant to dissect the defects of socialist state ownership. In a report (Ji et al. 1987, 4–15) written by a research team of the Chinese Economic System Reform Research Institute, China's state ownership was criticized as a system that discouraged enterprises by monopolizing ownership rights. It argued that ownership rights became meaningless when there was only one owner of property (i.e., the state). Only when enterprises became independent owners of property could they be concerned with efficiency and could their competition in turn generate optimal resource allocation. Wu Jiaxiang (1988, 4) emphatically stated that exclusivity was necessary for an explicit right of ownership. One major defect of China's state ownership, according to him, was the obscurity of property rights, stemming from the lack of exclusivity. The practice of separating ownership from operation rights did not solve the worst problems of state ownership caused by enterprises' deprivation of property rights. Rather, it created relative discretionary powers, which, unconstrained by property rights, tended to capture quick gains by misusing state property (*SJJJDB*, January, 1989, 12).

The Transferability of Ownership

Property rights economics emphasized the owner's right to transfer assets at mutually agreed upon terms. The transferability

116

CHAPTER 5

of ownership provides incentives for resources to move from less-productive to more-productive owners. China's prevailing state ownership, however, blocked any form of transferability of ownership and
thereby made optimal movement of productive factors impossible
(Tian and Zhu December 1988, 5). The concept of ownership transferability permeated Chinese economic thinking so deeply that many
people started to regard it as "an inevitable trend in the development
of the socialist commodity economy in China" (*XHS*, 11 January 1988).

In a conference held in Wuhan in January 1988, a consensus
was reached among officials, specialists, scholars, and entrepreneurs
that the property rights trading mechanism would provide extensive
opportunities for the growth of a contingent of outstanding enterprises and, thereby, make possible the efficient use of fixed assets
that had accumulated in China over the past thirty years (*ZGTXS*, 19
January 1988). In fact, property rights transfer among enterprises
materialized into a policy at the local and ministerial levels. Beijing,
Shengyang, Wuhan, and other cities opened enterprise auction markets. The Ministry of Light Industry issued documents to encourage
well-managed enterprises to buy those that suffered losses (*ZGTXS*,
19 January 1988).

Transaction Costs

Transaction costs are the costs of all the resources required to
transfer property rights from one economic agent to another.
Property rights economists evaluate the efficiency of an institutional
arrangement by measuring the transaction costs involved. While
admitting that transaction costs are high even under capitalism, property rights economists assert that private owners have both the right
and the incentive to reduce them. Yet, a socialist state-run economy
has an inherent tendency to increase transaction costs by (1) prepar-
ing economic plans; (2) monitoring their execution; and (3) cheating
and lying to bureaucratic superiors (Pejovich 1990, 110). These arguments were echoed in the criticisms of state ownership by Chinese
commentaries. Some pointed out, for example, that the enterprises'
efforts to appeal to the government for more supplies or favorable
conditions increased transaction costs. In addition, in order to main-
⋯al treatments of enterprises with different conditions, the
⋯ner of property had to assign a different tax rate

to each enterprise. The negotiation between the state and numerous enterprises for a mutually acceptable tax rate involved very high transaction costs (Yang and Xu 1989, 25).

Property rights economics provided Chinese economists with an entirely new conceptual tool and approach to assess China's economic system and, more importantly, with strong arguments for a radical change in state ownership. Before 1987, reformist leaders and intellectuals basically identified the reform of state ownership as a managerial problem. From 1988, they started to appeal to a fundamental restructuring of the property rights system. Some of them even urged a "property rights revolution" (Chen, *SJJJDB*, 24 October 1988, 4).

Three major alternatives emerged from the strong consensus that a new property rights system should be established. One was to displace the old state ownership with a joint-stock–like system in which property rights would be shared by enterprises, as well as by the central and local governments. The state remained a major, but no longer the sole, owner of property in a state-run economy. In other words, the state possessed the major portion of shares, while enterprises were also shareholders. This would break the unitary form of the prevailing property rights system in a state-run economy.

The second proposed alternative was to change state ownership into enterprise ownership, in which enterprises became legal entities (*faren tuanti*) and were responsible for enterprises' property. To complete a transition from state ownership to enterprise ownership, a trust investment bank should be set up to temporarily perform the function of the owner on behalf of the state.[9] The relationship between the trust investment bank and the enterprises was no longer one of owner and user. Rather, it became a relationship between the two powers, united in the enterprises with equal status. That is, the trust investment bank should be gradually run as an enterprise, and the funds officially owned by enterprises should be regarded as loans rather than as the government's investment. The relationship between the trust investment bank and enterprises might be "completely transformed in the future into the one of liability" (He, *JJXZB*, 3 January 1988, 2).

The third alternative was total privatization. Some of its advocates, basing their arguments on Marxist historical materialism, justified private ownership as more suitable relations of production than public ownership for China's lower level of productive forces at the current stage. For others, drawing on Western liberalism, private ownership provided both freedom and the incentives for individuals to engage in behavior that moved the economy in the direction of efficient allocation of resources. It therefore represented the most effective and also the simplest property rights system. This alternative not only was based on economic analyses of the advantages of private ownership, but was also stimulated by the successful experiments of private economy across various parts of China.

Despite their differences, all three alternatives moved away from the fundamental principle that who (or which class) controlled the means of production was determinative, and all of them treated ownership as an institution whose primary function was to create an efficient economy. Except for those who openly embraced a Western liberal ideology, most reformist officials and intellectuals tended to justify the new concept of property rights in "fundamental" terms. However, as these instrumental principles tended to highlight the role of property rights in creating wealth, their boundary with capitalism blurred. The experiment with the shareholding system, aiming at clearly defined property rights relations, epitomized the conceptual erosion of China's socialist state ownership.

The Shareholding System

In 1984 when China began the experiment with the shareholding system, no clear distinction was made between equity and debt. While the beginning of the shareholding system was initially related to the issuing of bonds by enterprises, the latter nevertheless became a preparation for the emergence of the equity market. Bond issuing was initiated by local state-run and collective enterprises as a measure for fund raising. A few enterprises in Shanghai began issuing bonds in 1984 among their own employees to raise funds to set up service programs. The advantages of bond issuing in raising capital soon captured the attention of municipal officials and academics. The system was tried in more enterprises after 1986. According to He Gaosheng, the director of the Shanghai Economic System Reform Office (*SHJJ*, 30 September 1988, 3), until 1988 nine medium-sized and large state-run economic units in Shanghai (including enterprises, commercial units and a bank) were transformed into standard shareholding companies. They sold bonds and stocks to the public. By the end of June 1988

Shanghai had 1,255 enterprises that issued shares worth one billion yuan. Thousands of other state-run enterprises were involved in bonds sales to their own employees. The experiment was also undertaken in other cities. According to official statistics in early 1989, there were more than six thousand shareholding enterprises throughout the country, and most of them were in Shanghai, Beijing, Shengyang, Wuhan, and Guangzhou.[10] China's official news agency reported on 23 August 1986 that workers in three of Guangzhou's larger state-run enterprises bought 30 percent of the shares of their enterprises over the last six months. Altogether, workers invested 6.63 million yuan ($1.79 million) in these three enterprises. In these plants, between 70 percent and 90 percent of the workers participated, each buying an average of more than 1200 yuan ($324) in stock.

Generally speaking, there were three kinds of shares, depending on the enterprise: (1) the state share, namely, state investment in enterprises; (2) the collective share, or accumulated profits retained by enterprises; and (3) the private share owned by employees. Profits were mainly distributed in the form of dividends and extra dividends. The method of imposing restrictions on the amount of dividends and extra dividends varied in different localities. In some cities no ceiling was set, while in others the amount was not allowed to exceed 20 percent (Beijing) or 15 percent (Wuhan) of capital stock. Distribution of dividends of government shares also varied in the localities. In Shanghai they were turned over to the state-owned asset management department at the same level while in Beijing they went to finances of the state and then were partially was allocated to enterprises by the state as development funds.

Although the inception of the shareholding system did not purposely aim at the restructuring of property rights, its evolution and the debates on its applicability to the socialist economy convinced the reformers that it could be a remedy to China's current state ownership system. As Wu Jinglian (SJJJDB, 4 April 1989, 10), a well-known economist involved in reform programs at the central level, disclosed, when the contract system was bogged down in late 1986, a consensus emerged between the Office of the Party General Secretary and the Office of Premier of the State Council that the shareholding system should be the next step for the reform of SOEs. In fact, under the sponsorship of both offices, economists had worked out a plan to transform state ownership into a sort of shareholding system. According to this plan, the state would retain 70 percent of shares, while 20 percent and 10 percent would go to enterprises and employees, respectively. For unclear reasons, this plan was not brought into effect. Nevertheless, reformist leaders continued maintaining a positive attitude toward the shareholding system. Zhao Ziyang (1987), while asserting the significance of the ICS in the Thirteenth National Party Congress, affirmed that the shareholding system was "an organizational form of property in socialist enterprises" and encouraged continuing to experiment with it. In his talk with Milton Friedman on 19 September 1988, Zhao further indicated his determination to promote the shareholding system as a way to "clearly define the property rights of SOEs."[11]

Although the central government never formulated any concrete policies specifically in favor of the shareholding system until 1992,[12] as it did for the ICS, appeals to expand the shareholding system gained momentum as more and more people realized its implications for restructuring the property rights system in the state economy. In a symposium held in Shengyang on 23 August 1988 (*XHS*), sixty entrepreneurs, financiers, and theorists from various provinces reached a consensus, after studying the experiments in Shanghai and Shengyang, that the shareholding system had produced better economic returns. They therefore urged the implementation of the shareholding system for large state enterprises. Li Guixian, then governor of the People's Bank of China, was present at the symposium and affirmed the shareholding system as "an effective way to promote optimum distribution of social resources, improve management of state-owned properties, invigorate enterprises, and deepen the reform of the financial system" (*XHS*, 23 August 1988).

Not surprisingly, experiments with the shareholding system involved more extensive ideological reformulation with regard to ownership. For a long time the shareholding system had been related to capitalism or the "old China" (i.e., pre-1949 China). There was strong skepticism about its applicability to a socialist economy. Opponents questioned its compatibility with socialism (cf. Fan and Lin, *JJYJ*, 20 January 1986; Jiang 1986; *BR*, 5 October 1987). Their opposition centered on the following themes. First, only the socialist state represented the interests of the whole people; the introduction of the shareholding system in SOEs would lead to the gradual disintegration of ownership by the whole people. Second, the shareholding system was synonymous with the "capitalist system"; a transformation of SOEs into the shareholding system, which followed the principle of distribution according to capital shares, constituted capitalist restoration. Third, the shareholding system would give rise to a parasitic social stratum that lived on dividends and bonuses. In short, as Jiang Xuemo pointed out, to practice the shareholding system meant a retrogression from socialist public ownership.

In the face of the opposition, which emphasized the capitalist nature of the shareholding system, the ideological argumentation for the shareholding system focused on its neutralization and the establishment of its compatibility with socialism.

Neutralizing the Shareholding System

The first and most important strategy employed by reformist leaders and intellectuals in justifying the shareholding system was to detach the shareholding system from capitalism. For some commentators (e.g., Guo 1986), a shareholding economy and a capitalist economy were two different categories, though the former's developed form existed at the mature stage of capitalism. They argued that the shareholding system represented a type of cooperative economy—a necessary result of the socialization of production and an advanced commodity economy. In other words, the shareholding system was an economic organization related only to the development of production rather than to any specific economic system. Thus, as an entrepreneur said in a Shengyang symposium of 23 August 1988 (*XHS*), "Shareholding is not a patent of capitalism." A similar argument was reflected in Zhao Ziyang's report at the Thirteenth National Party Conference, which explicitly stated that the issuance of bond and stockissuing was not unique to capitalism; it necessarily emerged accompanying the socialization of production and the development of a commodity economy (Zhao 1987, 25).

Establishing the Compatibility of the Shareholding System with Socialist Economy

After being detached from capitalism, the shareholding system was regarded by reformers as an economic organizational form that could serve both capitalism and socialism. In other words, China's socialist economy could also benefit from the shareholding system in terms of aggregating floating shares, importing investment efficiency, and facilitating economic cooperation. (see Guo 1986). Some Chinese theorists (e.g., Zheng et al. 1987; Xiao, *SJJJDB*, September 1988, 13) even emphasized the linkage of the shareholding system with socialism by citing Marx's remark that the shareholding system created a transitional economic form from the capitalist mode of production to an associated one.[13] Along the same line, Li Yining (*SJJJDB*, 30 January 1989; May 1989) argued that the shareholding system was a "feasible method" to turn state-owned enterprises into people-owned ones.[14] Contending that the shareholding system would make "people-owned enterprises" meaningful by spreading property rights to people, Li suggested that the shareholding system was closer than state ownership to socialism. Such a system, it seemed to him, could give tangible forms of ownership to people and therefore represented what he called a "new public ownership" or "social ownership."[15]

How many shares the state should control under the shareholding system was a disputed issue, however. Many who supported the shareholding system or who at least agreed to give it a chance for trial were in favor of a dominant state share in enterprises. Indeed, there were some real difficulties, such as very low levels of personal income, that forced some people to be cautious as to how to transform the hundreds of billions yuan assets from state-owned enterprises into individual shares. On the other hand, fundamental ideological principles were always subtle but strong factors that came creeping into policy inquiry. A critical question some people raised was how China's economic system could still be called a public ownership if most of the shares in state-owned enterprises went to individual hands. Thus, as Liu Guoguang (*JJRB*, 4 January 1986, 3), the vice president of the Academy of Chinese Social Science and a leading party economist who supported limited practice of the shareholding system, asserted that to allow individuals to hold a major portion of shares would ruin public ownership and surely did not conform with the socialist nature of Chinese society. Apparently, the fundamental principle underlying Liu's argument was that state control was the leading form of public ownership and thereby the guarantee for socialism. Quite a few supporters took a similar position on the shareholding system, cautiously avoiding breaking the taboo that the state's control over the means of production was imperative for socialism.

Some of those who opposed state control over shares justified their argument by redefining public ownership. For them, the long-assumed identity of state ownership with public ownership was erroneous. As an article (*JJXZB*, 3 January 1988) argued, state ownership came along with the emergence of a state and was thus not an indicator of socialism. Enterprise ownership, it seemed to the author, was closer to real public ownership—"the association of free people"— because an enterprise was where the laborers and the means of production got integrated. Li Yining's "new public ownership" proposition was also an effort to detach public ownership from state ownership. For him, the shareholding system was a more appropriate form of public ownership than state control, though he suggested a gradual diminution of state shares in enterprises.

In a symposium "The Crisis of State Ownership," in April 1989 in Beijing, Yu Guangyuan (*SJJJDB*, 3 April 1989, 10),[16] a senior party liberal theorist and the former vice president of the Academy of Chinese Social Science, strongly opposed the state's continuing control over enterprises by holding the major proportion of shares. Yu contended that for a long time China's existing socialism had negated the importance of "associated individuals"—a genuinely Marxist idea. He seemed to believe that the shareholding system could be a right form of "associated individuals," which meant a negation of state ownership.

However, for some advocates of the shareholding system, unlike those who attempted to incorporate it into a socialist tradition, the relevance of the shareholding system to any "ism" was no longer important. For example, Guo Shuqing (*SJJJDB*, 3 April 1989), the deputy bureau head of the State Planning Commission, stated that it was simplistic to label shareholding enterprises "capitalist" or "socialist." These economists favored the shareholding system, not because it could produce better economic returns while being able to accommodate socialism, but because it represented a vital, if not the only, alternative to the current state ownership system that "had reached its final stage" (*SJJJDB*, 3 April 1989). They primarily endorsed the shareholding system as an efficient property rights institution. This system, as some commentators argued (e.g., Su and Jiang 1989), had a twofold function that could create truly autonomous enterprises. First, the system would lead to a thorough and complete separation of ownership from management, because shareholders as the owners of property virtually had nothing to do with the micro-operations of enterprises. Second, because shares were not "refundable" and shareholders could not withdraw their investment, enterprises became "a body corporate," which had real rights to dispose of property. This arrangement, many believed, could produce "hard budget constraints" that would strengthen enterprises' incentives and responsibility for the rational use of property.

Some local government officials emphasized the positive function of the shareholding system in diminishing state control over enterprises. For example, in summing up Shanghai's experience with the shareholding system, He Gaosheng (*SHJJ*, 1988, no. 2) pointed out that the chief merit of the system was to clearly define property rights relationships (*mingqu chanquan guanxi*) between different parties, such as central and local governments, enterprises, and individuals. Under this system, he went on, the state would function primarily as the "social regulator" or "tax collector" rather than as the owner of enterprises.

It was too early to evaluate the impact of the shareholding system on the state economy as a whole. After all, the practice of this system was still limited and was not institutionalized yet. Nevertheless, the ideological implication of this system was more obvious than its economic impact: The presumed linkage between state ownership and socialism had been broken. An economic institution prevailing in Western capitalism was recognized by many people as compatible with socialism and, hence, as a solution to the problems created by socialist state ownership. However, pragmatic justification for the shareholding system engendered some corollaries that were hard to incorporate into the CCP's fundamental ideology. This system was predicated on the recognition of private property rights, which were the target of socialist revolution. Although its advocates had tried to differentiate between the practice of this system and privatization, the fact was that this system transferred some portions of state property to private hands. The debate on how many shares the state should control indicated a dilemma confronting the leadership: too many shares in the hands of the state would continue to restrain enterprise autonomy, whereas too few meant a virtual dissolution of state ownership. Thus, how far and on what scale the shareholding system should be carried out turned out be an ideological issue about whether the CCP could still claim a socialist economy if the real owners of property rights were located in stock markets.[17]

The CCP's ideology became profoundly affected. Quite clearly, the policy tendency and ideological discourse that had emerged since 1984 increasingly emphasized the instrumental dimension of the ownership system. Moreover, the experience that had loosened state control over enterprises in turn encouraged a further demand for diluting state ownership. However, a search for the justification of the shareholding system stimulated people's interest in private ownership. Although the practice of private ownership was not preceded by the shareholding system, the theoretical justification for the latter led to a reassessment of private property rights. The arguments presented by many social scientists and entrepreneurs for the shareholding system were actually used to support the privatization of enterprises in the first five months of 1989. The concept of property rights, introduced to justify the shareholding system, was logically used to appeal for private ownership. Indeed, there was only a very small step from legitimating the shareholding system to justifying private ownership. Thus the practice of the shareholding system opened up the path toward the conceptual disintegration of socialist state ownership.

6
Justifying the Private Economy

Capitalist private ownership was the main target of communist revolution. Marx's vision of the new society rested upon a total rejection of capitalist private ownership once it had fulfilled its "historic mission" of developing society's productive forces. Marx regarded private ownership of the means of production as the only source of antagonistic social relations. It gave rise to exploitation and, together with the development of the productive forces, was responsible for the growing alienation of workers. As Engels wrote in *Anti-Duhring* (1935), the abolition of private property would amount to "the genuine resolution of conflict between man and nature and man and man." In short, a revolutionary eradication of capitalist private ownership was to put an end to all social problems. Thus, as Marx and Engels stated in *The Communist Manifesto* (1985), "The theory of the communists may be summed up in the single sentence: abolition of private property." Indeed, this has been the core of communist ideology.

China's socialist transformation wiped out private ownership of the means of production, or the private economy (*siying jingji*). As we showed earlier, it not only uprooted capitalistic private ownership, but also reduced the individual economy (*geti jingji*) to a minimum (in 1978, only 150,000 self-employed laborers were left in the whole country, see table 2.4.). In China's official ideology, private ownership had long been described as related to exploitation, anarchical competition, destructive cyclical crisis, class conflict, and all other kinds of social evils. Private ownership was also considered the most fundamental barrier to the productive forces because of its anarchical nature in production. The individual economy, though seen as less evil than the private economy, was viewed as erosive due to its spontaneous tendency toward capitalism. Thus, China's ownership system since 1949 had followed the line of *yida ergong* (larger size and higher degree of public ownership), which excluded the practice of the private economy and minimized the individual economy.

However, after a three-decade socialist transformation, the post-Mao era saw a resurrection of the private economy. Though limited in scale, China's private economy has become the most active and thriving sector in society.[1]

China's rising private economy was mainly composed of four parts: completely private enterprises (including those owned by foreign capital), shareholding private enterprises, enterprises that nominally belonged to collectives but were actually owned and controlled by individuals, and self-employed individual commercial and service businesses. The rise of the private economy was apparently a result of the CCP's pragmatic economic policy which reflected a significant reformulation of the CCP's ideology. That is, the rise of the private economy could not have happened without a substantial overhaul of the previous ideological framework. In any sense, privatization was the institution least compatible with CCP's ideological fundamentals. The CCP's policy toward private economy typically reflected the tension between fundamentals and instrumental principles that paved the way for the emergence of capitalist economic institutions.

The Urban Individual Economy: An Initial Step toward Privatization

Revival of individual business was a preliminary step toward the revival of the private economy in post-Mao China. Nevertheless, the CCP's policy shift to recognize the individual economy in 1979 was entirely expedient. It was a measure to meet a practical pressing need, that is, to solve the serious problem of urban youth unemployment. Mao's policy during the CR period to rusticate urban youths ended up, after his death, with the flooding of a great number of young people back into urban areas. This mounted unprecedented pressure on the government for employment and, indeed, became a thorny social problem. Deep resentment with their unemployment had brought thousands of youths to the streets in several major cities (Seymour 1982). But China's state economy was not able to absorb such a great influx of labor. By the time the Gang of Four was arrested, the CCP had acknowledged that China's national economy was virtually in crisis. To alleviate the problem of youth unemployment, the CCP in 1979 adopted the policy of encouraging the growth of collective as well as individual businesses to absorb unemployed urban youths. The Central Employment Work Conference in 1980 endorsed a policy of "self-looking-for-employment" (*zimou jiuye*), explicitly encouraging self-employed individual businesses (*ZYWX*, 1987, 87). This policy was further sanctioned in one of the most important party documents in post-Mao China, *The Solution on Certain Questions in History of Our Party since the Founding of the PRC*.[2] The individual economy was justified as a complementary part of socialist public ownership and formally put on the agenda of the CCP's reform programs. Emphasizing the importance of compatibility of production relations with productive forces, the document implied the fitness of the individual economy with China's current level of economic development (*ZYWX*, 1982, 787).

The CCP's new policy soon led to rapid growth in the individual economy. By the end of 1980, the number of people involved in individual businesses in urban areas shot up to 806,000 from 150,000 in 1978.[3] Most of them engaged in commerce, the service industry, and handicrafts. However, one problem stood out as the individual economy prospered: Was an individual businessperson allowed to hire workers?

The problem of labor hiring (*gugong*) emerged with the expanded scale of the individual economy in many areas. Undoubtedly, this was a challenge to the fundamental principle that considered the private hiring of labor as exploitation. Official reaction to labor hiring wavered. The document coissued by the Central Committee and the State Council on 17 October 1981,[4] briefly addressed the problem of labor hiring. According to the document, an individual businessperson was allowed to hire at most two helpers (*bangshou*); those who had special skills were permitted to hire no more than five apprentices (*xuetu*)(*ZYWX*, 1987, 91–92). The decision to restrict the amount of labor hiring stemmed from ideological considerations. It obviously intended to limit the scale of any single individual business in order to prevent it from becoming a capitalist private enterprise. On the other hand, the document did not put a ceiling on the income of individual businesspeople, as long as their activities remained legal. Another significant change in CCP policy toward the individual economy was that it defined individual businesspeople as "socialist laborers," recognizing their work as "necessary for socialism" and therefore "glorious." This perceptual change was embodied in an unprecedented decision by the CCP, that is, to allow individual businesspeople to join the party or Youth League organization, if they were politically qualified (*ZYWX*, 1987, 91–92).

It was clear that the CCP's initial motive for fostering the individual economy was to alleviate the youth unemployment problem. This policy proved effective: 1,471,000 jobless people were absorbed into the individual economy from 1978 to 1982 (Wang et al. 1989, 270). The individual economy produced some other positive results. It invigorated and improved the service sector, which had long been the weakest part of the national economy. It provided people with various kinds of services that the state had failed to offer. It also diversified commercial channels. Thanks to its flexibility and relative independence, individual business contributed to the formation of some interregional or even nationwide commercial networks, speeding up the growth of the market of daily consumer goods in China.

The rise of China's individual economy did not involve too many ideological contentions. The individual economy, after all, did not pose any significant challenge to the prevailing ownership system. But some conservatives still accused the development of the individual economy of "giving the green light for capitalist restoration" (Wang et al. 1989, 271). Thus, theoretical justifications with regard to the individual economy followed. First of all, the leadership picked up the necessity of the coexistence of different forms of ownership systems, a policy that was formulated in the "Common Programme" in the early years of the People's Republic but soon abandoned. Then, the CCP's documents interpreted the rationale for encouraging the individual economy as ranging from solving practical problems (namely, unemployment) to following Marxist principles (namely, the compatibility of production relations with the productive forces). However, the official justification of the individual economy implied a fracture of the sole legitimation of public ownership. Three problems soon challenged the CCP's ideology. First, the individual economy contrasted with the deteriorating efficiency of the state sector and therefore caused popular as well as intellectual skepticism about, and criticism of, the latter. Second, the individual economy demonstrated a strong but natural tendency toward expansion, which provided opportunities for the emergence of a capitalistic private economy. Third, the individual economy created a social stratum that was distinct from others in terms of income level. To categorize this stratum as "socialist laborers" contradicted the egalitarian distribution principle defined by the CCP's ideology. These problems became even more salient as the private economy rose by leaps and bounds from 1984 on in various parts of China.

The Private Economy as a Supplement to Socialist Economy

The rapid development of the individual economy put a considerable amount of wealth into individual hands. By the end of 1985, according to the statistics provided by the General Office of the State Council, 11,710,000 licensed individual businesspeople possessed 16.4 billion yuan in funds, averaging 1,402 yuan per person.[5] The accumulation of capital in private hands was even more rapid and striking in some areas. In Wenzhou, for example, it was not rare for individuals to hold from tens of thousands to two or three hundred thousand yuan.[6] The accumulation of capital in private hands, generated by the individual economy, prepared for the emergence of private enterprises, characterized by large-scale labor hiring.

Labor hiring basically took three forms (Mo 1986). First, there was seasonal hiring. It took place mainly in the rural areas, where some peasant households hired laborers for harvesting. Employers themselves also engaged in labor. Second, there was apprentice hiring. In this form, individuals with special skills hired apprentices while passing on their skills to the latter. Apprentices were paid low wages, or in many cases only stipends. Third, was wage labor hiring. This was a common capitalistic practice in which employers hired workers to make profits. Employers were not involved in direct labor but only in operation and management. Of these three forms, the third one was the most controversial. It involved the question of how much the means of production were allowed to be privatized, since capitalistic private enterprises were inherently expansionist.

Officially, private enterprises differed from individual business in China by hiring more employees to work for profit. The CCP's document regarding the hiring problem in 1981, as mentioned above, put a ceiling on the number of hires (two to five employees), with a clear intention of deterring the formation of private enterprises. However, the spontaneous expansion of the scale of the individual economy quickly broke this limitation in many localities. The leadership was obviously caught in a dilemma: It wanted to keep the individual economy going because it contributed so much to China's economic revival, but it also had to confront leftist criticism that the capitalistic nature of the emerging private enterprises was self-evident.

A Party Central document in early 1984 provided a solution that clearly exhibited the CCP's predicament in balancing its practical needs and its ideological commitments. According to this document, a private enterprise was legal if its hired workers numbered no more than seven. Why did the leadership specifically set seven as a limit? The story was that, at the request of the leadership, some ideologues tried very hard to search for theoretical grounds and finally dug out Marx's quotation that said that an enterprise with seven or fewer employees was a "workshop"; it became a capitalistic enterprise as more workers were hired (see Ding 1988, 1130). Thus, the CCP seemed to be comfortable with the acceptance of seven as a legitimating number for hiring since Marx affirmed its noncapitalistic nature. This artificially drawn line pointed to the fact tha, at the early stage of the experiment of the private economy, the CCP deliberately limited the scale of the private sector mainly out of ideological considerations.

For a time this policy discouraged the expansion of private enterprises. Fear of being labeled "capitalist" forced many private business owners to avoid overstepping the "line of seven." As a Jiangsu entrepreneur said, "I have engaged in private business for five years. In terms of my operational conditions, I could enlarge my business. But according to Marx's 'final conclusion' (dinglun), I have strictly complied with `hiring seven as a maximum.'"[7] A local investigation showed that the major reason for self-limitation by private entrepreneurs was that "they were not willing to become capitalists."[8]

However, the limit of seven was gradually overstepped, overtly or covertly, and several factors accounted this. First, the social climate of reform was favorable for individual pursuit of wealth. The official slogan "to be rich is glorious" motivated many to make money by various means. People became emboldened when they tasted the "forbidden fruit" of profit without being punished. Second, local governments acquiesced in the breaking of the rule because their revenues increased through taxation of private enterprises. Third, a large number of local bureaucrats were personal beneficiaries of the bribery of private businesses that needed their help for access to resources and markets. Finally, and most important, although the central government set the limit on the number of hired hands, its measures against violation of the rule were not very effective; no harsh punishment was inflicted on those who went beyond the limit.

Thus, from 1985 on, many private enterprises expanded the scale of production. A national sampling showed that by the end of 1985 there were forty thousand private enterprises that hired more than eight workers. Some private enterprises even had hired hundreds or thousands of workers.[9] For example, a privately run coal mine[10] in Fangshan County, Beijing, hired more than a thousand workers and was one of the largest private enterprises at that time. Contending policy recommendations arose as private enterprises spread and expanded. Some officials preferred to eliminate these "exploitative practices" (Ding 1988, 1130). But others advocated a more liberal policy. In a research paper based on a national survey, policy analysts from the State Council[11] explicitly proposed not to restrict the number of hired workers, asserting that such a restriction was inexpedient for solving the remaining unemployment problem. The municipal government of Tianjing (the third largest city in China) officially recognized the de facto existence of private enterprises by permitting the limit of seven to be broken.[12] However, quite a few local governments observed the center's policy. For example, Chongqing's municipal government appeared to be relieved that in its jurisdiction employers rarely exceeded the limit. The fourteen enterprises hiring more than seven workers were said to be transformed into cooperatives.[13] It was surprising that Shenzhen, the first Special Economic Zone in China, took a restrictive attitude toward labor hiring in 1986. A policy recommendation presented by an investigative team of the municipal government on this matter suggested specific hiring limits for different sectors, such as 3 to 6 workers for catering trade, or 1 to 2 for the grocery trade, and 1 to 2 for repair trades.[14]

Apparently the Shenzhen government prudently tried to avoid breaking the limit of seven. But it was very doubtful whether the implementation of the center's regulation was really effective, even in localities where the local governments openly claimed to comply with the center's regulation. There was plenty of evidence that, to avoid being suspected of engaging in capitalism, a large number of the private enterprises that had more than seven hired workers had camouflaged themselves with "cooperative enterprises." But the means of production in these cooperative enterprises were actually controlled by individuals.

Before the Thirteenth National Party Congress held in October 1987, which formally sanctioned the private economy, no top party leader publicly supported the de facto capitalistic practice. As the private economy flowered, what was going on among the party leadership behind the scenes was unknown to the public. But the fact that the government neither punished those who broke the regulation nor officially endorsed the private economy seemed to indicate that the party itself was uncertain about what to do with the development of the private economy. It was believed that the party was then conducting "investigations and studies" (*diaocha yanjiu*), based upon which it expected to make formal decisions. Although there was no official policy to sanction the private economy, ideological reformulation had already been under way in various official publications. Both the instrumental value of the private economy and its ideological legitimation were discussed in many articles.

In terms of its instrumental value, the private economy was supported by quite a few local governmental officials, policy analysts, and social scientists. They believed that it benefited China's national economy in several respects. First, the private economy, they argued, created job opportunities for the urban unemployed and also absorbed a large number of the surplus rural labor forces displaced by the household responsibility system. For a long time, the commune system had bound hundreds of millions of peasants to the limited arable land and was responsible for the grave "disguised unemployment" problem in China's countryside. The responsibility system, which imposed an efficient use of labor, suddenly threw thousands of peasants out of work and brought the problem of unemployment into the open. Since the capacity of the state economy to soak up surplus labor was very limited, the private economy provided an outlet for it. The limited experiment of private economy since 1984 had in fact demonstrated its effectiveness in absorbing rural laborers. By 1988, according to official statistics, 250 thousand private enterprises in the country had absorbed 4 million surplus laborers (Wang 1990, 279). In some localities private enterprises proved particularly effective in providing job opportunities. For example, the population of Cangnan County in Wenzhou was 185,000, with a per capita average of 4 *fen* (1/15 *mu*) of arable land. It was estimated that there were 40,000 surplus laborers.[15] Since the growth of the private economy, this county not only had reallocated its surplus labor but also had provided job opportunities for thousands of people from other areas. Thus, many agreed that the development of the private economy had generated a new productivity beyond the state's capacity.

Second, as some specialists pointed out, the private economy was superior to the individual economy because the former had the advantage of economies of scale. The private economy, they contended, created opportunities for a free combination of floating funds, surplus labor, and expertise that was not fully utilized by the state. In other words, the private economy could make use of resources that would be wasted under total state control. An individual named Jiang Tongjun, of Jilin, after accumulating a great amount of money via an individual business, set up the Changshan Construction Team by hiring about thirty technicians and engineers. Most of his new employees had either been out of work or had lain idle in their own units. In addition, 150 rural surplus laborers were hired.[16] Some people also argued that the private economy could serve large industrial sectors by processing small or labor intensive industrial parts for large industries.

Third, private enterprises could add more revenues to the state treasury than the individual economy could, since the former had larger, higher output value and greater turnover. For example, it was reported that Zhang Jingquan, the owner of a mechanical processing factory of some seventy employees in Jilin Province, turned over to the state 50,000 yuan each year,[17] an amount that any single individual businessperson could not make.

Although the advocates of private enterprises found it easy to justify the pragmatic advantages of the private economy, they had to wrestle with incorporating it into the prevailing ideology. Ideological reformulation with regard to the private economy principally focused on three questions:

1. *Why did China need private economy after three decades of socialist revolution?* A telling answer, found in most of the official publications favoring private economy, was that this type of economy fit the current level of productive forces. As some authors (Xue 1986; Jilin 1986) argued, the development of China's productive forces was extremely uneven. Whereas China had reached a certain level of industrialization, 80 percent of its population still engaged in manual labor. The coexistence of automatized, mechanized, semimechanized, and manual labor correspondingly demanded a coexistence of multiple forms of ownership. According to these scholars, the failure of a unitary public ownership to provide full employment and deliver consumer goods and services lay in that it exceeded the level of the productive forces. It seemed to them that the private economy could better accommodate a lower level of productive forces that was not yet ready for socialization.

The argument for the coexistence of multiple or diversified forms of ownership had been endorsed by several CCP documents. Although none of these documents considered the private economy as a legitimate economic institution, the advocates of the private economy found that the "coexistence" approach provided a starting point for justifying it. Their tactic was to emphasize the necessity of multiple forms of ownership first, then to include one more form— the form of the private economy. Thus, to raise private economy as an alternative was a logical extension of the "coexistence" approach.

To those who favored the private economy, its justification based on the compatibility of the productive forces and the production relations was very Marxist and, therefore, could stand up to conservative criticisms. Yet their argument actually rested upon a factually problematic assumption: that public ownership corresponded to a higher level of productive forces and private ownership to a lower one. Those who held this assumption failed, intentionally or not, to face the reality that the higher level of productive forces in the contemporary world was reached in the capitalist systems. Capitalism seemed to be more capable than the "existing socialism" to accommodate or generate technological innovations and progress. Whether there was any logical relation between the productive forces and public or private ownership was subject to debate. But a simplistic identification of capitalistic private ownership with a lower level of the productive forces derived from Chinese reformers' attempt to justify private economy in a framework of Marxist historical materialism.

2. *Would private economy undermine China's public ownership system? Would it lead to a restoration of capitalism?* It seemed hard to pretend not to notice the capitalistic nature of the emerging private enterprises in China. In 1986, this issue was publicly acknowledged in a variety of official publications. For example, some authors (Wang and Li 1988) asserted that an enterprise could be defined as capitalist as long as it met two criteria: (1) it hired a certain amount of workers, and (2) it used capital to earn profits. Unquestionably, a large number of enterprises in 1986 fell into this capitalist category. However, the question was: Would the spread of the capitalistic private economy shake the public ownership—the very foundation of China's socialist system? Some people thought it would and hence appealed for the elimination of such enterprises.[18] For reform-minded officials and intellectuals, on the other hand, private enterprises would not change the nature of China's socialist economy for three reasons.

First, some advocates of the private economy emphasized the external environment that prevented private enterprises from becoming the agencies of capitalist restoration. According to them, despite its capitalist nature, China's private economy fundamentally differed from its counterpart under capitalism in terms of the external environment. The predominance of state ownership in China determined that any other economies, private ones included, had to depend on the former in many ways. Private enterprises had to rely on the state economy as a supplier as well as a market. Thus the private economy could not survive and develop unless it subordinated itself to the state economy. In this sense, the private economy was only a bird in the "socialist cage."

Second, some policy researchers stressed the role of the state in confining the private economy to the socialist framework. For them, the state possessed adequate legal means and economic levers to directly or indirectly regulate the private economy and guide it to serve socialism. For example, by making laws, the state could define the domain of operations of private enterprises; by pricing, taxing, and lending, the state could adjust, restrict, or encourage their operations according to its will; by applying various regulations, the state could monitor their operations, scale and distribution. In short, the state could contain the activities of private enterprises, keeping them from overstepping certain boundaries set by the state and from undermining the socialist economy.

Third, those who favored the private economy maintained that the composition of the newly emerging employer stratum would have some positive effects on their activities in terms of restricting capitalism. The employer stratum was mainly composed of three groups of people: urban and rural youths who grew up under socialism, former government cadres and employees, and retired workers and intellectuals. Some of these employers were members of the party or the youth league.[19] Most of them were described as "educated by the party for many years" and "having a certain degree of socialist consciousness." Thus, although they became owners of private enterprises, they were believed to be different from capitalists in capitalist societies. Their willingness to accept the party's leadership, observe socialist moral codes, and comply with laws could make their enterprises less capitalistic.

It was not hard to conclude that in 1986 the supporters of the private economy were actually advocating a sort of "restricted capitalism." With a strong emphasis on the restraints on socialist production relations and on the guiding role of the state, their ideas approximated the official policy of state capitalism initially promoted in the early 1950s. Nevertheless, a fundamental difference existed. State capitalism of the 1950s was implemented as a transitional economic form aimed at transforming the remaining capitalist sectors. The goal of the advocates of private economy in the 1980s, however, was to develop the private economy as a viable economic form to solve the problems the public economy failed to solve. It was thus a partial reversal of the results of the socialist transformation. The state's role in handling capitalist economies in these two settings was radically different. Under the state capitalism of the 1950s, the state took a variety of measures to progressively reduce and finally eliminate the private economy. According to proponents of the private economy in the 1980s, however, the state was supposed to adopt policies favorable for private enterprises, though the state's responsibility to minimize their negative effects was also emphasized. Unlike in the 1950s', when state capitalism indicated a clear-cut and straightforward social and ideological goal (to eradicate capitalist remnants), the policy recommendation of private economy in the 1980s was more ambivalent. As a result, an intellectual vacuum ensued and provided opportunities for alternative interpretations to get in.

The argument for a "restricted capitalism" overlooked a possibility that later turned out to be a fact: that the practice of private economy would spread capitalist ideas. Although the state could restrict the activities of private enterprises, it would have difficulty restricting the ideas they bred. Property rights, the entrepreneurial spirit, wage differentials, market competitions—all of these quickly entered Chinese economic thinking as the private economy grew. It was not surprising, therefore, that in 1988 and early 1989 the idea of privatization was so appealing in the reformers' circle that it became one of the major targets of the hardliners' ideological attack after the Tiananmen Incident of 1989.

3. *Why was exploitation allowed to exist under socialism?*[20] One of the most controversial issues involved in the experiment with private economy was that it led to exploitation. A stated goal of the CCP since its birth in 1921 has been the elimination of exploitation in the world. This goal was declared by the CCP to have been realized in China in the socialist transformation of 1950s. The experiment of private economy in the 1980s, however, restored the capitalistic "exploitative practice." Considering it to be one of the worst sins in socialist China, some requested a ban by the government on exploitation. The advocates of private economy did not deny the existence of exploitation in private enterprises, but they claimed that wage labor under socialism differed from that under capitalism because those employed were not proletarians who possessed nothing but labor, and who could not survive unless they sold out their labor to capitalists, as was the case in capitalist societies. Instead, laborers chose to work in private enterprises for better benefits rather than for survival (Wenzhou Municipal 1986). Conceding that employers gained profits by exploiting surplus values, the pro-private-economy argument also suggested that a careful examination be made to distinguish between their legitimate incomes and profits from exploitation. It held that a fair proportion of their incomes, which could be very high, was justly earned by their managerial activities—namely, complex labor. Finally, the advocates of private economy believed that under socialism the negative effects of private enterprises could be controlled by the state. They claimed, "our working class regime will not allow employers to ruthlessly exploit workers" (Wenzhou Municipal 1986).

No matter from which perspective it was viewed, the "exploiting practice" was difficult to justify under socialism. Later developments demonstrated that it was more difficult to handle the "exploitation problem" than to simply recognize the existence of the private economy, though the former was an inevitable outcome of the latter. Exploitation had a much wider and more direct psychological impact on the average person and caused popular cynicism about the communist ideology that had denounced "class exploitation."

The Private Economy as an Agent of Modernization

From the end of 1986 through the first half of 1987, China's reform encountered a strong backlash, accompanied by the Anti-Bourgeois-Liberalism campaign. Hu Yaobang, the reform-minded party general secretary, was accused by conservatives of failing to deal harshly with liberal intellectuals and students, and was removed from power. Recommended by Deng Xiaoping, Zhao Ziyang, then premier of the State Council and another major reform-minded leader in the CCP, took over the Secretariat. Zhao was a firm advocate of economic reform, and his ascension reflected that Deng had no intention of stopping the ongoing reform. Deng's endorsement of the Anti-Bourgeois-Liberalism Campaign and his appointment of an economic reformer as the general secretary reflected his decade-long strategy of liberalizing economic policy while preserving Leninist political and ideological control (Hamrin 1990).

To counteract the conservatives' attack, the Secretariat under Zhao's control issued the CCP's Document no. 4 of 1987, which tried to confine the campaign to the party (dangnei) and the "thought domain" (sixiang lingyu). In other words, one unambiguous intention of Document no. 4 was to prevent the campaign from spreading to the economic sphere. Conservatives were upset with the document. They complained that "we are now only opposing those who were speaking of liberalization, not those who were doing liberalization." Asserting that "the deepest source of bourgeois liberalization comes from the economic sphere," they maintained that "to oppose political liberalization, we must also oppose economic liberalization" (ZYWX, 1987, 424). Thus, they urged the breaking of the limit set by Document no. 4 on the scope of the campaign. A clear signal of tightening up (shou) from the Party central propaganda organ, controlled by conservatives, threw many people, from local officials and owners of private enterprises to individual businesspeople, into confusion, uncertainty, and fear. Some local authorities reportedly began closing private enterprises, while many private entrepreneurs and self-employed people considered shutting down their businesses.

Facing the increasingly strong conservative backlash, Deng Xiaoping called in Zhao Ziyang on 28 April 1987, and asked him to speak out to affirm the economic reform (Chen 1990, 22). As a result, Zhao made his famous 13 May Speech, which reiterated that the Anti-Bourgeois-Liberalism Campaign should not be extended to the economic sphere. As he stated,

> Current [economic] policies are formulated by the Center and have nothing to do with liberalization. If the current polices were labeled as liberalization, people would be be terrified, production stopped, business closed, trees cut down, and pigs killed, who would take the responsibility for all this? (ZYWX, 1987)

Zhao rebutted the conservatives' arguments for extending the campaign to the economic sphere as "irresponsible" and "politically incorrect," and warned that these arguments had produced considerable negative impacts on the economic reform. To keep the economic thinking favorable for the reform, Zhao specifically warned against the danger of "a notable phenomenon," namely,

> Some comrades label as capitalist the things that have been proved conducive for emancipating the productive forces and facilitating socialist construction of modernization, while regarding as socialist those which fetter the productive forces (ZYWX, 1987).

Although Zhao did not specify what was conducive or harmful to productive forces, he made it explicit that all the policies of the economic reform should be continued. In an impressive display of political agility, Zhao, with Deng's backing,[21] worked successfully to keep the campaign from thwarting economic reform, and then shut down the whole campaign.[22]

The reformers' upper hand rescued many ongoing reform programs, the private economy included. Even though some private enterprises were affected by the campaign, due to local officials' instinctive response to the "political wind" from above or to their own fear as owners of private enterprises, the majority of them pulled through the crisis.

The year of 1987 was a turning point for the development of China's private enterprises; for the first time the CCP officially sanctioned the private economy. In his work report presented to the Thirteenth National Party Congress on 25 October 1987, Zhao Ziyang made the following statement:

> Under socialism private economy is necessarily connected with the dominant public ownership system and subject to the enormous influence of the latter. Our experience has demonstrated that a certain degree of development of the private economy helps promote production, stimulate markets, increase employment, and better satisfy the different needs of people's livelihood. [Private economy] is a necessary and useful supplement to public ownership. [We] must make policies and laws concerning private enterprises as soon as possible to protect their interests and strengthen the guidance to, supervision over, regulation of private economy (Zhao 1987, 32).

It is true that there was virtually nothing new in Zhao's statement; the bold arguments had been made in various official publications in 1986. What Zhao did was only to confirm some components of these arguments and translate them into official policy. The compatibility of Zhao's statement with the pro-private-economy arguments indicated that the ideological ferment in 1986 was a theoretical preparation for the legitimation of the private economy. The leadership's eventual sanction of the private economy was based on its belief that some important ideological issues on the private economy had been basically clarified and a general consensus within the party had been reached in terms of the utility and neccessity of private enterprises to China's modernization. Another factor leading to the CCP's formal endorsement of the private economy was Zhao Ziyang's ascendancy. As Premier, Zhao once sponsored the General Offices of the State Council to do research on the private economy and to examine its applicability and feasibility to China's socialist economy. With the relative weakening of the positions of conservatives after the unpopular and short-lived Anti-Bourgeois Liberalization Campaign, Zhao captured the opportunity to further liberalize the economy and publicly put the experiment of the private economy on the reform agenda.

Following Zhao's official approval of the private economy at the Thirteenth National Party Congress in 1987, the first session of the Seventh National People's Congress, held in 1988, amended the Constitution to legitimize the private economy. The new article added to the Constitution was basically an echo of what Zhao stated at the party's congress.[23]

The relatively liberal atmosphere of 1988 brought about a rapid development of private and individual economies. Statistics showed that by 1988 China had 225,000 private enterprises (Fang 1988). Private and individual economies possessed 2 percent of the total national fixed assets and employed 4.2 percent of the national workforce[24] (*GMRB*, 29 October 1989). Although still small, these figures were not insignificant, given the fact that in 1978, when the reform began, there were only 150,000 self-employed people and not a single private enterprise existed in the whole country.

The leadership's sanction of the private economy encouraged and, indeed, stimulated a new surge of change in ideological discourse.

Private Economy and the Rural Natural Economy

Unlike those whose arguments had emphasized only its expedient nature, Fang Gongwen (1988), the deputy chief editor of the *Guangming Daily*, suggested a transformative role of the private economy in the restructuring of China's economy. For Fang, in the rural areas China's economy was confronting an important transformation: from a "natural economy" (namely, a self-sufficient or semi-sufficient economy) to a "commodity economy."[1] The importance and urgency of the transformation, according to Fang, was that socialism could not be built upon a natural economy.

The commune movement, according to Fang, lay in a futile effort to build socialism upon a natural economy. If the fact that about half of China's workforce was still trapped in a natural or seminatural economy constituted a great obstacle to China's socialist modernization,[26] how could China overcome it and rapidly "commoditize" the rural economy? Fang presented four alternatives. The first was to rely on a spontaneous commercialization of agricultural production. In this process most of the petty commodity producers would go bankrupt in competition, while the survivors would engage in a larger-scale commodity economy. Although this process was already under way in rural areas, Fang saw it as being too slow to transform China's rural natural economy and also as too painful for the peasants.

The second alternative was to take the land away from the peasants by coercion and force them to work for capitalist factories and farms, as happened in the "enclosure movement" in Great Britain in the eighteenth century. But this method of primitive capital accumulation, for Fang, contradicted the nature of China's socialist regime.

The third alternative was to dismantle the natural economy by cooperatization or collectivization. This was what the CCP had done after assuming power. This strategy needed a certain level of productive forces, on the one hand, and massive state assistance in terms of funds, technology, and managerial expertise, on the other. Both, however, were scarce in China.

The fourth alternative was to encourage the private economy, which meant allowing those households or individuals that had become rich in past years to convert part of their income to investment for rural industries. If this were done, most rural surplus labor could be released from the fetter of the natural economy and transferred to the nonagricultural sectors. An article in *The People's Daily* (16 March 1988) pointed out that there were still 150 million rural surplus laborers that the state was unable to absorb. If the portion of the private economy in the country's gross industrial output value could increase to 10 percent (it was then 1 percent), 36 million surplus laborers could be absorbed into the nonagricultural sectors. Fang pushed this hypothesis further by suggesting that when the private economy accounted for 20 percent of the country's gross industrial output value, half of the rural surplus labor could go to industry. This would decisively change China's rural natural economy. Fang believed that this was a speedier and less painful way for the transformation of the rural economic structure, because it would not drive peasants into bankruptcy or deprive them of land.

In any case, Fang's argument presented a capitalistic solution to China's rural structural problem. Its core was to transform self-sufficient peasants into wage laborers through a massive penetration of capitalistic enterprises into the rural areas. Although Fang still affirmed "cooperatization" in positive terms, he considered it to be not as feasible or effective as the private economy. But this argument

did not sufficiently assess the long-term impact of rural class disparity on China's socialism.

Socialism and Capital

Whenever the word *capital* is mentioned, a famous saying from
Karl Marx occurs to many Chinese: "Capital comes dripping from
head to foot, from every pore, with blood and dirt." Indeed, this quotation could be found in every official textbook of political economy
in China. For party officials and intellectuals who had basic Marxist
training, it was not hard to understand that capital embodied capitalist relations of production and was a means through which capitalists exploited the working class. But once the private economy
was legitimated, a reevaluation of capital was inevitable. Was there
any room for capital to exist in socialist China? According to an internal study document prepared for party cadres by the Shanghai Party
School (1989), capital should be checked, rather than eliminated, at
the preliminary stage of socialism. The reasoning underlying this
argument derived from the productive forces criterion. The
author(s) denied that China's socialism was a "qualified" socialism
in terms of its level of productive forces. This was because China's
productive forces not only lagged far behind those of contemporary
Western capitalism, but were far below the level that "many other
countries" had reached under capitalist conditions.[27] The low level
of China's productive forces was implicitly attributed to an insuffi-
cient development of modern capitalism. For the author(s), the
development of capital would provide the necessary material conditions for the socialization of the means of production. In other
words, capital could be eliminated only on the basis of its sufficient
development. In a less industrialized socialist country, a prompt
action to expropriate capital and to wipe out private ownership , as
China did, could only destroy the productive forces. An evaluation
of capital in moral terms, it seemed to the author(s), was simplistic
and superficial. Capital had a dual role in both exploiting labor and
promoting the productive forces. It symbolized a specific developmental stage of the productive forces, and an artificial jump over
could be counterproductive. The logical conclusion was that capital
should be allowed to continue its role in promoting the productive
forces in China.

This argument brought back a long-debated theme of the transition for less-developed countries to socialism in general and questioned the Chinese socialist revolution in particular. By appealing to classical Marxism, which emphasized the determining role of the productive forces in social transformation, the argument justified a compromise with capital and a retreat from a socialism that had jumped over the necessary stage of the productive forces. But the question left unanswered was how much room capital should be given in the economy and how to reconcile the operation of capital with socialist commitments and policies. Quite a few scholars and officials who supported the practice of private economy affirmed the dominance of public ownership. This might be due to the fact that a naked argument for a primary role of capital in the economy was politically risky or to a genuine belief that socialism and capital could peacefully coexist. But capital had an inherent tendency to expand, and its expansion might erode public ownership. Thus, the argument or the policy favoring the introduction of capital in a framework of a communist system generated conflicts for ideology and social institutions.

Private Economy and Commodity Economy

One of the stated goals of China's economic reform was to establish a socialist commodity economy. In the Resolution of the Third Plenum of the Twelfth National Party Congress held in 1984, a sufficient development of the commodity economy was interpreted as "an impassable developmental stage of socialist economy" and "a necessary condition for economic modernization" (ZYWX, 1987, 237). The policy goal was reemphasized at the Thirteenth National Party Congress in 1987 (see Zhao 1987, 26). The original intention of this policy was to relax China's rigid planning system and revitalize the state-run economy. But in 1988, this "socialist commodity" approach was used by the reformers to vigorously support private economy. Many considered the growth of the private economy to be a catalyst for the development of the commodity economy. Several reasons were highlighted (see Wang and Li March 1988; Fang 1988). First, because private enterprises mainly relied on markets for their operation and hence were real commodity producers, their very existence and growth inevitably would enlarge the scale of the commodity economy. Second, the private economy stimulated the movement of labor and converted labor into a factor of the commodity economy. Third, the private economy entailed a real commodity exchange relation with the state economy and thereby forced the latter to adapt to the commodity economy. Fourth, the private economy, as mentioned earlier, drove millions of the rural population into commodity production and profoundly enlarged the commodity economy on the basis of the erosion of the natural economy.

The positive relationship between private sectors and the commodity economy indicated the importance of clearly defined property rights to the development of the commodity economy. The commodity economy originated from a mutual need for goods belonging to different and independent owners. Commodity exchange, in the final analysis, was an exchange of rights of ownership. When the state was the major owner of everything, the commodity economy existed only in name and lost its meaning; when property rights were ambiguously defined (as under the industrial contract system), the commodity economy created chaos in the market. Thus, clearly defined property rights were the prerequisite for a functioning commodity economy. It certainly did not mean that only private sectors represented clearly defined property rights, which in fact could take various forms, ranging from cooperatively owned to community-owned property. However, in 1988 there was a visible consensus among reformers that the commodity economy could not work well without clearly defined property rights. This realization came to the intellectual and policy circles particularly when the economic reform was increasingly exhausting its options.

The Private Economy as an Alternative Economic Institution

The phenomenal growth of private enterprises in 1988 was unfortunately paralleled by mounting difficulties for economic reform, especially in the urban areas. The reform of the state-run economy, while considerably improving industrial efficiency, brought the property rights problem to the surface (see chapter 4) but did not provide any solution to it. The ambiguously specified property rights that emerged with the ICS were believed by reformers to be a contributing factor to the stagnation of industrial reform. Some behavior of state enterprises, such as making blind investments, pursuing quick profits, and expanding consumption funds (which led to skyrocketing inflation in 1988), were attributed to the absence of constrains on property rights. The market disorder and corruption were regarded as the results of discord between the continuing dominance of state ownership and the so-called dual-price-track system. Government officials, still controlling major economic resources in the name of the state, greatly profited by selling state fixed-price commodities at free-market prices, which were usually more than three times higher than the original price.[28] Worse, such governmental corruption was no longer confined to individual officials; it was commonplace that many governmental departments were involved (Gong 1993). In addition, private enterprises' heavy reliance on the state economy (more accurately, on the officials or the departments that had access to resources and markets) as a supplier and a market induced various types of corruption, ranging from embezzlement to bribery.

The year 1988 also witnessed a worsening social mood,[29] caused by a sense of normlessness, because the economic reform was leading nowhere.[30] Three alternatives were proposed to deal with the crisis (see Gong and Chen 1990): (1) Further liberalization: Liberal intellectuals and officials believed that the current crisis was rooted in China's political and economic institutions. Hence the fundamental solution should be a further liberalization of political and economic structures. (2) Restoration of central planning: Contrary to the liberals, conservatives believed that economic and political liberalization tended to trigger economic imbalances and social crises instead of mending them. Thus they proposed to restore the political and economic order of the pre–Cultural Revolution period. (3) Neo-authoritarianism: This approach suggested promoting a liberalized economy under a strong central government. Its core was to use an "open economy plus closed politics" formula to prepare for the transition to a full democratization.

The voice for privatization from the latter half of 1988 through the first half of 1989 came mainly came from liberal circles, though neo-authoritarian advocates also endorsed it. The pro-privatization ideas in that period showed some critical differences from those of previous years. First, as we have seen, the previous arguments proposed to create private economies outside the state economy. Their central idea was that the state concede the right to individuals to have their own businesses and permit the formation of private ownership outside the boundary of the state economy. This was actually what China had done with its early experiment with private economy. But now quite a few economists openly suggested a more radical step— to sell state assets to individuals, namely, to privatize SOEs. Second, while giving a positive assessment of it, the previous arguments basically looked at private ownership as a necessary evil, or as an institution connected with the lower level of the productive forces. The intellectual discourse on this subject after late 1988, however, tended to consider private ownership as an institution that better suited modernization. Some people even regarded private ownership as an alternative to state ownership and as a solution to serious problems that emerged due to the halfway reform of the ownership system.

Whereas in previous years people in reform circles had attempted to put private ownership into the framework of historical materialism, they now tended to justify it in terms of Western classical, neoclassical, or property rights economics. Rather than relating private ownership to the lower level of the productive forces, many interpreted it as an institution that was essentially superior to state ownership in terms of efficiency. A party study document issued in Shanghai in 1989 identified four merits of private ownership. First, owners of private enterprises were motivated by profit maximizing and therefore responsive to market signals. Thus, their operations of production were best suited to the market mechanisms that the reform sought to establish. Second, private enterprises could create a desirable combination of ownership rights, management rights, and decision-making rights. Such a combination would give enterprises real autonomy and flexibility in their operations and effectively diminish transaction costs. The separation of these rights had been perceived by reformers as a fundamental defect of the ICS. After the experiment with the contract system, many people thought that this defect was incurable within the framework of the state economy. Third, the private economy could breed an entrepreneurial stratum, characterized by a strong consciousness of competition and efficiency, a sensitivity to market signals and information, and a high motivation to innovate. Such a stratum was believed to be a dynamic agency of economic modernization.

The theoretical embrace of private ownership was accompanied by a policy recommendation to sell state assets. It was reported that "a central leading comrade" had suggested, at a symposium in

Shanghai in October 1988, that small state enterprises be sold to individuals. To be more explicit, he had emphasized that this suggestion referred to selling ownership rights to individuals rather than just contracting or leasing management rights to them. He believed that even if all small state enterprises were sold to individuals, the nature of the socialist economy would not be changed, because the state still controlled the major industries (*TGXX*, November 1988). But for some others, the medium and large state enterprises were also subject to sale. Hua Sheng (February 1989) argued for a complete sale of state assets to different parties, ranging from local governments to privately sponsored investment trust companies. Given a very low individual income level in China, Hua suggested that nonofficial (*minjian*) financial investment organs be set up to accumulate private capital and therefore be able buy shares from state enterprises.

Some of the most radical recommendations in publications for the privatization of state enterprises were put forward not by Chinese within China but by overseas Chinese scholars. Perhaps an open advocacy of the privatization of state enterprises still presented political risks to Chinese residing in China. Nevertheless, a systematic publication of articles by overseas Chinese appealing for a comprehensive privatization program undoubtedly reflected a domestic intellectual ferment and was part of a domestic ideological reformulation. All of these articles prescribed thorough privatization as the only and final solution to China's ailing state economy. According to Huang Youguang and Yang Xiaokai (*SJJJDB*, 6 and 20 February 1989) from Australia, economic scarcity in socialist countries was not a reason for state control over resource allocation. Resources were always scarce in any society, relative to the demands of human beings. It was the "scarcity" that made private property rights necessary, for private property rights provided a foundation for free price mechanisms, which would make possible the rational allocation of resources. Without an order defined according to property rights, in their words, chaotic and disruptive scrambles for resources were unavoidable, and therefore scarcity would be exacerbated. China's industrial contract system, rather than solving the problem, created what they called "truncated property rights," meaning that the income level of those granted the right to dispose of property and the outcomes of their disposal were disjointed. Under such an arrangement, property rights were further obscured, and irrational resource allocation intensified. Huang and Yang argued that the party's ideological paranoia was the major obstacle to pursuing privatization in order to escape the current predicament of the state economy. Total privatization, after all, would destroy the party's self-respect by discrediting the achievements of socialist revolution.

In an article entitled "Without the Privatization of Enterprises, There Will be No Real Commodity Economy" (*SJJJDB*, 29 August 1988), Xiao Jingru, from America, ascribed undesirable outcomes of the contract system to the absence of unambiguously specified property rights. In his view, the contract system did not solve the problem of who should take the real responsibility for state assets. Rather, it produced an institutional arrangement under which managers and workers could cooperate to encroach on state assets. Thus, he suggested, except for a few sectors, such as energy, mining, and railways, all other state industries should be privatized. State assets should be converted into shares and sold to individuals. In order to neutralize bureaucratic resistance, a certain proportion of shares should be granted to officials in enterprises and industrial departments to buy them off.

In January 1989, eleven Chinese economists in the United States presented a formal proposal to Chinese leaders. This proposal, *The Privatization of State Assets: Tendencies of and Alternatives of China's Economic Reform*, was published in *World Economic Herald* (*SJJJDB*) on 27 February 1989. According to the proposal, there could be three alternatives to privatization. First, there could be a fair redistribution of state assets. Although this measure seemed to be simpler and to be able to realize privatization immediately, the proposers thought it unrealistic because a comprehensive value assessment of state assets was technically difficult, if not impossible. Without an objective value assessment of the state assets, an equitable redistribution was impossible. Second, they proposed to encourage further development of the individual and private economies until they eroded and replaced most parts of the state economy. However, this process, the proposers argued, would be too slow to cure the ailing state economy. They predicted that the national economy could crumble before the reform of the state ownership was completed. According to the third alternative, China's privatization could begin with an encouragement of individual savings. When the amount of savings reached a certain level, individuals could be allowed to obtain loans from banks to buy real estate. After some time, individuals could raise a mortgage on their real estate from banks to buy state assets. The proposers found this incremental strategy of privatization to be realistic and feasible, and they appealed to Chinese leaders to take this measure for the sake of national rejuvenation.

International comparisons were also a factor stimulating new enthusiasm among Chinese reformers for the private economy in 1988 and 1989. Specifically, the economic success of the "four little tigers" in East Asia (South Korea, Taiwan, Hong Kong, and Singapore) was frequently mentioned to back the argument for privatization. China traditionally regarded itself as the most advanced country in East Asia. But its poor economic performance relative to that of the rest of region was particularly galling. Many Chinese intellectuals attributed it to the flawed economic system. As one author argued (*SJJJDB*, 14 March 1989), the most important factor behind the success of Asia's newly industrialized economies was that they "offer considerable economic freedom to their residents and strictly enforce the system of private ownership of property." The biggest problem for socialism, he went on, lay in the inability of public ownership to sustain economic growth. By comparing the "four tigers" with other Asian countries enforcing state ownership, such as Burma and Vietnam, another author (Zhu, *SJJJDB*, 29 August 1988) made a quick generalization that third-world countries with dominant state ownership developed much more slowly than did those with a prevalence of private ownership. Thus, he asserted, in terms of promoting productivity, private ownership demonstrated a progressive role that was unavailable under state ownership.

The advocates of a private economy also attempted to strengthen their arguments by highlighting the worldwide trend toward privatization. Some authors emphasized that in both developed and less-developed countries, it was commonplace that governments chose to privatize their state sector as a strategy to solve national economic problems ranging from deficits, inefficiency, and waste to poor competitiveness. The experience of privatizing public sectors in Britain, France, Italy, West Germany, and Japan, or in third-world nations, was frequently referred to by many articles to show that the movement toward privatization was international. For example, some writers (Cha and Li, *SJJJDB*, 29 August 1988) cited that Britain had improved its economy in the past ten years by reducing the state sector in the national economy from 11 percent to 6 percent.

Contrasting the situation in Eastern European countries with the stories of successful privitization elsehwhere, they argued that the economic stagnation in these countries stemmed from the fact that they had confined their economic reform to repairing state ownership rather than to fundamentally changing it.

In a national symposium held in Qinghe of Hebei Province in 3–9 March 1989, private economy was further acclaimed by hundreds of participants from central, provincial, and local governments, academia, and the press (SJJJDB, 1 May 1989). Qinghe used to be a county that had to rely on state subsidies for survival. After a four-year experiment with private economy, 99.5 percent of its industry and commerce were controlled by individuals, who were able to turn over 10 million yuan annually to the state. Impressed by the successful experience of Qinghe, some viewed privatization as an effective method of eradicating poverty and even concluded that where there was private economy, there was a rapid economic growth. Others claimed that privatization was the hope for rural modernization. Still others maintained that if we admitted that the socialist economy was a commodity economy, we should implement a private economy because privatization was best suited to commodity production.

A general consensus reached in this symposium was that private ownership was the form of property rights that was most imperative for a modern economy. With the appreciation of private economy, the criticism of state ownership by the participants was intensified and, indeed, radicalized. For Zhang Weiguo,[31] "public ownership had eroded the entire nation, the entire society, and the entire ranks of cadres," in the sense that it stifled creativity, innovations, and progress. He held the dominance of state ownership directly responsible for China's poverty and backwardness. The criticism of state ownership reached a peak when an anonymous "Declaration of Private Ownership—China's Hope" was widely circulated in some major cities in April 1989. The declaration listed ten major charges against state ownership, ranging from "restricting the development of the productive forces," "causing astonishing waste," and "checking working efficiency" to encouraging bureaucracy and leading to autocracy. The declaration also linked private ownership to China's democratization by stating, "China cannot have genuine democracy and freedom and cannot become strong unless public ownership, the root of trouble, is eradicated" (FBIS, 6

December 1989, 38). Understandably, the argument for encouraging a private economy in order to foster a Western-style political system was later seen by hardliners as a serious threat to the party's legitimacy.

It should be pointed out that the pro-privatization arguments in 1988–89 were largely derived from reformers' frustration with the program for reforming the state economy. A deep sense of hopelessness with the state economy impelled them to seek more-radical remedies. Thus their vision of private economy was, to a certain extent, idealized. Some of them even perceived the private economy as a panacea for China's economic problems. While they fixed their eyes on Western laissez-faire economics, they paid little attention to some established criticisms against it. They seemed unaware of, or not to care about, the adverse effects of private economy. Few seriously asked if China could sustain a total privatization. But for some others, China had to pay a price for its transition from a "distributive" system to a "productive" one. They did not deny the need for an active role of the state in a privatized economy, but they believed that a system in which the state was a major owner of the means of production and producer, manager, distributor, and regulator was fundamentally different from a system in which the state intervened in economies while guaranteeing private property rights and market mechanisms.

The ideological discourse on private economy typically pointed to the process in which instrumental principles, once they deviated from fundamentals, could evolve into alternative ideologies. As we have seen, the justification for a private economy initially was placed in the framework of socialism. But private economy was capitalistic in nature. Its justification would unavoidably stimulate capitalistic thinking that clashed with fundamental principles of the official ideology. The CCP thus put itself in a dilemma: On the one hand, it needed private economy as a supplementary means to overcome economic difficulties, and therefore it opened up this "forbidden zone." On the other hand, it could not identify itself with the ideology embodied in private economy. The leadership felt comfortable when the private economy issue was justified in "fundamental" terms. However, as the issue was increasingly defined in a way that was virtually leading to capitalism, the leadership felt that the system's legitimacy was threatened. This resulted in the ideological crackdown on the proponents of privatization after 4 June 1989.

Reconciling the Socialist System and a Private Economy:
A Problem Unsettled

Ideologically, right after the Tiananmen Incident of 1989, the CCP leadership showed the tendency to restore the tradition that based instrumental principles on fundamentals. Consequently, the pro-privatization argument defined in liberal terms was accused by the hardliners of attempting to restore capitalism. A large number of articles appeared in the official publications rebutting privatization and defending state ownership. The criticisms were of two main types. One was to recast a bad image of private economy, a strategy scholars termed "negative legitimation" (Shlapentokh 1986). By using this strategy, conservatives connected the private economy with the worst social maladies. An article in *Liberation Army's Daily* (2 November 1989), for example, linked privatization to economic fluctuation, a high unemployment rate, high stagflation, and unfair distribution. Enforcing privatization, the article argued, could only result in a system in which "the majority of our people will fall back into poverty, and a very small number of people would get rich." Thus, it meant nothing but a retrogression into the old China (*FBIS*, 12 December 1989, 20). While making a theoretical attack on private economy, conservatives also disparaged private enterprises in China. A *Guangming Daily* article (He, GMRB, 27 October 1989) portrayed owners of private enterprises as using all kinds of means to undermine the state economy and infringe upon public interests; For example, the article claimed they competed with state enterprises for productive materials and markets by bribing or giving high commissions to those in charge, they bought off skilled workers and professionals from state sectors by offering higher wages, and they cheated consumers by selling adulterated goods. More seriously, according to the article, more than 80 percent of private enterprises and individual businesspeople evaded taxation. Many of them were claimed to have made profits and to have accumulated personal wealth by illegal means. In short, private economy was cast as a cause of, rather than a solution to, China's economic chaos.

Another category of criticism was to focus on defending China's public ownership. One argument in various official publications was that China's public ownership was created out of historical necessity. Conservative defense of public ownership mixed economic and political justifications. By refuting the argument that public ownership was not suited for China's low productivity, conservatives asserted that to judge whether or not productive relations were suited to China depended not on the absolute level of the productive forces they generated but on the relative speed of development they brought about (*GMRB*, 7 October 1989, 7). From this perspective, they argued, China's public ownership was superior in terms of promoting productivity, given the very low starting point of the development of the productive forces in 1949. But such an economic interpretation was apparently inconsistent with classical Marxism, according to which China was far from economically mature enough to enforce public ownership, which must be based on a high level of productive forces. Realizing this, conservatives explained public ownership as an "inevitable outcome of the sharpening of class contradictions between the Chinese people and imperialism, feudalism, and bureaucratic capitalism" (*GMRB*, 1989, 7). Public ownership was seen as the only alternative for the CCP to solve social and class contradictions and therefore as politically necessary (*RMRB*, 2 December 1989, 1, 2). However, the proposition that public ownership was a result of political necessity seemingly contradicted the one that stressed public ownership as an outcome of advancing productivity. This had actually been a theoretical as well as a practical dilemma confronting the CCP since it took power. Edward Friedman (1984, 11–46) called it a "socialist conundrum" that could be a deep source of ideological and policy conflicts in China or other state socialist countries.

After the Tiananmen Incident, conservatives also rebutted the argument that only privatization was best suited for commodity production. It contended that there were two types of commodity economies, which were respectively determined by public and private ownership. Under different ownership systems, the commodity economy could assume different characteristics. Conservatives believed that China could have its own commodity economy (namely, a commodity economy with Chinese characteristics) without private property rights. This commodity economy, it seemed to conservatives, would be more benign than the capitalist one. But the question of by what mechanism this "socialist commodity economy" could work was evaded. Initially, a stated goal of China's reform was to establish a "planned commodity economy," that is, a reconciliation of public ownership with a market economy. As the reform deepened, however, the conflictual nature intrinsic to this goal became so apparent that the demand for a more radical restructuring of the economy was inevitable. After all, commodity economy had its own logic, which, once set in motion, would either push the economy to adapt to it, which meant a disintegration of state socialism, or cease working (or work in a distorted form) if structural restrictions were not removed. The failure of economic reforms in Eastern Europe had proved that the linkage between state ownership and a commodity economy was very weak. As Kornai (1990, 58) pointed out, based on his longtime observation of economic reforms in Eastern Europe, "It is futile to expect the state unit will behave as if it were privately owned and will spontaneously act as if it were a market-oriented agent. It is time to let go of this vain hope once and for all." But the CCP leadership needed both state ownership and a commodity economy. Its effort to continue to base instrumental principles on fundamentals, however, retained all the potentials that had led to China's crisis in 1989 and to the collapse of communism in Eastern Europe and the Soviet Union.

In parallel with the CCP's ideological reorientation, the most notorious policy move against the private economy was the CCP's decision to bar private entrepreneurs from joining the party. This new order was contained in the internal Document no. 9, 1989, issued by the party's Organization Department (*South China Morning Post*, 2 October 1989, 1). Disseminated to local party cells, this document asked local party branches "not to absorb heads of private enterprises into the party." This move, the document claimed, was to "preserve the purity" of party cells and to ensure that party members remained the "pioneers" of society. When the rule took effect, according to the document, entrepreneurs who had been party members would be entitled to an income only roughly equivalent to pay received by cadres working in state enterprises. Those who failed to obey the new regulation would be expelled from the party. This rule reversed the previous policy, supported by Zhao Ziyang, that party members were allowed to operate private enterprises and that private entrepreneurs could be recruited into the party. However, localities seemed unenthusiastic about this policy. In a speech to the National Conference of the Heads of the Provincial and Municipal Party Organization Departments, Song Ping, the head of the CCP's Central Organization Department, complained that some localities even prevented the document from passing on to the grassroots level because they were afraid that it would offend private entrepreneurs. Song Ping affirmed that this policy must be resolutely carried out.

Otherwise, he warned, the private economy could become a political force that would eventually shake China's socialist system. The intention of this policy, therefore, was obviously to prevent the private economy from seeking representation within the party.

With the drastic change of the political climate, the official policy toward the private economy was also tightened up. The purpose, as Jiang Zemin, the new general secretary, stated explicitly, was that the CCP would never allow the private sector to "curtail or abolish the predominant position of the state economy" (FBIS, 2 October 1989, 47). Thus, the State Council stipulated that state-run enterprises would be given priority access to raw materials, energy, and transportation facilities, a move aimed at reversing the reformist policy that private enterprises were encouraged to compete with state ones for resources in markets. Private enterprises were subject to harsh restrictions in many ways, and some were even forced to close as a result.

Although the private economy was drastically affected by the shift of the "political wind," it did not suffer total liquidation. The CCP still affirmed the need of the coexistence of private enterprises with the state economy. After all, to ban the private economy would mean massive unemployment, a great loss of state revenue, and many inconveniences for consumers—all of which could cause popular discontent and social instability. Thus, the policy to continue the private economy, which was, however, subjected to strict state supervision, was a result of political calculation. Deng Xiaoping's personal commitment to the economic reform might also account for private economy's having survived the political storm. Despite hardliners' attempts to push a total reversal of the ten-year reform, moderates, mainly Deng Xiaoping, insisted that the economic reform be continued. On a private occasion, Deng reemphasized the productive forces criterion, pointing out that "whether our policies or work are good or not, correct or incorrect, depend upon whether they are conducive to the development of the productive forces" (South China Morning Post, 4 July 1990). Thus, although the morale of private entrepreneurs was drastically hurt in the days immediately following the Tiananmen Incident, they generally could continue their business later on, with a careful eye to governmental policies that were subject to fluctuation at the time. At the ideological level, however, the liberal justification for the private economy simply disappeared. Private enterprises were strictly defined as only supplementary to the state economy. The CCP's "anti-peaceful-evolution" campaign, started after 4 June 1989 and intensified after the collapse of communism in Eastern Europe, and especially in the Soviet Union, made any idea favoring private economy heterodox. Thus, the CCP deeply trapped itself in the predicament of sustaining the private economy in practice while staunchly fighting for the preservation of the communist system.

7
The Distribution Issue in the Economic Reform

This chapter deals with the CCP's ideological reformulation regarding distribution. It shows that as egalitarianism proved detrimental to economic development, the leadership sought to pursue economic efficiency at the expense of distributional equality. As the implementation of measures to boost the economy enlarged income differentials, equality as a fundamental goal of socialism eroded. Reformers' efforts to justify distributional inequality within a socialist framework have substantially diluted the CCP's ideological fundamentals and, indeed, stimulated capitalistic alternatives. However, the CCP, as a Leninist party that still officially commits itself to socialism, is politically vulnerable to the growth of inequality in the society it rules. Thus, although the CCP has adopted a pragmatic distribution policy in favor of production, socialist equality (or "common prosperity," as defined in China's official publications) remains only symbolically important for the CCP's legitimacy. Nevertheless, as the following analysis shows, this proves to generate crises.

Egalitarianism: Theory and Practice

Marxist ideology holds that the ownership system of the means of production determines the distribution system. As Marx stated, "The prevailing distribution of the means of consumption is only a consequence of the distribution of the conditions of production themselves" (quoted in Xue 1981). One of the fundamental socialist rationales for public ownership is that the latter could wipe out exploitation and lead to distributional equality. This was the purpose behind China's socialist transformation. Chinese Marxists perceived the establishment of public ownership as a decisive means of realizing socioeconomic equality. As Xue Muqiao (1981, 68) claimed, "Under the socialist system, the means of production are the property of the whole society or that of a collective, namely, property owned jointly by a group of working people. Laborers are the owners of the means of production and are no longer separated from them." Such a system, he continued, "rules out the exploitation of man by man," which was at the root of capitalist socioeconomic inequality. In addition, public ownership of the means of production makes it possible for a society to allocate resources in favor of the majority of the working people, and hence constitutes a prerequisite for socioeconomic equality.

It should be noted, however, that the founding fathers of communism did not anticipate that socialism would usher in an era of social leveling. On the contrary, Marx believed, that some form of inequality would remain for a long time, even after exploitation was exterminated. As Marx asserted in his *Critique of the Gotha Programme,* the persistence of the "bourgeois right," largely manifested in the process of distribution, was a major feature of the socialist mode of production. "To each according to his work," the socialist principle of distribution according to Marx, did not create a genuine equality because laborers with unequal productive capacities did not receive equal pay, and it was thus the "bourgeois right" in nature. Nevertheless, Marx emphasized the transitional nature of the "bourgeois right" and believed that it would be eliminated in full communism.

The CCP's pre-reform vision of distribution highlighted the egalitarian element of Marxist ideology. To Mao Zedong and his followers, it was the historical mission of the Chinese communists to push forward and accelerate the transition of Chinese society to communism. Thus, a historical initiative should be taken by the communists to create conditions for the transition. The complete elimination of the bourgeois right, therefore, was regarded by them as the animus of the socialist revolution (Joseph 1984). Consequently, egalitarianism became a basic component of Maoist ideology that dominated China's distribution policy for two decades.

The pre-reform ideology rejected individual material interests. For Mao (1977, 129), making "an absolute out of concern for individual materials interest" was "bound to entail the danger of increasing individualism." And "To treat distribution of consumer goods as a determining motive force is the erroneous view of distribution as determinative." He also criticized the assertion in a Soviet economics textbook that "socialism is fundamentally superior to capitalism because wages steadily rise."

The pre-reform ideology denounced distributional inequality that emerged in socialist societies as a departure from socialism or, more seriously, as a symptom of capitalist restoration. The Nine Commentaries (jiuping), which served as a theoretical weapon during the Sino-Soviet ideological debate in the 1960s, systematically and vehemently accused the Soviet Union and Yugoslavia of restoring capitalism by widening income disparities in both societies. Due to the "lesson" of "capitalist restoration" in the Soviet Union and Eastern Europe, and the prevalence of Maoist socialism, egalitarianism was further highlighted during the CR period. For the Maoist leadership, egalitarianism was necessary both for preventing capitalist restoration and for speeding up the transition to communism. Mao's emphasis on the importance of egalitarianism in combating capitalistic tendencies was clearly reflected in his *Latest Instruction on the Question of Theory*, publicized in 1975 (*BR*, 17 February 1978), a year before he died:

> In a word, China is a socialist country. Before liberation it was much the same as capitalism. Even now she practices an eight-grade wage-system, distribution to each according to his work and exchange by means of money, which are scarcely different from those in the old society. What is different is that the system of ownership has changed.
>
> Our country at present practices a commodity system, and the wage-system is unequal too, there being the eight-grade wage-system, etc.; these can only be restricted under the dictatorship of the proletariat. Thus it would be quite easy for people like Lin Biao to push the capitalist system, if they came to power.

Here Mao himself sounded as though he advocated distribution determinism, for he believed that distributional inequality, even unrelated to the ownership system, might provide a social and economic foundation for capitalist restoration. Mao also displayed here his suspicions about the principle of "To each according to his work." For him, inequality could be entrenched if the bourgeois right, mainly embodied in the principle "To each according his work," was not deliberately restricted. In fact, Mao's emphasis on restricting distributional inequality to arrest capitalistic tendencies was hailed in the pre-reform ideology as a contribution to the development of Marxism (Christensen and Delman, 1983, 9–20).

Shaped by Mao's ideology, pre-reform China pursued a basically egalitarian distribution policy.[1] According to a report by the World Bank (1983), gini coefficients for urban income inequality in China in 1980 were 0.16, while the urban average for other developing countries was 0.43. The lowest gini coefficients of a developing country on record (Pakistan, 0.36) were more than twice those of China. Several factors accounted for the low degree of inequality in China's urban areas. First, there were no property-based incomes (such as rent, dividents, and profits) except interest from savings. Second, no private businesses existed. Third, the wage system was basically equal; the wages of managerial, technical, and professional personnel were far lower than those of their counterparts in developing countries. Slightly higher gini coefficients in China's rural areas, according to the World Bank report, could be attributed mainly to spatial differentiation (also see Selden 1988). Even so, the report indicated that gini coefficients of China's rural income inequality in 1979 (0.31)[2] were still lower than those of other developing nations included in their survey (India, 0.34; Bangladesh, 0.33; Indonesia, 0.4; Malaysia, 0.5; Thailand, 0.39; the Philippines, 0.39; Sri Lanka, 0.35; only Pakistan's, 0.3, were lower, but they were very close to China's).

For a long time, Western critics, from both the right and the left, were doubtful that communist regimes in the Soviet Union and Eastern Europe carried out the promise of an equal society. They believed that a privileged stratum, composed of party and government officials, managerial officials, and professionals, had formed in these societies and that they lived a life that was inaccessible to the majority of people. This criticism was reinforced by the analyses of the privileged stratum done by those who used to be part of these communist systems (for example, Djilas 1957; Sik 1975). But Mao's China was perceived as different, particularly by those on the left who were deeply disillusioned with Soviet society (for example, Sweezy and Bettelheim 1972). For them, Mao's egalitarian strategy maintained the tradition of socialism, while Soviet bureaucratism perverted it. However, the negative side of China's egalitarianism was neglected. While maintaining distributional equality, this type of egalitarianism led to passivity, inertia, and a mentality of poverty in equality. In other words, equality was sustained at the tremendous cost of productivity. Even some official data in China (Liu 1983) demonstrated that two sharp declines of national labor productivity during the pre-reform period were related to the prevalence of egalitarian policies. In 1958–60, the piece-rate wage and bonus were eliminated in state enterprises. As a result, the annual average wage of employees in state enterprises dropped by 17 percent, from 637 yuan in 1957 to 582 yuan in 1960. In the countryside, "communist wind" (*gongchengfeng*)[3] led to a 14 percent fall of rural annual per capita consumer expenditure, from 79 yuan in 1957 to 68 yuan in 1960. The dire economic situation of that period was officially attributed to natural disasters and a sudden withdrawal of Soviet economic aid. The party did not admit that human errors and internal mistakes were the principal factors contributing to economic failure until the years of economic reform.

The deleterious consequences of the Great Leap Forward on the economy were followed by a short period of policy adjustment in the early 1960s, when "to each according to his work" was emphasized. However, Mao's egalitarian ideology did not lose strength and soon reached its zenith again during the CR period. With a second elimination of the piece rate wage and bonus and the strict restrictions on the rise of wages, the per capita annual income of employees in state enterprises fell to 605 yuan in 1976 from 652 yuan in 1965. In parallel with this was a 10 percent drop in the rate of productivity. In the countryside, egalitarian distribution took a form in which 70 percent of grain, vegetables, firewood, and other agricultural and sideline products were distributed according to the number of family members, while the remaining 30 percent were distributed according to work points for labor. That is to say, whether or not people worked hard, they received roughly the same pay. The result of such egalitarianism, as we have mentioned in chapter 6, was the stagnation of China's rural economy.

Rehabilitation of "To Each According to His Work"

The CCP's ideological reformulation began with a "rehabilitation" of the principle "To each according to his work." Before officially resuming power, Deng Xiaoping (1983, 98) addressed this problem. In his talk with the head of the Office of Political Research of the State Council, Deng emphasized the need to restore "to each according to his work" as a socialist distribution principle. This principle, as Deng understood it, meant distribution according to the quantity and quality of work. Those who worked hard, had good working skills, or made special contributions to scientific and technological inventions should be awarded a higher wage. Moreover, he argued, material incentives, such as the bonus system and invention awards, should have a position in China's socialist economy. All of these, he claimed, served one aim—to encourage people to do better. What Deng said was not qualified as a theoretical justification for a distributional inequality under socialism. But he straightforwardly raised the association between "to each according to his work"—the socialist distribution principle—and income differentials. His message was clear: Not only would income differentials be an unavoidable outcome of the socialist distribution, but they also were necessary for and conducive to the socialist economy.

In parallel with Deng Xiaoping's policy suggestion, many theoretical works and articles appeared in 1979–80 to justify income differentials and material incentives. One influential work was Xue Muqiao's *China's Socialist Economy* (1981), which devoted a chapter to the distribution issue. As a veteran party Marxist economist, Xue justified income differentials strictly within a Marxist framework. According to him, a socialist society in which the productive forces were not yet fully developed was not able to provide its members with a free supply of all necessary means of subsistence. It could only pay each laborer on the basis of the quantity and quality of labor he or she performed, leaving it to the laborer to work out a family budget. Practicing the system of "To each according to his work" meant recognition of unequal pay for laborers with unequal productive capacities and unequal labor contribution. Xue argued that distributional inequality was inevitable, because the socialist system, as Marx claimed, tacitly recognized the unequal productive capacity of the worker as a "natural privilege" (69). According to Xue, unequal pay for laborers with unequal productive capacities underlay the material interests of the individual and material incentives. Thus, to him, it was rational that the greater one's ability and contribution were, the greater one's pay should be. While affirming its "historical inevitability," Xue also pointed to the defects of "To each according to his work," which were nevertheless unavoidable in socialism. He noted that the principle meant both equality and inequality, because, first, ability (and therefore pay) varied from individual to individual, and second, the number of one's dependents (and therefore the standard of living) varied from family to family. However, Xue contended, because this inequality played a positive role in the development of the productive forces at present, the principle must be defended (75).

However, as a leading party theorist, Xue seemed reluctant to fully endorse material incentives. For him, the principle "To each according to his work" "lies within the narrow confines of `bourgeois right'" (77), and placing undue emphasis on material incentives to the point of neglecting political-ideological education would encourage "bourgeois individualism." Thus, he suggested that adherence to the principle "To each according to his work" should be coupled with regular socialist education of working people.

Xue's elaboration of "To each according to his work" in fact added little to Marx's *Critique of the Gotha Programme*. However, in contrast to Maoist ideological argumentation, which stressed the egalitarian tenet of Marx's work and advocated a progressive restriction of distributional inequality, Xue interpreted Marx's theme of the bourgeois right "fatalistically," namely, as something inevitable at certain stage of socialist development. But there was a more significant difference between Maoist and Xue's interpretation of Marx: Maoist ideology negatively perceived any form and any degree of distributional inequality as a catalyst for capitalism, whereas Xue positively considered inequality in some forms as a stimulus to productivity. Thus, the argumentation presented by Xue and many other official theoreticians represented an important reformulation of the official ideology. However, the distributional inequality in Xue's and many others' views at that period referred only to a moderate income differential stemming from individual laborers' capacities or from the different performance of enterprises. Their theories immediately became inadequate, because they ruled out any sharp increase in income gaps, gaps that later arose due to the emergence of private property rights, labor hiring, joint ventures, and market speculation. In fact, as the economy was increasingly liberalized, the sources of individual income multiplied; some of them were beyond governmental control. Thus, while justifying distributional inequality as necessary for production, the CCP's ideology came to encounter the problems of how much and what kind of inequality would be tolerated.

The New Dimensions of Distributional
Inequality in the Rural Areas

The growing income disparity emerged first in China's rural areas. Before 1979 the most significant differentials were those between localities with different ecological conditions or proximity to urban markets, whereas income in villages was evenly distributed (Riskin 1987, 10). However, the state had implemented policies to equalize income differentials by raising the accounting level, which obscured existing differences in earning power and long-term subsidization of one village by another. Since 1979, however, large gaps had appeared within, as well as between, localities. The rural income inequality was a direct result of the implementation of *chengbao*. As the means of production were contracted out to individual households, the incomes of individual households came to conform more closely to their particular characteristics (labor power, skills, education, and social connections) without the equalizing intermediation of a common work-point system and central distribution.

Accompanying *chengbao* was the CCP's new policy of helping (or allowing) some peasants to prosper first, which deliberately encouraged distributional inequality. The party's Document no. 75 of 1980 indicated that the party would support all kinds of *chengbao* systems as long as they increased income levels. Also, as shown in chapter 6, because *chengbao* was defined in party documents as a practice of "To each according to his work," the income disparity caused by it was legitimated. Deng Xiaoping personally advocated the "some-to-prosper-first" policy. In a conversation with officials from the State Planning Commission, the State Economic Commission, and the Agricultural Ministry, he said, "[We] should allow some people to prosper first in both rural and urban areas. Getting rich through diligence is justified" (Deng 1987, 21).

The households that were first to prosper in the rural areas were called "specialized households" (*zhuanyehu*). These households typically developed out of an expansion of household sidelines into a large-scale operation involving the full-time labor of one or more family members. There was a rough national guideline for classifying specialized households: A family was a specialized household if 60 percent of its economic activity was in a single specialized line, 60 percent of its labor power was engaged in this activity, and 60 percent of the product or service produced by this household enterprise was sold as a commodity (Johnson 1986, 23). Economic activity that did not reach these standards was categorized as an ordinary household sideline.[4]

Although there were no official figures on the number of specialized households, Chinese authors often cited 20 million or 13.6 percent of peasant households as the approximate number of specialized households (*JJRB*, 22 February 1984). According to a survey (Lin 1984) of tens of counties and prefectures in over ten provinces, the percentage of specialized households varied from 5 percent to 40 percent, depending on conditions such as local resources, transportation, and distance from commercially developing cities. In terms of the activity of specialized households, Howard's study (1988) showed that in early 1984 most specialized households were concentrating on grain or cash crops, livestock, poultry, or fish. Over one-third were specialized in field crops. In South China, 20 to 30 percent of the rural labor power was handling the agricultural production formerly done by 70 to 80 percent (*China Daily*, 29 February 1984, 4). A large number of peasants freed from the land chose to engage in a variety of "specialized activities," covering afforestation, production of animal proteins,[5] construction, transportation, mining, service industries, and running clinics, nurseries, schools, and entertainments.

Specialized households still constituted fewer than 15 percent of rural families in 1985, but their output in certain sectors was out of proportion with their numbers. For example, according to Howard (1988), there were about 3.35 million households that specialized in livestock and poultry production. In one year they increased the national supply of poultry three and a half times. Although the average household kept no more than a dozen fowls, specialized households raised hundreds. Tianjin, the third largest city in China, used to import 90 percent of its egg supplies from outside the municipality. By 1984, thanks to specialized households, a very small percentage of local families supplied 60 percent of the city's eggs.

The emergence of specialized households had many positive effects on China's rural development. It provided an outlet for surplus labor power released by *chengbao*; it facilitated the commercialization of the rural economy and supplied urban areas with abundant products; it popularized agricultural technologies; and more importantly, it substantially raised the living standard of the peasant households involved. However, the development of specialized households also brought income polarization. While Chinese peasant households as a whole benefited from *chengbao*, specialized households took a larger share of the economic growth. In other words, much of the increase in inequality was caused by the rising income of the successful specialized households. The incomes of specialized households tended to be double, triple, even ten times the incomes of village families that were not specialized. Particularly, as the scale of operation expanded, quite a few specialized households began to hire labor and develop into capitalistic enterprises. Their income could be a hundred times those of average households. "Ten-thousand-yuan household" (*wanyuan hu*) was a catchword the Chinese media used to designate households whose annual income was over ten thousand yuan.

Selden (1988) found that gini coefficients of intrarural income inequality based on government surveys, had risen from 0.22 in 1978 to 0.27 in 1985, these figures indicated a small but steady increase in income differentials, although its degree remained low by international standards (see table 7.1).

Table 7.1 Rural Per Capita Net Income, 1978–85
(Percentage Distribution)

Income Group	1978	1980	1981	1982	1983	1984	1985
Over 500 yuan		1.6	3.2	6.7	11.9	18.2	22.3
400–500	2.4	2.9	5.0	8.7	11.6	14.1	15.8
300–400		8.6	14.4	20.8	22.9	24.5	24.0
200–300	15.0	25.3	34.8	37.0	32.9	25.6	25.6
100–200	49.2	51.8	37.9	24.1	19.3	11.3	11.3
Below 100	33.3	9.8	4.7	2.7	1.4	0.8	1.0
Average Income	133.6	191.3	223.4	270.1	309.8	355.3	39716
Gini coefficient	0.2281	0.2448	0.2502	0.2528	0.2683	0.2666	0.2718

Source: State Statistical Bureau (cited from Selden 1988). Data for 1979 are not recorded.
Note: Net income is based on a calculation of the value of income in kind plus cash income.

A report based on a national survey of rural development (1987), sponsored by the Research Office of Rural Policy of the Secretariat of the CCP Central Committee from late 1984 to early 1985, also demonstrated rural income differentials. According to the report, for 37,422 households under survey, the income of the richest one-fourth accounted for 51.7 percent of the group's total income in 1984, compared with 47.7 percent in 1978, while that of the poorest one-fourth dropped from 9.2 percent in 1978 to 8.2 percent in 1978 in 1984. Some local data confirmed the same tendency. In the prefecture that pioneered the IHC, Chuxian in Anhui Province, rapid growth of incomes was accompanied by increased differentiation. By 1981, 1.2 percent of families had moved up to the level of 500 yuan per capita income, while another 5 percent earned less than 60 yuan—a gap believed to be significantly higher than before (Riskin 1987). In Jiangsu's Sugan County in 1982, about 3,400 households out of a total of 200,000 earned more than 1,000 yuan; at the same time, 5 percent of households' per capita income was less than 100 yuan per capita (*BR*, 28 November 1983, 48).

Many factors contributed to the rapid income increase in some peasant households. Among others, two were significant. First, as the means of production were dispersed among the peasants, how to effectively and efficiently use them turned out to be the key for the peasants to get rich. Some of the peasant population—former brigade and team cadres, educated youths and demobilized soldiers, skilled craftspeople, and individuals with "commercial minds"—proved more able than others to use the means of production to make profits.[6] The means of production alone, which were roughly evenly contracted to the households, were not sufficient for bringing in a higher income. Political influence, social connections (*guanxi*), administrative skills, technical know-how—all were necessary resources for making wealth; they were nevertheless distributed unevenly. Those who possessed these resources tended to make their fortunes faster. Second, the government deliberately adopted policies in favor of specialized households. According to the *Central Committee Circular on Rural Works in 1984* (ZYWX, *1987*), all levels of government should support specialized households, providing necessary services for them, and satisfying their demands for loans, information, supplies and marketing, and technical advice. In many localities, governments signed contracts with specialized households, guaranteeing necessary materials, and providing interest-free loans, various technical advice, and purchasing agents to ensure speedy delivery of products to city markets. In a "scarcity economy" with an undeveloped market, the government's "rich first" policy fostered a fast accumulation of wealth in the hands of peasants who were favored.

By international standards China's rural income differentials as a whole might seem unimpressive. But compared with China's egalitarian past, the change in distribution was significant. Moreover, considering the striking contrast between "ten-thousand-yuan households" and those households that were still struggling with poverty, it appeared obvious that a fundamental change toward distributional inequality was taking place. Confronted with this, the CCP was compelled to seek new ideological justifications.

The "Rich First" versus Common Prosperity

A salient ideological issue raised with the emergence of the rural inequality was the nature of the "rich first" policy: Was a policy that encouraged distributional disparity still socialist? There seemed to be strong doubts about it. Some worried that if some households got rich before others, it would be more difficult to achieve socialist prosperity for all. Worse, they argued, such a policy would lead to class polarization and the emergence of a new bourgeoisie (FBIS, 8 January 1980, Q3). Others accused the "rich first" policy of encouraging people to seek private interests and deviate from socialism (FBIS, 25 May 1982, K17). The People's Daily reported a typical case (RMRB, 20 May 1982, 1) that showed local resistance to the "rich first" policy, due to ideological confusion. Zhang Xiangheng, a peasant who got rich by engaging in diversified household economy, was publicly denounced as "taking the capitalist road." The authorities of the Sanjing administrative district of Nanzhang County in Hebei Province, where Zhang was living, called more than a thousand people to participate in a mass accusation rally to criticize Zhang's capitalistic deeds. An Pingsheng (JJGL, 5 Marcy 1983, 7), Yunnan's party secretary, wrote in an article that many comrades had asked him in his inspection tour whether the "rich first" policy was going to produce class polarization and a movement toward capitalism.

The theoretical justification for the "first rich" policy focused on the following questions:

The Meaning of Common Prosperity

Common prosperity (gongtong fuyu) was defined as a goal of socialism and was used to oppose the "rich first" policy, so its reinterpretation became crucial for justifying the emergence of distributional inequality. Proponents of the "rich first" policy did not deny that common prosperity was a basic socialist goal. However, they argued, common prosperity did not amount to a simultaneous or an identical prosperity. According to a pamphlet (Xie et al. 1982) specially written for rural cadres, common prosperity was a long-term goal, which could be reached only through the process of some peasants becoming well-to-do first. A simultaneous or identical prosperity was practically impossible, for two reasons. First, there were spatial differentials, shaped in large measure by ecological factors, including terrain, climate, soil quality, precipitation, and access to water, transportation, and urban markets. These differentials, which could not be eliminated in a short time, determined substantial differences in per capita income and opportunity among villages. Second, the principle "To each according to his work" unavoidably generated distributional inequality, because (1) the amount of labor that peasants could provide was different, and therefore their incomes were different; (2) the amount of labor power each household had was different, which brought different income levels; and (3) even with roughly the same amount of income, the living standard of households could be drastically different due to the number of nonlabor members each family household had to support. As a result, common prosperity would not be a process in which each household could get rich simultaneously. Instead, it could only be a process in which economic benefits were diffused among peasants at a different pace. The "rich first" policy, hence, was a recognition of objective constraints and a realistic step toward a common prosperity.

In redefining the meaning of common prosperity, some commentators criticized past policies that had pursued common prosperity by preventing some peasants from becoming prosperous first. As one author (FBIS, 17 May 1979, L8) pointed out, there were cases in which peasants in better-off villages were deliberately held to a poor standard of living to narrow the gaps among peasants in a certain area. The result was disastrous. Peasants in better-off villages were reluctant to increase production, and peasants in worse-off villages lost interest in improving their conditions. A strong argument echoed by many authors was that the past practice of pursuing common prosperity had led to dead-end common poverty. To many advocates of the "rich first" policy, the correct way of realizing common prosperity was to allow some peasants to receive more income and live better lives first so that they could serve as examples for the rest (*FBIS*, 23 February 1979, E12). Here we may see an important assumption underlying the "rich first" policy, that is: the "demonstration effect." Deng Xiaoping (1987, 15) made an assertion that clearly reflected his belief in the "demonstration effect":

> The fact that part of the population gets rich first inevitably exerts an enormous demonstration force, influencing their neighbors, and driving people in other areas and units to learn from them. Thus, the whole national economy will be promoted and the whole people of the country will get prosperous faster. Thus, this is a major policy, a policy that can spur on the whole national economy.

The assumption of the demonstration effect actually prevailed in all official publications that favored the "rich first" policy. Indeed, for those who were apt to encourage distributional inequality, this assumption seemed to provide the strongest linkage between the "rich first" policy and the goal of common prosperity. With this assumption, the current inequality was justified by an eventual coming of common prosperity that would be stimulated by a demonstration effect.

Common Prosperity and Egalitarianism

Differentiating common prosperity from egalitarianism was a major task of ideological reconstruction. While conservatives rejected the "rich first" policy as opposing socialist common prosperity, reformers claimed that common prosperity pursued by the past leadership had been perverted into egalitarianism. Common prosperity, as Yu Guangyuan (1985) analyzed it, was interpreted in the previous ideology as an equal distribution of the means of consumption and departed from the principle "To each according to his work." Rather than being compatible with scientific socialism, Yu argued, egalitarianism was an ideal of the petite bourgeoisie and represented a destructive, reactionary, and backward factor in the socialist economy. With an equal distribution of income among people regardless of the amount of their labor, egalitarianism as such actually meant that some social members could freely own others' labor. Such a practice, Yu continued, did not foster common prosperity; instead, it abetted laziness, passivity, irresponsibility, and low morale, and seriously hindered the development of productive forces and technological innovations. Indeed, Yu pointed out, egalitarianism had proved most detrimental to productivity. Thus, common prosperity based on egalitarianism, as the authors of the pamphlet mentioned above asserted, could end up leading to common poverty (Xie et al. 1982:, 7).

"Rich First" and Polarization

In China's economic thinking, polarization was usually related to capitalist systems, where, as it was said, the rich got richer and the poor got poorer, due to an unequal distribution based on private ownership. It was thus not surprising that polarization became a major conservative argument against the "rich first" policy. For those who favored distributional differentials, the "rich first" policy would not produce a polarization. As some commentators argued, (Xie 1982) the main reason was that in China, the root of polarization—private ownership—was eliminated. Distributional polarization, according to the authors of the pamphlet mentioned above, was a manifestation of unequal distribution of the means of production, which had not existed in China since the collectivization. Even though chengbao contracted the means of production to the peasants, the peasants were not allowed to use the land and other major means of production to exploit others. They still had to rely on their own, rather than others', labor as the source of income. According to the pamphlet, the income differentials stemming from labor fundamentally differed from income polarization based on private ownership of the means of production. A similar view was expressed by reform leaders. In his report at the Central Rural Work Conference, Wan Li (BR, 1984, 27) argued that worries about polarization were unfounded, and that the emergence of the current rural differentials was just a question of "some folks getting rich first" and "not the result of some people having exploited other people." Citing some local data, Wan emphasized that getting rich through labor (laodong zhifu) was the mainstream in the countryside. Most "rich first" peasants, he said, were those who were well educated, skillful, business oriented, and "good at combining various productive factors"; they became well-to-do through their own labors. The message Wan conveyed to the public, as manifested in numerous official publications, was that income differentials derived from labor would not produce class polarization.

However, the ideological reformulation regarding the "rich first" policy did not fill the gap between an emerging inequality and the official commitment to socialism. The "rich first" policy was flawed because it overlooked the dynamics of distributional inequality of the emergence of a de facto exercise of private property rights. It was perhaps right that, as long as individuals were alientated from property rights, "To each according to his work" would not lead to growing distributional inequity. Labor separated from control or exercise over property rights would hardly generate polarized income differentials. However, with the development of the IHC and specialized households, private ownership of property became a factor that could considerably polarize income differentials.

Private property rights generated a widening income gap in the rural areas mainly through two channels. First, without involving any exploitation, some households, relying on exercises of private ownership of property, accumulated wealth at a speed that was virtually impossible, no matter how hard they worked, in the absence of property rights. For example, in March 1983, William Hinton (1983) found a peasant in Fengyang County, Anhui, who owned two tractors, each of which could earn 1,000 yuan per month, thus paying for itself in six months. Another peasant had become a trader, distributing locally woven reed mats to purchasers in the northeast. He made 20,000 *yuan* in a single year, paid three-fourths of it in income tax, and still ended up with fourteen times the country's average income. Similar cases could be found nationwide.

Second, the exercise of private ownership of property was directly related to capitalist exploitation, which was apparent in rural private enterprises. Private entrepreneurs, as we showed in chapter 5 and will examine in the following analysis, had reached an income level high enough to separate them as a special social stratum from average people. Both developments demonstrated that, with the emergence of private ownership of property, the "rich first" policy went beyond the principle "To each according to his work," and in many instances, became "To each according to his property."

By maintaining the collective or state ownership of the land, reformers believed that capitalist exploitation could be averted. The possible threat of class polarization the allowance of private capital accumulation and inheritance posed was avoided in the reformulated ideology. Yet, as Kenneth Lieberthal pointed out,

> [The] logic of current policy is that a new rural elite stratum will emerge that will enjoy leverage across many aspects of rural life. The new policy permits peasant families that have prospered to use their surplus capital to acquire more extensive and holdings, to set up transport companies, to invest in local enterprises, and so forth. Such wide-ranging economic activity will inevitably produce pressures for enhanced social and political power (1985, 109–10).

Thus, in restructuring China's rural economy, the CCP's leadership encountered a dilemma that many third-world countries had faced in pursuing modernization—growth versus equality. The leadership seemed to be convinced that the spectacular growth of the rural economy indicated that income differentials could play a positive role in boosting the economy. The official criticism of egalitarianism indicated the leadership's orientation toward growth at the expense of equality. Even though the initial reform of distribution was limited to a full play of "To each according to his work" (the so-called bourgeois rights), it soon exceeded the boundary as rural property relations were adjusted. The result was that property, not simply labor, began to determine the income levels of peasant households. Such a practice in fact had broken the principle "To each according to his work," though the CCP still interpreted it as a form of socialist distribution. Thus, the CCP created a contradiction that confused both itself and the society about what socialist distribution really meant. This contradiction was intensified when an acceleration of economic liberalization began in urban areas in 1984 and when some new institutional structures emerged to widen distributional inequality on a larger scope.

The Emergence of Urban Distributional Inequality

Distributional inequality did not stand out as a salient issue in urban areas until 1986, when, with economic liberalization, various kinds of opportunities arose for the accumulation of personal wealth. Three official policies contributed to the emerging urban inequality. The first was a partial privatization, which included permission for individual economy first and then for private enterprises. Privatization, though limited, created a social stratum whose income level exceeded that of the rest of society. The second was the industrial contract system. By linking income with enterprise performance, this system encouraged intraenterprise inequality and forced enterprises to choose measures, such as layoffs, to pursue efficiency at the expense of equality. The third was the dual-price system, which produced opportunities for individuals to make enormous profits by taking advantage of the gap between plan and market prices. All of these were related to the weakening of the state's control over the means of production. Indeed, the decentralization of the means of production, as we will show, introduced new distribution mechanisms that further enhanced income disparities.

Privatization

The emergence of an urban individual economy (*geti jingji*) first created significant income differentials between a small group of people who were involved in individual businesses, and the majority, who lived on state wages. A survey in 1985 of more than 50,000 individual businesspeople across the country conducted by the Research Office of the State Council (General Office of the State Council, 1986) showed that 51.1 percent of them earned more than the average urban annual income (1,500 yuan). Of these, 18.3 percent earned 3,000 to 5,000 yuan, whereas 7.1 percent earned 5,000-10,000 yuan. The richest 5.7 percent earned more than 10,000 yuan per year, nearly ten times more than the average urban annual income. Local data also demonstrated a significant income increase among those who engaged in individual business. For instance, in 1985, of 377 individuals in a small commodity wholesale market in Shanghai, 43 percent earned 5,000 to 1,000 yuan per year, whereas 19.4 percent earned more than 10,000 yuan. In Qiaotou town of Wenzhou, about 100 individuals broke the of 100,000 yuan-per-year level.

Capital accumulation in private hands through the individual economy fostered the formation of private enterprises, which in turn generated income differentials. Though there were no national statistics to show the overall effect of private enterprises on the country's emerging distributional inequality, some locally based data confirmed the tendency of rapid accumulation of wealth in the hands of a few. In Beijing, for example, some private owners of department stores made a 1,000 yuan profit per month, and some of them were able to make a profit of 30,000 yuan per month; however, the average wage of their employees was 100 to 250 yuan per month. The profit of a private owner of a small coal mine in Fangshan County, Beijing, was over 100,000 yuan in 1986, 185 times the wage of his employees (540 yuan) (Lei 1989). A survey of 10 big private enterprises in Jiling Province found that per capita capital was 372,000 yuan, while per capita income was 40,000 yuan. The richest owner made 85,000 yuan per year (Jiling 1986). It was reported that among 971 registered private enterprises in Shanghai, the annual income of most owners was between 5,000 and 10,000 yuan. Some earned 40,000 yuan yearly, while a minority of them reached above 100,000 to 200,000 yuan (Li, W. 1988). A striking income gap between employers and employees was found in 50 private enterprises in Hebei Province, where the income of the former was 226 times those of the latter (Wang 1989, 285).

Another major source of nonlabor income (*fei laodong shoulu*) came from the stock exchange. By Western standards, China's stock market was still in an embryonic form. However, many Chinese had known how to enrich themselves through stock speculations. A few of them became extremely wealthy. It was reported (*LW*, 9 September 1991, 13), that Yang Huanding, a worker in Shanghai, had increased his savings to seven digits through stock exchange.

Another significant source of income differential arose between private and state enterprises. Generally speaking, private enterprises could pay a higher wage to their employees than state enterprises could. Private enterprises were more efficient in productivity and enjoyed more discretionary power in distribution. To strengthen competitiveness, private enterprises were willing and able to "buy off" technical and skilled personnel with high pay. According to a study conducted by a team of economists from Fudan University (Wang, Z. K. et al., ed., 1989), the annual income of technicians and managerial personnel in private enterprises could be 3,000 to 7,000 *yuan*, three to seven times higher than that of state enterprises. As for ordinary workers, a survey conducted by the State Administration for Industry and Commerce showed that the overwhelming majority of individual business people and workers in private enterprises received an average income of 3,000 to 4,000 yuan, or about twice the average of 1,400 to 1,500 yuan workers in state-owned enterprises

(*BR*, 15 August 1988, 4–5). The immediate outcome of this income disparity was that a large number of technical, managerial, and skilled personnel chose to quit their jobs in state enterprises and work for private ones. Meanwhile, state enterprises no longer found it as easy as before to recruit youth workers in urban areas. For example, with 150 positions open in 1985, the Beijing Fifth Construction Company only received 37 applications; twenty of the new hires quit within a month of recruitment. A rubber product factory in Qingdao planned to recruit 35 workers in 1988; only 4 applied, and one of these did not show up at the last moment (Ying and Geng, 1989, 393).

In short, with the development of individual and private economies, a social stratum had arisen—a stratum that enjoyed a very high standard of living that even overshadowed that of high governmental officials. The rise of this stratum posed a major question for the CCP: How much distributional inequality could a socialist system sustain?

The Labor System of Reform

The emerging distributional inequality in reforming China had another feature: Although what stood out about it was the higher income of a minority of people, which sharply contrasted with the lower income of the majority, it was also the case that a large number of people lost their jobs and no longer had a secure source of income. Ironically, state enterprises were producing most of the unemployment. After the implementation of the industrial contract system, state enterprises were compelled to pay attention to efficiency. Reducing surplus labor became an important measure for improving efficiency. In 1984, a pilot reform program of the labor system was implemented in several cities, resulting in layoffs of workers for the first time since 1949. During the same time, the government began to experiment with "contracted labor" in some selected enterprises, which was later formalized by the State Council in 1986 as a universal policy for all state enterprises (*XHS*, 17 June 1984; 9 September 1986). This signaled the end of the lifetime employment policy that had been practiced for many years in China's state enterprises.

From 1987 on, layoffs were no longer rare and in fact became a legitimate source of power for state enterprises. Layoffs in China's state enterprises were carried out in the name of optimal combination (*youhua zuhe*), that is, the optimal readjustments of the ratio between the means of production and the labor force. As a result of such a practice, many workers were thrown out of work. Unemployment, which used to be regarded in China as only associated with capitalism, now became a fact of life for many Chinese. According to official statistics (*XHS*, 8 August 1988), by August 1988 more than 300,000 workers had been fired by state enterprises nationwide. Most of these jobless people were kept in a "labor market" within enterprises for six months, receiving 50 percent of their regular wages, accepting technical training, and waiting for an opportunity to be "recombined." If they failed to be "recombined" in six months, they had to leave the enterprise and receive unemployment insurance (30–40 yuan per month) from their residency districts for one to two years. Aside from a few lucky ones who were able to find opportunities with other enterprises (state, private, or joint venture) in a short period, or to start individual businesses, most of the unemployed remained unemployed. For them, life was not secure anymore. The following is a case that pointedly reflected the plight of the unemployed (Ying and Geng 1989, 412). A woman worker in Shanghai was fired by a state factory due to her illness and, as a result, she could no longer enjoy full medical insurance. According to policy, 70 percent of her medical expanses could be covered by unemployment insurance within a year of her termination. However, her condition deteriorated, and she needed to be hospitalized when her unemployment insurance expired. Her cry for help to get 5,000 yuan in advance for hospitalization was turned down by all relevant agencies: her former employer rejected her because she was fired; Shanghai Labor Service Company, an agency with a twenty-million yuan unemployment insurance fund, rejected her because her insurance had expired; the Civil Administration Bureau rejected her on the grounds that her case was beyond its jurisdiction; and an unemployment relief foundation affiliated with the Trade Union rejected her for fear of involving more money in treatment. As the head of the foundation complained, there were already several tens of thousands of unemployed in Shanghai waiting for help, so how could we afford to spend a large amount of money on one worker?

Compared with capitalist or former socialist societies, China's unemployment problem is far from acute.[7] But when layoffs began, China's socialism came under serious challenge. For three decades before the reform, the CCP attributed unemployment to capitalism. How then could people distinguish unemployment in socialist China from that in capitalist countries? Unemployment intensified distributional inequality and harmed the weak in the society, which was contradictory with the fundamental principles of the official economic ideology.

Dual Price System

China's reform of its price system, started in 1984, resulted in a dual-price system composed of several forms of prices—state-set prices, floating prices, and market prices. In theory, these prices were restricted to their respective spheres: state-set prices for capital or intermediate goods distributed according to mandatory planning; floating prices for goods under guidance planning; and market prices for products not subject to state control. The coexistence of plan and market prices produced a situation in which identical items (such as tons of steel) could sell at prices that differed by more than 20 percent. The disparities between plan and market stimulated rampant rent-seeking behavior among governmental officials who had access to scarce materials. Many officials developed ways to acquire items at plan prices, sell them at market prices, and use a part of the phenomenal profit to make payoffs to cover their deeds. Also, tens of thousands of administrative corporations emerged. These were usually run by cadres, or their relatives, who, by relying on their official contacts and by acting as go-betweens in market exchanges, were able to make huge profits. This practice, called "official speculation," led to a speedy accumulation of wealth in the hands of a few officials and their relatives and contributed to distributional inequality. There were too many of these cases to be cited. According to a leading Chinese economist, rent-seeking activity by officials involved some three billion yuan per year (see Lieberthal 1993, 27). However, Qian Jiaju (*ZYRB*, 25 October 1991, 4), another prestigious Chinese economist,[8] suggested that the number could be even higher.[9]

We may never know the total amount of money that went to the private pockets of officials and their relatives and contacts. But a privileged social group definitely arose with an excessively high income drawn from private transactions of state-owned resources. These people were able to live the extravagant life and open savings accounts in foreign countries, though their nominal wages were similar to those of other Chinese.

Justifying a Market-Driven Distribution of Income

Many ideological questions arose as urban inequality grew. Obviously, it was difficult to explain the emerging distributional inequality in terms of "To each according to his work." Distributional inequality was more related to exercises of property rights, control over resources, and various social powers, than to labor. Distribution also began to be subject to the pressure of market competition, which demanded efficiency at the expense of equality. Thus, the CCP was confronted with how to reconcile socialism with a growing property-based and market-driven distributional inequality, which had for a long time been interpreted as a malady of capitalism. Consequently, the following issues became the foci of ideological reformulation with respectto accommodating the emergence of widening distributional urban inequality.

Redefining Equality

For those who favored distributional disparity, a major short-coming of the previous ideology lay in its identification of socialist equality with "equal outcome" (jieguo pingdeng), which meant that everybody should obtain an equal share in the distribution of income. The pursuit of "equal outcome," as criticized by a party study document (Shanghai Part School 1989), in fact did not create an egalitarian society as the party anticipated. Privileges based on political power persisted in the postrevolutionary society. Those who were close to the center of power took a much bigger share of economic benefit, though the majority of average people received a roughly equal distributional outcome. Moreover, equal outcome did not bring an egalitarian lifestyle for people, because many other factors could counteract "equal outcome." The only consequence of "equal outcome" was retardation of productivity. Thus, the author(s) of this document suggested that the reform of the distribution system should focus on two aspects: (1) the equality based on "equal outcome" should be replaced by the equality stressing equal opportunity, and (2) the distribution according to political power should give way to the distribution based on economic capability.

For some other Chinese commentators, even "equal opportunity" was not a feature of socialism at its preliminary stage. Although, as Zhang (1988) argued, a shift from the pursuit of "equal outcome" to the endorsement of "equal opportunity" represented progress, the latter was still wishful thinking and an unrealistic goal in current Chinese socialism. There were two reasons for this: First, unequal ownership relations, now acknowledged as part of socialism, necessarily favored some people while disfavoring others; those who owned or were able to exercise real control over the means of production enjoyed more opportunities than those who owned nothing and lived on salaries. Second, the uneven development of productive forces determined a hierarchical economic structure that distorted economic opportunities among people. Thus, according to Zhang, it was misleading to believe that socialist distribution could provide an "equal opportunity" in the sense that everybody ran from the same starting line. If equal opportunity had any realistic meaning in China's current reform, he contended, it should mean permitting everybody to participate in open competition.

In reinterpreting equality in China's preliminary socialism, Zhang contended that certain types of unequal economic relations were rational because they promoted productivity. For example, unequal returns brought about by unequal possession of technology and managerial skills were rational because they would stimulate improvements in technology and management. Unequal distributional outcomes stemming from returns of private property rights (private enterprises, stocks, and so forth) were also rational, as long as private property rights had a positive role to play in fostering production. He asserted that all rational unequal economic relations should be allowed to exist and should be protected.

Maintaining a balance between equality and efficiency was never an easy task for any government. It was particularly difficult for a regime that still needed to define equality in terms of socialism. While preliminary socialism provided a flexible framework within which to interpret equality, it also obscured the meaning of equality under socialism. Indeed, as "equal outcome" and "equal opportunity" were taken away from socialist distribution, what socialist equality meant became increasingly ambiguous in ideological discourse.

While reformers claimed that neither equality nor efficiency could enjoy absolute priority in China's economy, they believed that efficiency should be a basis of equality (*RMRB*, 23 July, 1988). However, efficiency did not automatically bring equality. As inequality widened with economic liberalization, China's socialism encountered a system-damaging crisis, which raised the question of how much inequality could be incorporated into a system that still called itself socialist.

Reassessing Wage Labor and Exploitation

It was widely agreed that as a major source of income disparity, China's newly emerging private enterprises accumulated wealth through exploiting labor. At the beginning of the economic reforms, the CCP sought to draw a line between exploitative and nonexploitative practices by defining seven as a permissible number for hiring labor (see chapter 5). This line was soon broken as private enterprises demonstrated strengths in boosting the economy, and by 1985 there was no officially fixed upperlimit for the number of hires. As a result, a stratum of private entrepreneurs emerged, with extremely high incomes coming from, in Marxist terminology, the exploitation of surplus value. Thus, to justify distributional inequality under socialism, exploitation had to be justified first. It should be noted that some social scientists tried to avoid acknowledging exploitation in China's private economy by defining the high income of private owners as rewards for their managerial and risk-taking activities (for example, Wan 1988). But quite a few people tended to face the existence of exploitation and seek theoretical legitimation for it.

A systematic reassessment of exploitation could be found in officially sponsored research conducted in 1987–88 by a team of economists from Fudan University, Shanghai (Wang, Z. K. 1990). According to this research, three points of view must be taken into account in evaluating exploitation in private enterprises. First, as a historical phenomenon, exploitation should be assessed in terms of production rather than ethics. Thus, the "exploitation" that was conducive to production should be regarded as positive and historically progressive, albeit morally reprehensible. Judging from the primacy of production, the research asserted that exploitation had not lost its progressive role in China's context because it had proven effective for production. Second, though a goal of socialist revolution, the elimination of exploitation had to be based on a highly developed productive force. The existence of exploitation was an objective manifestation of a less-developed productive force. Hence, the research argued, in order to eventually do away with exploitation, China might have to make use of it first to facilitate production. In other words, the elimination of exploitation had to be a result of its development. Third, to address the accusation that the permission of exploitation meant an abandonment of socialist and communist goals, the research emphasized the importance of a differentiation between socialist goals and the means to realize these goals. According to the research, China's private economy was never a goal. It was only a means to serve a fundamental task of China's preliminary socialism—to boost production.

From 1988 through early 1989, justifying exploitation in terms of its positive role in production became a prevalent trend in China's ideological discourse on distributional inequality. Many Chinese theorists believed that their defence of exploitation was legitimate because they based their arguments on historical materialism. But the practical reevaluation of exploitation tore the CCP's ideology apart. Acknowledgment of the "historical progressiveness" of exploitation raised the question of whether the extermination of capitalism by the Chinese revolution was premature. Some commentators argued that ending exploitation required certain conditions and that China lacked these conditions when it started to wipe out exploitation (*ZGJJWT*, March 1988, 12). Thus, the necessity of socialist revolution was put in doubt. Furthermore, justifying capitalist exploitation in terms of production suggested an ideological plight in assessing capitalism in a more general sense: Was contemporary capitalism progressive, since it was still able to promote production? More specifically, was capitalist exploitation in Western countries, say, the United States, France, and Great Britain, also progressive? In fact, in seeking a legitimation of exploitation, socialism as an alternative to capitalism was thrown into question. As Fudan's (Wang, Z. K. ed. 1990, 97) research project stated:

> Today, most areas of the world still have exploitation systems, including mainly the capitalist wage labor system. The antagonism between capital and labor has not yet been eliminated but it has not become the fetter to productive forces either. On the

contrary, the wage labor system continues to provide a strong momentum for the development of social production in capitalist countries. On the other hand, the social and economic development in the countries where a socialist system has been established is not very successful. The founding fathers of Marxism would not predict that, after a half-century of practice, socialism would not find a concrete form of public ownership able to promote productive forces and to inspire the enthusiasm of workers.

It might be improper to interpret such a statement as advocating total restoration of the capitalist wage labor system. However, a message embodied within this document seemed to be that wage labor could be a cure for the system that had aimed at eliminating exploitation. To reduce tensions between official socialist commitments and the need for exploitation, some Chinese social scientists and policy specialists proposed to confine exploitation to certain spheres, especially where productive forces were at a lower level, while others suggested a "moderate exploitation" so that an excessive distributional inequality could be avoided. Thus, when policy makers had to balance between making use of exploitation and preserving a socialist image, they were bogged down by definitions of "legitimate" and "reasonable" exploitation. In fact, the CCP had been contradicting and confusing itself in the issues such as these: How much exploitation in a particular enterprise could be seen as "moderate" or "reasonable"? Why was private ownership allowed to enter into some spheres while denied entry into others? What criteria were used? There was no consensual solution. Policy orientations fluctuated between justifying practical needs and maintaining the fundamental principles.

Commodification of Labor Power

Orthodox Marxist Chinese economic thinking denied labor as a commodity. It asserted that the commodification of labor was a unique capitalistic phenomenon that could happen only when laborers who lost the means of production had nothing to sell in markets for survival but labor. The socialist economy was believed to have put the means of production under the control of laborers themselves and therefore to have ended the history of labor as a commodity. In parallel with this doctrine was a three-decade labor system in which free mobility of individuals was restrained.

With the liberalization of the economy, a flexible labor system was developed to accommodate other reform measures. At the outset, the reform of the labor system was aimed at encouraging the "mobility of skilled personnel" (*rencai liudong*), which meant to reallocate, by administrative means, personnel that were professionally misused.[10] As the reform went on in depth, a further deregulation of the labor system was put on the governmental agenda. The new developments, such as private labor-hiring, contract labor, layoffs, and more individual freedom in job choice, indicated that the state's overall control over the movement of labor was crumbling, and consequently, an introduction of market mechanisms into the allocation of labor power became necessary. An increasingly free movement of labor was a contributing factor to widening distributional inequality.

To incorporate these new developments into the official ideology, reformist intellectuals and policy specialists proposed to redefine the nature of labor under socialism—that is, to recognize labor power as a commodity. A vigorous effort as such was presented by a research project sponsored by the Shanghai Municipal Government in 1987.[11] Theoretical justifications for the commodity nature of labor in the socialist economy constituted a substantive part of this project. To begin with, reform theorists attempted, as they did in many other controversial issues, to detach the commodification of labor power from capitalism. As Jiang (1988, 253) argued, the separation of labor from the means of production under capitalism was not the sole condition that generated the commodification of labor power. As long as the combination of labor and the means of production in socialism took an indirect and incomplete form, which excluded universal public ownership of the means of production, the commodification of labor power could not be avoided. Xu (1988, 284) suggested two explanations of the commodity nature of labor power in socialism. First, socialism did not eliminate the individual ownership of labor power, which thus entailed the applicability of market principles to the use of labor power. Second, if a product was a commodity, then the productive factors that made up this product must also be commodities. Acknowledging certain productive factors (such as material inputs) as commodities while denying others (such as labor) was self-contradictory.

Some writers emphasized the difference between commodification of labor power in socialism and capitalism. As W. He (1988, 266) contended, while the exchange between labor and capital under capitalism did not violate the principle of exchange of equal values, capitalists, with ownership of the means of production, exploited surplus values created by labor. In socialism, however, though laborers sold their labor power for the exchange of income, the value created by their surplus labor (here, the author deliberately avoided using the concept of surplus value, which was thought to exist only in capitalist societies) went to public use, from which laborers themselves would benefit. Thus the commodification of labor power in socialism did not involve exploitative relations.

The commodification of labor power, to researchers of this project, had broad practical advantages (Shanghai Municipal Personnel Bureau 1988). It could facilitate an optimal combination of labor with the means of production by moving labor to its best use. With labor power being evaluated according to market value, laborers could get paid the equivalent of the amount of labor they put into production, and thereby "To each according to his labor" could be better implemented. Also, the commodification of labor power, by encouraging a "horizontal" movement of labor, would break China's administratively run economic institutions, reorganize economic structures, and promote the growth of a national market.

With the emergence of the need to legitimate private enterprises, however, the socialist labor market became penetrated by capitalistic commodification of labor power. Many scholars and policy specialists tended to recognize that, in many ways, there were no differences between workers in China's private enterprises and in capitalist societies. The former, similar to the latter, had to make a living by selling their labor to capitalists, who exploited surplus value. The income level of China's private employees, as that of their counterparts in capitalist societies, was determined by supply and demand of labor power. Such a capitalistic commodification of labor power, as seen by some specialists, was unavoidable as private enterprises became an integral part of the national economy. Moreover, a labor market became increasingly necessary for allocating surplus labor power released by the IHC in rural areas and the labor system reform in urban areas.

If marketization was a general goal of China's economic reform, then the commodification of labor power was natural and, indeed, inevitable. However, the commodification of labor power discredited a fundamental socialist commitment—working people were the master of the country. Such a commitment had never been put into practice. Both Marxist and non-Marxist scholars in the West had characterized labor relations in socialist systems as alienated or clientelist. Nevertheless, China's previous economic system apparently distinguished itself from the capitalist one by ending the commodification of labor, which, in Marx's terms, was the root of capitalistic alienation. Thus, the problem with the legitimation of commodification of labor in China was not that it brought alienation, which, to many Chinese and foreign commentators, had existed in its own forms in socialist economies; rather, it blurred the distinction between two opposite economic systems, one of which claiming laborers to be the owner of the means of production and the other subordinating laborers, just as any other goods, to market laws. Whereas the former, to a large extent, was only a fallacy, the introduction of the latter shattered a basic promise upon which China's socialism was based.

The Conflict between Ideology and Practice: What are Its Solutions?

Due to a deficiency of aggregate data it is difficult to make an overall assessment of China's emerging distributional inequality at the national level. But it is safe to say that the emerging differentials became so tangible in 1987 and 1989 in daily life, and so exposed to the public by various publications, that serious resentment arose in Chinese society. Reformers continued to defend distributional differentials. They attributed social resentment to "the fetters of old concepts," which they believed constituted "an ideological obstruction to the people's correct treatment of the current issue of income distribution" (LW, 22 August 1988). Instead of blaming distributional inequality, some suggested that the problem lay in "a psychological adjustment" to it. As Gao Shan pointed out in an article in People's Daily (23 July 1988, 1), the community's psychological capacity had to be developed in order to withstand the strain in distribution, which was a necessary price to pay for the reform. To strengthen his argument, he even cited Shang Yang, a reformer in ancient China, who asserted more than two thousand years ago that people would like to enjoy the fruits of any of their undertakings, but they would not like to give thought to the problems involved in starting them. Thus, Gao appealed to changes in value, through ideological work, to make people psychologically more capable of bearing distributional differentials.

From the perspective that distributional inequality was a necessary price for reform, reformers were inclined to treat it as a policy issue separate from ideological fundamentals. Thus, their recommended solutions were more welfarist than socialist. For example, some suggested the establishment of a social insurance and relief system and subsidies for low earners (*FBIS*, 24 May 1988, 23; 16 August 1988, 36). Others proposed to improve China's tax system, through which some redistributional functions could be introduced (*FBIS*, 16 August 1988, 37). As for distributional inequality caused by official speculation, reformers believed that the best way to undo it was to deepen market reforms, thereby expediting the transition to a single price determined by the market (*FBIS*, 16 August 1988, 37; 9 September 1988, 46).

While Chinese economic thinking about distribution turned away from socialist egalitarianism, property and power increasingly became determining factors in distribution. The official communist ideology, however, remained symbolically important. This irreconcilable clash set a background in which popular discontent found its way into the streets in the spring of 1989. By international standards, the emerging distributional inequality in China might be far less acute than that of many third world countries. It had nevertheless contrasted sharply with the CCP's communist image. To a certain extent, popular resentment against distributional inequality was mainly psychological, as many reformers pointed out. Whereas a few who were advantaged by opportunities got richer and richer, the majority did not become poorer and poorer. In fact, the livelihood of most Chinese had simproved teadily since the reforms. Thus, rather than being a grievance against a deepening poverty, the popular feeling was ridden with what sociologists called "relative deprivation" (see Gurr 1970). People were more inclined to compare their livelihoods with those of other reference groups than with their own past. Thus, although no vicious poverty had yet occurred, the fact that a few got too rich dissatisfied many. Popular frustration was intensified, particularly as the CCP's communist commitment was contrasted with the reality of growing inequality. It was not surprising that, as reported (Ying and Geng 1989, 409), when an old worker was fired, he scolded the factory manager, "How can you be a communist manager? You are obviously a capitalist!"

Reformers' attempt to stimulate productivity by enlarging the income gap was doomed to be conflict generating in a polity that was officially committed to socialism and communism. It was practically difficult to define how much inequality was reasonable, and to draw a line between rational and irrational distributional differentials. If, as some argued (Zhang, *GMRB*, 2 July 1988), incomes, no matter how high, were rational as long as they were legally earned, then any high income could be rational, given that private enterprise was legal. As individuals made as much income as they could through operation of their private property rights, a capitalist institution emerged. One proposal was to limit the wages of private managers to an amount that was no greater than ten times the average wage of their employees (*FBIS*, 16 August 1988, 37). But this might damage the entrepreneurship that the reforms sought to revive.

Although China's emerging distributional inequality was not as serious as that of some third-world countries, its increasing tendency to rely on the market for distribution was unavoidably increasing inequality and would intensify it in coming years. Some Chinese reformist intellectuals thought that there was nothing to fear. For example, Wu (1986, 102) cited the arguments of Western development economists, to emphasize the inevitability of growing income differentials in a country's early stage of modernization; he believed that a trickle-down would happen eventually. The point Wu and many other theorists missed, however, was that as an alternative to capitalism, socialism was believed to be a social institution that could generate modernization without inducing class inequality. The basic rationale of socialism would be thrown into question if China had to pursue modernization at the expense of equality.

Some reformist intellectuals and policy specialists seemed to try to redress the distributional inequality problem in a way that was closer to the one practiced in Western welfare states.[12] This, however, entailed a fundamental ideological change that could accommodate the dominance of the market institution and a liberal democracy. With this kind of change, socialism would be no longer an alternative to capitalism. Rather, socialism would become certain "policy measures" to remedy the unjust and inhumane aspects of unfettered capitalistic markets. Certainly, such a change would mean relinquishing the CCP's official ideology and the party's status as a Leninist institution.

Those who advocated new authoritarianism in China suggested a market-oriented development with state intervention. They held up Taiwan and South Korea as cases that showed that, through some proper governmental policies, equality would not be necessarily a casualty of economic growth. But this option would be unacceptable to the CCP in two ways. First, though unequal income distribution in China was not as serious as in some third-world countries, especially in Latin America, the cases of Taiwan and South Korea still revealed the dependence of those countries on capitalistic economic institutions. China's formal communist ideology excluded what prevailed in both areas, such as the formation of a strong capitalist class that controlled a huge amount of wealth. An emulation of Taiwan and South Korea thus could eventually lead to a dismantling of the communist system. Second, following the examples of Taiwan and South Korea would discredit the CCP by demonstrating to the public that there was a better alternative than socialism in sustaining both equality and economic growth. Thus, in the final analysis, the CCP's fundamental ideology, designed as an alternative to capitalism in the first place, was not able sustain market-driven and property-generated distributional inequality without a loss of its identity. It could do little to solve capitalist inequality without destroying capitalist institutions.

As shown previously, China's official ideology did lose much of its identity by incorporating elements of capitalist ideology. The sociopolitical crisis of 1989, to a large extent, was attributable to conflicting policies caused by ideological disarray. The coexistence of a commitment to socialist common prosperity and the rise of an economically privileged social stratum disoriented the society. Fearing that the clash between ideological commitment and deviating practice was undermining its legitimacy, the party leadership had to reassert the ideological fundamentals regarding distribution. Indeed, by 1989, so manifest was the confluence of various crisis elements generated by the conflict between the communist system and capitalist practice, the party was forced to choose either overall legitimation of capitalistic practice or reemphasis of ideological fundamentals.

The post–June Fourth leadership reaffirmed the importance of distributional equality. In his speech on the fortieth anniversary of

National Day, Jiang Zemin, the new Party General Secretary, declared that "we must guard against and correct unfair social distribution" and stressed that "unfair social distribution is not only an economic question, but a social question as well" (*FBIS*, 28 November 1989, 39).[13] An internal study document (September 1989) issued by the Party Central Propaganda Department linked (legitimately, indeed) the problem of distributional inequality with the prospect of capitalist restoration. The document accused those who advocated widening income gaps of subverting socialism. According to the document, the liberal claim that China needed a middle class (namely, a capitalist class) was to prepare a social foundation for a bourgeois republic. In a more moderate tone, some party theoreticians appealed for a fair distribution. But how should *fair* be defined? He Jianzhang (*GMRB*, 27 October 1989) proposed that, because public ownership was the dominant form of China's economic system, the income level of employees in state enterprises should be used as a chief reference point to judge whether social distribution was fair. Although he did not specify how much higher than that of a worker in a state enterprise a private entrepreneur's income could be and still be treated as fair, his proposal strongly implied a leveling of incomes of nonstate sectors to those of state enterprises and thereby implied a return to a more egalitarian distribution.

Whereas the post–June Fourth leadership brought back the rhetoric of "fair distribution," it could do little to change the current distributional structure. The forms of China's ownership system had been so diversified that, unless they were reunified, a return to a monolithic socialist egalitarian distribution would be difficult, if not impossible. An imposed return could only be counterproductive. Nevertheless, the reassertion of ideological fundamentals by the leadership did block the continuation of a problem-solving process that had been set in motion in the reform and whose logic contradicted communist principles. Thus, while China's economy and society were facing mounting problems due to the nature of the semi-reformed economy, the leadership prevented enterprises from a more thorough disengagement from the state and the land from being owned by the peasants. One underlying consideration was that doing so would intensify polarization. But then why were practices such as private enterprise, contracting, leasing, "rich first," and the like, encouraged in the first place? It might be possible that at the outset the CCP did not expect that these practices could lead to serious distributional inequality. In other words, although the CCP was relatively comfortable with allowing capitalist measures to boost the economy, it was ill-equipped for bearing their social consequences. However, China's reforms seemed to have reached the point at which, to solve emerging problems, the reform measures had to be pushed to their logical extent. The dilemma for the CCP was that its ideology had exhausted flexibility in accommodating itself to more radical reform policies. It was difficult for party hardliners to realize that the prevailing but crumbling ideology was not necessarily able to solve distributional inequality, but that it would necessarily hinder economic development.

8
Conclusion

With the fall of communism in Eastern Europe and the Soviet Union, the CCP becomes the last major Leninist institution in the world that still formally claims its commitment to communist ideology and that tries to keep that ideology relevant. But as the preceding chapters have shown, , Because of the fundamental-instrumental discrepancy, China's official economic ideology has significantly diverged from the core values of communism. The current official economic ideology, in many ways, is indistinguishable from its antithesis—capitalism. Certainly, the fundamental-instrumental discrepancy does not betoken a formal abandonment of ideological fundamentals. Rather, it is a political strategy to practice pragmatic and divergent ideas while maintaining the formal legitimacy of ideological fundamentals. However, the fundamental-instrumental discrepancy has minimized and undermined the role of fundamental principles in the economic domain and has opened the way for the emergence of a new economic discourse that has profoundly reoriented economic policies.

It seems that in the immediate future, China's leadership will continue in two seemingly contradictory tendencies that result from the fundamental-instrumental discrepancy: its aggressive practice of capitalism and its insistence on fundamental principles for its self-

197

legitimation. However, it is questionable whether the CCP will be able to sustain the fundamental-instrumental discrepancy in the long run. Despite its short-term utility for pragmatic problem solving, in the long run the fundamental-instrumental discrepancy is crisis generating because it shakes and erodes the ideological fundamentals upon which the CCP depends for political legitimacy.

The implications of the fundamental-instrumental discrepancy for China's future are enormous. Not only has it revealed profound dilemmas confronting China's leadership in its pursuit of modernization, it has also forced China to the threshold of a more fundamental transformation.

Marxism and Underdeveloped Socialism

The fundamental-instrumental discrepancy unmistakably implies a crisis of state socialism. Its deep roots lie in the fact that Marxist ideology fails to give solutions to China's problems with economic modernization. If the Marxist model could be regarded as an alternative to the capitalist economic model, it might work as its designers anticipated, but only under the conditions of mature capitalism. Socialist transformation, according to Marx, could proceed only when the "historic mission" of developing productivity had been accomplished by capitalism. But this century has witnessed a socialist revolution that would "turn Marx on his head" because of its success in underdeveloped regions. Consequently, rather than being a historical successor to capitalism, socialism has become a historical substitute (White 1983, 3). Marxism, in its original meaning, is more a theory of social transformation based on prescribed material conditions, rather than a practical model of economic development. It does not designate socioeconomic development in regions where the necessary materials conditions for socialism are not in place. Ruling Communists in these regions have been forced to take on the dual tasks of promoting economic development and maintaining socialist structures; they have created their own "Marxist models" of development. However, in the late 1970s, three visions of socialist development—Stalinism, Maoism, and Titoism—plunged into crises (Solinger 1984). They all failed to realize one of the dual tasks—fostering economic development.

The fundamental-instrumental discrepancy in the post-Mao period pointed to the dilemma that has confronted the CCP in steering post-revolutionary social development. As a Leninist party, the CCP needs to uphold its revolutionary momentum in order to keep socialism vital and hence maintain its own legitimacy. Tremendous scarcity of material conditions, on the other hand, compels the CCP to focus on economic modernization. Mao Zedong, pursuing the first goal at the expense of the second, believed that incessant revolutionary change would bring about economic development in the long run. From the Great Leap Forward to the Cultural Revolution, however, these ideas repeatedly proved unworkable and disastrous.

The post-Mao leadership's reversal of Mao's lines has been a response to what could be called a "crisis of development in socialism," which has been manifested in sluggish economic growth, stagnant living standards, and lagging scientific and technological progress. For the post-Mao leadership, the development of material productive forces was an essential prerequisite for social and intellectual change; socialism could not continue without a solid material base. The primacy of production was therefore necessary for building this base. In order to put "economy in command," it became necessary for the CCP leadership to apply non-Marxist solutions to economic issues, because Marxist solutions seemed less able to tackle immediate economic tasks. Thus the CCP had to incorporate into its ideology the instrumental principles of capitalism in order to redress its formidable economic problems. By doing this, the gap between the non-Marxist practices and the Marxist principles widened—a process that has deprived Marxism of its persuasive power and made it less relevant in the economic domain.

The Irreconcilability of the Fundamental-Instrumental Discrepancy under Communist Systems

This leads to a second implication of the fundamental-instrumental discrepancy: the reconcilability of communist ideology with capitalist economic thinking. Most reformers have justified instrumental principles in terms of fundamentals (namely, the official ideology), but they are borrowing from liberal economic ideas. Reformers justify integration of capitalist elements in an essentially socialist structure by creating the concept of socialism with Chinese characteristics. However, this has proven futile. The heart of the problem here is whether there can be any workable programs based on a combination of communist goals and capitalistic methods. Ten years ago Alec Nove (1983), in search of a "feasible socialism," argued that there was no alternative to the market as a basis for running an advanced economy and ruled out the possibility of a third way, such as "democratic planning." The changes in Eastern Europe and the former Soviet Union seemed to reinforce the notion that there were no socialist economics, there were only economics (Ash, quoted in Callinicos 1991, 96). This study shows that Chinese economic thinking has progressively approached economic laws that are based on modern capitalism. Indeed, many of the CCP's practical principles have nothing to do with socialism and communism. They are simply following the capitalist principles that have been operating in the West. The point here is not whether laissez-faire or private ownership is best, but that the CCP's instrumental principles (manifested in policies such as contracting, leasing, private enterprises, privatization of land use, income differentials, and the like) have sharply contradicted and diluted its fundamental principles, and that they have given rise to a legitimate concern whether China can find any noncapitalist high road to economic growth and prosperity. The fact that the CCP has to reformulate its instrumental principles by borrowing from other theoretical contexts suggests that its fundamental principles have lost much of their relevance to contemporary economic problem solving.

The attempted incorporation of capitalist elements into communist ideology undermines the force of the latter. Communist ideology is essentially a self-enclosed system in the sense that it claims an undisputed command of social and historical truth and hence absolute superiority over other ideologies. Thus, its ruling power depends on its ability to convince society that it represents the best alternative to societal development. Because this proves questionable, the CCP leadership believes that a cautious manipulation of capitalist economic ideas could serve socialism. But this implies that the ruling communist ideology is only partially true or selectively applicable, and an ideology as such could "have no significant power in exercising moral sanctions in a society where all institutions have been justified solely by this total ideology" (Ding 1988). Therefore, it is not surprising that the fundamental-practical discrepancy has so profoundly disoriented the party's theoretical foundations and confused its policies that the official ideology's credibility and the party itself are seriously compromised.

The fundamental-instrumental discrepancy has produced socioeconomic consequences that are difficult to handle within the current ideological and institutional framework. For example, the expansion of private enterprises has posed a serious dilemma for the leadership: limiting them is counterproductive, whereas encouraging them undermines China's socialist structure. Income differentials and social class polarization have embarrassed the CCP's in its official commitment to socialism. The introduction of capitalistic institutions, such as contracting and leasing, have encouraged many state enterprises to pursue rapid profit maximization rather than long-term investment—a tendency that erodes the foundation of the socialist economy. All of these problems indicate that the fundamental-instrumental discrepancy has gone both too far and not far enough— too far because it challenges the current system by bringing in capitalism and not far enough because it has not brought an ontological breakthrough by which the leadership could seek more thorough ways to solve economic problems. Thus, reforms have been trapped in a limbo of unreconciled contradictions where liberal policies and ideas fight with socialist ideological and institutional structures.

The Fundamental-Instrumental Discrepancy and Ideological Transformation

A third implication of the fundamental-instrumental discrepancy is that it provides a perspective for understanding the pattern of ideological transformation in a communist system. As China's prevailing ideology is losing much of its relevance to newly identified efforts that focus on economic modernization, many in the party and intellectual circles believe that Marxism-Leninism must be supplemented with Western ideas. Although it borrowed extensively from the West, both in terms of ideas and technology, ideological reformulation was at the outset an attempt to generate a convincing alternative to the failed models of socialist development (especially Stalinist and Maoist) and to find a feasible socialism.

Official tolerance, and even encouragement of, the fundamental-instrumental discrepancy allowed a flow of liberal economic ideas into China's policy thinking. Although instrumental principles have been interpreted as being compatible with fundamental principles, their intellectual linkage to the latter is tenuous at best and nonexistent at worst. The cumulation of instrumental principles tends to erode the conceptual hegemony of the official ideology. As this study has shown, instrumental principles regarding the ownership system have at various times appeared to be making a sharp break from one fundamental principle to another. In the end, the basic premises of socialism have been worn away. This process characterizes an evolutionary transformation of the official economic ideology: The party initially permits the fundamental-instrumental discrepancy by integrating liberal economic ideas (in the form of instrumental principles) into its ideological framework; then instrumental principles, with their own logic, gain momentum for evolution on their own; and finally, instrumental principles challenge and break with fundamental ones. The point here is that the evolution of instrumental principles could be the major source of alternatives to the prevailing ideology. As instrumental principles evolve to the point of an "ontological breakthrough," they themselves could turn into fundamental principles (namely, the new ideology) that could redefine the Chinese polity.

Three ideological trends that evolved from instrumental principles aimed at fostering market-oriented reform have emerged in China. Although the elements of each of the three have already been reflected in the official economic ideology, none of them as a whole has taken command in China. Nevertheless, these three trends may represent different visions of China's postcommunist development.

Capitalist Vision

Advocates of the capitalist vision are composed mainly of three groups of people: (1) intellectuals who are exposed to Western liberal economics (either through self-learning or foreign training); (2) private entrepreneurs who benefit from privatization and managers of state enterprises who become quasi-private entrepreneurs with the implementation of contracting and leasing systems; and (3) policymakers who are totally disillusioned with the semi-reform of state-run enterprises within the framework of state socialism.

These groups of people begin with the selective application of capitalist concepts for economic problem solving and propose to take this line of thinking to its logical conclusion: privatization. Their criticism of the state economy focused initially on its low efficiency, irrational resource allocation, tremendous waste, and entrenched bureaucratism, and it paralleled the orientation of the liberal faction of reformers who advocate transforming Chinese society from a distributive one to a productive one. However, the social and economic pathologies caused by semi-privatization, or the state's partial disengagement from the economy, soon convinced this group that a comprehensive privatization was not only necessary but was the only way out of China's recurrent economic problems. There is no alternative, they now believe, to institutions such as the market and private property rights to move the country's economy ahead. A half-way reform, they argue, could only result in a juncture of defects of both market and planning that would disorient the economy. They criticize the state form of social and economic management because it tends to disenfranchise the population from effective participatory democracy and to enhance political dictatorship. They predict that dispersion of property rights among the population will decentralize political power and therefore will lay the foundation for democracy.

Ironically, such criticisms and policy proposals were initially made within a Marxist framework (particularly with respect to the compatibility between productive forces and the relations of production). But it became clear by the late 1980s that the radical pro-privatization proposal no longer fit within Marxism, and it was dislodged from its fundamental principles. Since then the proposal's advocates have been citing works from Adam Smith to Milton Friedman, thereby revealing their intellectual affinity with the ideology of laissez-faire. Their criticisms of the socialist state economy sound like the New Right critique of the welfare state in the West.[1] Their policy recommendations—comprehensive privatization, deep marketization, and income differentiation—unmistakably indicate their preference for laissez faire oriented capitalism.

Apparently, this vision is driven both by the newly formed social interests that are major beneficiaries of privatization and by the intellectual disillusionment with China's socialism. As the previous chapters have shown, a new social stratum has emerged from market-driven reforms and, particularly, from privatization. The members of this stratum have accumulated enormous personal wealth through capitalist practices. However, their entrepreneurship is still constrained by the semi-reformed state socialism in which the frequent distortion of market rules tends to raise their transaction fees. A more radical liberalization of the economy, therefore, is vital to them if they are to maintain profits and advance business.

The capitalist vision also arose out of a deep disillusionment among intellectuals and policy specialists with past failures of the state economy in sustaining growth. Pessimism about the current practice of a mixed economy also contributed to the formation of the radical solution. An idealized vision of laissez faire might be a catalyst for more capitalism. Many reformers believe that capitalist efficiency and prosperity can be attributed to private property rights and markets, both functioning under less state intervention than is the case in the current system. It might be unfair to accuse all of them of turning a blind eye to the negative features of unfettered capitalism. In fact, some of these radical reformers have recognized the inevitability of capitalist maladies, such as unemployment and social polarization, that would occur if their policy recommendations were put into practice. But their belief in the primacy of productivity has led them to insist that these are the necessary costs of economic modernization.

Although its elements have undeniably penetrated China's economic policy-making process at both central and local levels, this vision as a whole is politically and ideologically unacceptable to the CCP because it poses a threat to the foundation of the political system. Moreover, given China's current conditions, this vision, if realized, could be socially unbearable and technically difficult. A high unemployment rate might destabilize Chinese society, in which there are few social security nets. In the overpopulated rural areas, land is so scarce that its concentration (or privatization) in a few hands (given that industrialization would not be fast enough to absorb rural surplus labor), might lead to class polarization, which was an underlying cause of rural rebellions throughout Chinese history and of the Chinese Revolution itself. In addition, the sale of state assets could be severely constrained due to the low income level of the Chinese people. State assets are very likely to be transferred into the hands of a few governmental officials, and their relatives, who have accumulated personal wealth through official speculations. Finally, China also lacks the infrastructure (namely, a legal system, a price system, a national market, and so on) necessary for comprehensive privatization. In short, this radical alternative could encounter more problems than its advocates expect, even in a postcommunist context.

Social Democratic Vision

It may be premature to use this term to identify a systematic set of thought and to relate it to any particular social interests in China. But we may reasonably regard the social democratic vision as representing an emerging societal concern with the balance between equality and efficiency. The starting point of this alternative is a rejection of state monopoly of the economy. According to the social democratic vision, diversified forms of property rights operating in a market-dominated environment are desirable. This implies that although state sectors have to be limited, they do not have to be eliminated. However, this vision distinguishes itself from the official ideology in that it does not perceive state sectors as related to, or part of, some ultimate goal. Rather, its view on state sectors is instrumental: State sectors are regarded as necessary to deal with the problems that markets fail to solve. In other words, they are useful as problem-solving means rather than as ideologically imperative for social development. Thus, state sectors should and may continue to operate in providing public goods; the state has the right to control strategic industries such as steel, shipbuilding, mining, oil, and the like. However, the state should resolutely disengage itself from the management of most remaining enterprises and let them be privatized (or become cooperative property). Though in favor of privatization (or cooperatization) in general, this vision differs from the liberal capitalist vision with regard to distribution. According to the latter, with the implementation of privatization, only the market would determine distribution. The social democratic alternative, however, proposes a positive role for the state in distribution because it considers social polarization a potential problem that would threaten social stability, this vision favors a welfare state that could alleviate inequality and insecurity caused by the functions of property rights and markets.

Marxism was used initially in the justification of this alternative. Its proponents attempted to find a liberal interpretation of Marxism, which would allow a necessary retreat from the prevailing ownership system while regulating possible adverse consequences of the retreat. But this vision later was inspired by Western social democratic ideas. It undoubtedly rejects the notion of the ownership system defined by the prevailing ideology, but it also questions unfettered capitalism. It represents an effort among reformers to seek an equilibrium between efficiency and equality. Certainly, this vision retains elements of socialism. It nevertheless reduces the role of socialism from ideological fundamentals to a set of values and policies that promote the humane management of market economies. The existence of the state sector, in this vision, is tied to its specific functions in solving specific socioeconomic problems, rather than in its embodiment of certain advanced ideals that predefined a superior social order that China should pursue.

The social democratic vision mainly represents those intellectuals and policymakers who are aware of the defects of China's current state socialism and unfettered capitalism. They seem to be seeking a new social and institutional arrangement to guarantee basic equality in a market-dominated economy. In this sense, they might speak for those people, such as employees of state enterprises and the retired, who have become the major casualties of market-driven reforms.

Viewed from a broader socioeconomic perspective, this vision might look more feasible than the liberal capitalist vision. But this vision entails a democratic structure characterized by procedural legitimacy, and thereby demands the abolition of communism as the ideological truth, upon which the CCP has claimed absolute leadership. Its practice thus requires that the party change its legitimating foundation and therefore fundamentally change itself.

Neo-authoritarianism

This vision was suggested by some younger intellectuals who were actively involved in the policy-formulation processes by virtue of their participation in the think tanks (such as the Research Office of the General Office of the CCP Central Committee, the Rural Policy Research Office of the Secretariat of the CCP, and the Institute of Economic System Reform) that were associated with reformist leaders. In essence, neo-authoritarianism is not different from the developmental state solution mentioned before. The neo-authoritarian vision is inspired by the experiences of newly industrializing countries (NICs) of East Asia. Its basic argument is to use centralized state power to promote a market economy. In this vision, economic growth is the first and foremost priority of state goals. Thus, the GNP, productivity, efficiency, and competitiveness are the criteria by which to measure the performance of regimes and therefore are the basis of their legitimacy. This vision favors capitalist economic institutions, such as markets and private property rights, in order to foster growth.

However, the neo-authoritarian vision differs from the liberal capitalist vision in that it suggests strong state intervention in the economy. Positive state intervention, in this alternative, arises out of a three-fold necessity: First, given the predominant nonmarket structure in China, the state is instrumental in removing the obstacles to a market economy and in creating and redefining property rights. Second, the state confronts a competitive international environment; hence, it is obligated to strengthen competitiveness in industry and trade by employing monetary and financial levers and by adopting certain investment and trade policies. Third, the state should play a key role in fighting inflation, unemployment, corruption, and income disparity while Chinese society is shifting to a market economy. However, this vision proposes coercive or even repressive measures by the state in order to enforce developmental policies; an authoritarian political structure is necessary for the transition of China's economy from a nonmarket to a market economy and its politics from dictatorial to democratic politics. Moreover, this vision distinguishes itself from the prevailing ideology in that it tends to base a regime's legitimacy on its performance rather than on its ideological claims. The right to rule, in other words, depends on the job a regime does, not on the "privileged knowledge of truth" it claims to have. The neo-authoritarian alternative is intended to transform China's Leninist state into a developmental one, maintaining authoritarian governmental power only for the purpose of promoting economic development.

The ascendancy of the neo-authoritarian vision in the late 1980s reflected a complex coalescence of a vision of democratic transformation with certain vested interests. Quite a few Chinese intellectuals, working both inside and outside of the policy center, believed that Western-style democracy was not suited for China at that stage because of China's lack of basic democratic infrastructures (as was apparent in China's, economic backwardness and its limited market competition and private ownership, massive illiteracy, incomplete legal system, and the complete lack of a civil society). Thus, for them, neo-authoritarianism seemed to represent a more realistic transitional stage to democracy—a stage in which authoritarian modernizers would use state power to demolish barriers to, and create conditions for, democracy.

Behindehind this line of thinking, however, we can detect new political interests that have emerged. Some of the most enthusiastic advocates of neo-authoritarianism worked for, or had close connections with, the center of political power. They were young, well-educated, and politically ambitious. Their personal political careers were tied to their perceived neo-authoritarian leaders, such as Zhao Ziyang. They might have had a good chance to play an important role in Chinese politics if this vision had been adopted. It is thus legitimate to suspect that their insistence on reform under an authoritarian leadership, or reform within the system (*tizhi nei gaige*), was due partly to the fact that they would be political beneficiaries if it occurred. Taken in a broader sense, the neo-authoritarian alternative might also conform to the interests of a younger generation of leaders (at both central and local levels many of them were children of the first revolutionary generation),and technocrats who rose to power in the reform. They were devoted modernizers but might have something to lose if democratization took place.

For the top leaders who endorsed this vision,[2] neo-authoritarianism might provide a solution that would allow them to put market-oriented economic development at the top of the agenda while preserving party monopoly of political power. Deng Xiaoping, in many respects, represents a continuity of an intellectual tradition in late nineteenth century China that defined wealth and power (*fuqiang*) as the top national goals. These two goals, according to Deng, could be reached only under a strong national leadership—the CCP's leadership. Deng believes that democracy would create chaos and therefore would thwart economic modernization. However, he understands that without market-driven reforms wealth and power are unattainable. He thus might well perceive neo-authoritarianism to be a way that could sustain market-driven modernization in a Leninist system and hence achieve wealth and power. In this sense, the neo-authoritarian alternative conforms to the desire and interests of political leaders, like Deng Xiaoping, who are both modernizers and Leninists.

It seems to me, however, that this vision could not work well in a Leninist structure in the long term, becaise it is essentially inconsistent with the latter in two ways: (1) It resorts to means (especially private property rights) that discredit the ruling ideology; and (2) its emphasis on performance as a legitimating basis diminishes the relevance of the official ideology. Thus, this alternative requires that the

CCP redefine its foundation for legitimacy, which could destroy Leninism's dominance.

These three visons, as we have shown, originated from instrumental principles that were designed to solve economic problems and initially were interpreted by their advocates as compatible with ideological fundamentals. However, with the development of the fundamental-instrumental discrepancy, instrumental principles have been dissociated from fundamentals and have taken ideological forms on their own, which are contending with the dominant official ideology. The collapse of its cherished beliefs has thrown the party into theoretical disarray. The specter haunting the party leadership is that the fundamental-instrumental discrepancy means the demise of its ideology. The discrepancy, in other words, comes to mean not a better version of the existing model, but another model altogether. Indeed, the party has to rely increasingly on capitalist measures to keep the economy running, and this reliance is demolishing the official ideology. However, a Leninist party cannot escape a legitimacy crisis without a credible and functioning ideology in place. Hence, sooner or later, China's leadership will be compelled to solve the fundamental-instrumental discrepancy in order to prevent the systemic breakdown resulting from the tension between ideology and reality.

One solution is to return to the dogmatic pattern of ideological construction, that is, to bring instrumental principles closer to ideological fundamentals. But this is an unlikely scenario because it might be politically unpopular and economically counterproductive. Another solution is to reduce the discrepancy between fundamental and instrumental principles by breaking the "ontological block"—that is, by changing fundamental principles per se, and making them more compatible with instrumental ones. This would be difficult, for a total change of fundamental principles would shake the very foundations of the system.

Nevertheless, although the fundamental-instrumental discrepancy has created crises for the party, it has also brought opportunities for it. The evolution of instrumental principles may breed, and in fact has generated, new alternatives for future development. The above-named alternatives have penetrated, in different degrees, China's economic thinking. Which one of them will take the place of the crumbling though prevailing ideology might depend on various political factors. Of these, the critical ones are the party's redefinition of its ideology, its role in society, and its legitimating foundation. Without these, the party might face an eventual breakdown. The CCP stands at the crossroads.

NOTES

1. In this book the terms *capitalism* and *socialism* are used to refer to the two major alternative forms of economic organization in the contemporary world. Certainly these terms should be taken not as absolutes, but rather as "ideal types" that approximate, but do not fully represent, empirical reality. It is useful, as Peter Berger (1992) suggests, to think here in terms of a continuum, the two extremes of which are empirically nonexistent. For systems in the middle of the continuum, it may sometimes be difficult to decide which term to apply; most of the time, keeping in mind the concept of the "commanding heights," it is not difficult at all. Given the rapid marketization and expansion of private economy in China, which can be regarded as the "commanding heights" of a capitalist economic system, it is safe to say that China is moving toward capitalism.

2. According to Brzezinski and Huntington (1964), an ideological system is the one in which political leaders steer a society along the lines of their own political beliefs and aspirations. Ideology is the major source of the system's legitimacy. In contrast, an instrument system merely reflects the established social patterns and is designed to protect the existing character of a society and promote its growth along established, undisturbed paths.

3. It is safe to say, as many China scholars suggest, that with the deepening of China's economic reform, economic decision making has increasingly tended to be decentralized and dispersed among different actors, such

211

as provincial and local governments, ministries, and enterprises, as well as the central government. However, this has not changed the reality that the leadership still dominates certain economic policy issues it regards as crucial for its control over society. Ministries and local governments are virtually prohibited from taking initiatives on *key* policy issues that might conflict with the ruling ideology or might have systemic effects on the society. They have to wait for the "green light" from "above" (namely the central leadership) before acting, when these key policies are involved.

4. For example, Zaslavsky (1980) showed that a widening gap between the doctrine and the operation of ideology in the Soviet Union resulted in a "Soviet way of lie," a concept that served as a sort of middle-level theory to mediate the Soviet system's official ideology and its operating ideology.

5. Students of ideology have pointed out the importance of consistency and coherence in an ideology. For example, Willard Mullins (1972) posits that an ideology must have its own logic and "make sense," and Alex Pravad (1988) emphasizes that an ideology must maintain reasonable internal coherence.

6. For example, in his analysis of Taiwan's transition to democracy, Cheng (1989) argues that the principle of people's livelihood, on of the three principles of the people, espouses economic equality but does not specify any preferred means to attain it, such as social ownership or other redistributive policies. the KMT regime has adopted both private and state-owned enterprises as necessary to promote social welfare.

7. In China's orthodox economic theory, ownership is the core of the relations of production determining the nature of an economic system. According to that theory, the economic system, hence the entire society, changes when the ownership system changes.

8. I also assume that those academic articles that appeared in major official magazines and newspapers (such as *Hong Qi, People's Daily, Guangming Daily*, etc.) can be treated as representing official views.

CHAPTER TWO

1. The increase in the number of self-employed in 1961–1962 (table 2.3) was due largely to economic difficulties, when many people lost jobs in state or collective enterprises. In fact, about 70,000 people applied to operate individual businesses, but only 31,000 were given licenses.

2. Inheriting a schematic tripartition from Soviet Marxism, Chinese economists during the pre-reform period defined the relations of production as including three elements: (1) the ownership system, (2) mutual relations within procuction, and (3) the distribution system. However, ownership was considered the key element that determined the nature of the other two.

3. According to some studies (e.g., Selden 1988), however, the rural polar-

izization in 1955 was not as acute as Mao depicted. Thus, Mao's policy, to a great extent, was impelled by his own perception of an ideal society to be built.

CHAPTER THREE

1. The text of this speech was first made public by the Red Guard newspapers during the CR. It had circulated abroad about a decade before it was officially published in China.

2. According to the resolution of the Central Committee on 8 October 1976, the work on the editing of the selected works of Mao Zedong was "under the direct leadership of the Politburo of the Central Committee of the CCP with Comrade Hua Guofeng at its head" (see *People's Daily*, 19 October 1976).

3. On 4 April 1976, the eve of China's annual Qingming festival of homage to deceased ancestors, thousands of people gathered around the memorial to the martyrs of the Chinese revolution to the dead premier Zhou Enlai, who was regarded by many people as a symbol of an ordered lif and of a measure of decency in deeply troubled times of the Cultural Revolution. The mass gathering later turned to an anti-Gang of Four demonstration, which was dispersed by police forces and worker-militiamen under the order of Mao and the Gang of Four. Hundreds were arrested. Deng Xiaoping was denounced as responsible for the occurrence of this incident. On April 17, in the name of Mao and the Central Committee, Deng was removed from all his posts. On the same day, Hau Guofeng was named as the first vice-chairman of the CCP Central Committee (a position second only to Mao's) and premier of the State Council.

4. From August to November of 1978, all thirty provincial party secretaries, and fourteen regional commanders published articles in the *People's Daily* to support the practice criterion (see *HQRB*, 6 February 1989, 5).

5. "Returned students" were those young Chinese communists who had accepted training in Moscow in the late 1920s and returned China in the early 1930s. When backed by the Comintern, they took over the leadership of the CCP. They insisted that the Chinese revolution follow the Russian model and opposed guerrilla warfare strategy. Their political and military lines were said to lead directly to the defeat of the Red Army in the Jiangxi base area. This group, especially its leader, Wang Ming, was later accused of making dogmatic mistakes and deprived of leading positions in the party.

6. Hu Yaobang said in an internal speech at the Conference for the Guideline of the Theoretical Work that there were tens of million of people who were in despair about the government (*HQRB*, 1 February 1989). Wan Li, an important reform leader, then a vice premier, said in a meeting of the State Council that if workers, peasants and intellectuals had known the details of how the government's irrational decisions had led to the economy's bad performance, it would be very surprising if the CCP were not overthrown (see Chen Yizhi 1990, 2).

7. In his political report delivered to the Eighth National Party Congress in 1956, Liu Shaoqi stated that, with the completion of the socialist transformation, large-scale and stormy class struggle was over and that the major social contradiction in China had shifted from one between capitalism and socialism to one between "the advanced relations of production to the backward productive forces." Thus, he emphasized the development of the productive forces as the primary task of the party.

8. Some internal official statistics that found their way aboard revealed the incredible economic losses caused by "waging revolution" during the CR period. According to the estimates of the CCP's Central Committee's Document Research Institute (CD, 6 July 1990), of 1.2 trillion yuan lost during the CR, 200 billion resulted from a loss of 1.4 billion industrial workdays that were devoted to various mass criticism meetings and political studies at enterprises; 200 billion resulted from a loss of 2 billion workdays, at state units, that were used for various mass rallies and parades; and 400 billion resulted from chaos, within enterprises, that was related to political campaigns and factional conflicts. We can question the reliability of these statistics because we do not know how they were calculated, but they roughly reflect the indisputable fact that the CR did serious damage to the productive forces.

9. Wu Jiaxiang's book, *Deng Xiaoping: Thought and Practice*, was scheduled for publication in 1989. It was censored in connection with his arrest after the Tiananmen Incident. Some of its excerpts, however, appeared in *Shijie Jingji Daobao* (World Economic Herald), a Shanghai-based liberal newspaper that was officially shut down in the summer of 1989 by the government for its connection with the June Fourth Incident.

CHAPTER FOUR

1. This chapter mainly focuses on changes in China's agricultural structure and does not discuss rural industry, much of which remains collectively owned.

2. Dazhai was a production brigade in Xiyang County, Shanxi Province. It was regarded by the Maoist leadership as a model of China's agricultural development during the CR period. Its practices included banning the cultivation of private plots by members as well as their household sidelines, introducing "political work points" (work points granted according to one's political attitude), and taking the brigade as an accounting unit.

3. Chen Yizhi went into exile in the United States after the Tiananmen Incident of 1989 and is currently the head of the Center of Modern China Studies, located at Princeton University.

4. For example, in Chaohu county of Anhui Province, peasants' per capita income in the 1930s was equivalent to 340 yuan in the 1970s, while it dropped to 80 yuan in 1978.

5. *Jin* is a Chinese measure of weight equivalent to 0.5 kilograms or 1.1 pounds.

6. In 1979 Wan Li, then first party secretary of Anhui Province, inspected Jingzhai County and found that peasants there resided in terribly shabby cottages and could not dress warmly and eat their fill. The worst thing he knew of was that some girls even did not have trousers. Wan Li wept and said, "Only by giving peasants enough to eat, trousers to wear and houses to live in, would we the communist party not let the peasants down" (Chen 1990).

7. According to a unofficial estimate, 18 percent of Anhui's rural population in 1959–62 died from starvation; 33 percent fled from home villages and lived by begging in towns and cities (Yang, April 1989).

8. This pledge, signed on 24 November 1978, is displayed now in the Museum of Chinese Revolutionary History.

9. Work points are units by which rural economic collectives record the amounts of labor put in by their members and work out their remuneration.

10. It was said that Wan Li replied to Wang's phone call by saying, "I don't care about three or four levels [of the means of production]. It is okay as long as the peasants can eat their fill. It is the best method that can let peasants eat their fill" (Chen 1990, 33–34).

11. For example, leaders of Heqiu County, Anhui Province, thought that the *chengbao* would be labeled as a capitalistic tendency again and re-merged the contracting groups. This created chaos among the peasants and resulted in a sharp drop in production (see Wang, et al. 1989, 240).

12. Private plots are small plots of collectively owned land set aside for private use. Usually between 5 and 15 percent of a plot ofcollective land was set aside for such private sideline production. Products from private plots were restricted to peasants' own consumption. Selling them to the market was illegal.

13. This refers to ownership by the commune, the production brigade, and the production team.

14. After the Third Plenum this document started to be circulated through party channels to the local levels and was officially passed at the Fourth Plenum on 28 September 1979. It was never published in the Chinese press.

15. The first one refers to the land reform in the late 1940s and early 1950s.

16. At that period, Hu Yaobang, Zhao Ziyang, and Wan Li entered the top leadership.

17. The office was disbanded after 4 June 1989 due to its alleged involvement in signing a statement appealing for a government compromise with students. It was accused by conservatives of being one of the "black hands" behind the student movement. Du was dismissed from the post and was said to barely survive the membership reregistration conducted by the CCP right after the June Fourth Incident.

18. Growth of agricultural production in the early 1980s could also be attributed to such factors as comparative advantage farming and procurement price increasses.

19. Many hydraulic specialists attributed the worst flood in the summer of 1991 to the neglect of rural hydraulic system maintenance, which had partially resulted from the IHC.

20. See Rural Policy Research Office of the Secretariat of the CCP and Rural Development Central of the State Council (1987, 35).

21. See note 19, this chapter.

22. The results of the research came out as a book in 1988.

23. Some statistics show that China's arable land decreased 6.6 percent from 1978 to 1984. That is to say, approximately 25 million *mu* of arable land disappeared annually (see He 1989).

CHAPTER FIVE

1. As Chen Yizhi (1990, 50) revealed, investment under China's state economy was unbelievably irrational: Of 600 billion yuan invested for capital construction from 1958 to 1978, one-third was totally wasted due to "blind" decisions (*mangmu juece*); another one-third was far from reaching the anticipated productive capacity; only the remaining third reached the designated productive capacity.

2. Riskin 1987, 345.

3. Janos Kornai 1980.

4. According to Wang Hongmo et al. (1989), the experiment with the contract system in some state enterprises in 1981 and 1983 did not produce the anticipated results, due to many institutional constraints on enterprise managers.

5. For the details of Ma Shengli's story, see Wang, et al. 1989.

6. For an analysis of the impact of the ICS on the inflation in 1988, see Wan Li et al. 1989.

7. According to the National Statistic Bureau's nationwide survey on state-owned enterprises, for every percentage of profit growth in 1987, the total wage went up by 1.72 percent and various kind of bonuses by 5.52 percent. For the 2,172 contracted enterprises included in the survey, the figures for the increased wages and bonuses resulting from the 1 percent profit growth were 1.24 percent and 4.68 percent, respectively.

8. In the late 1980s, Western property rights economists widely cited in Chinese publications included R. Coase, O. Williamson, G. Stigler, and C. Schultze.

9. According to He Wei's article in an influential Beijing newspaper, *Beijing Jingji Zhoubao* (Beijing Economic Weekly), the tasks of trust investment banks in the transitional period are the following: first, to thoroughly separate the enterprises from the government at various levels on the basis of making an inventory and assessment of the enterprises' property, and to invest in the enterprises; second, to safeguard the safety of public property and to ensure that public assets will not be encroached upon; third, as the contract holder and leaser, to organize invitations for contractors and leasers

through public bidding and to supervise the implementation of contracts; fourth, to separate profits from taxes and to collect interest from contracting enterprises and rents from leasing enterprises in the capacity of owner; and fifth, to retain profits in accordance with a certain proportional rate and to hand over the remaining sum in full to the state. (See He Wei [1988, 2]).

10. Official statistics shows that by the end of June 1988, Shengyang had 707 enterprises which issued 147 million yuan in shares; and Guangdong Province (not including Guangzhou and Shengzheng) had 290 enterprises, which pooled 210 million yuan by issuing shares. Wuhan had 133 enterprises which issued 147 million yuan in shares. (See *Zhongguo Jingji Tizhi Gaige* [Chinese Economic Sytem Reform], 1, 23 June 1989).

11. For a detailed description of the conversation between Zhao Ziyang and Milton Friedman, see Chang Wu-chang, *FBIS*, 2 February 1989. Chang Wu-chang is an American-educated and well-known property rights economist in Hong Kong. He was said to have a close relationship with Zhao Ziyang and frequently advised him on economic affairs when Zhao was in power. Chang was present at Zhao's meeting with Friedman in 1988. According to Chang's record, Zhao was apparently dissatisfied with the current property rights system in the state economy. He complained that there was no definite answer as to whether the property of state-owned enterprises should lie with the Ministry of Finance, the Planning Commission, or anyone else. He believed that a shareholding system could clearly define property rights and said that it should be clearly stated which shares are held by a particular department, local government, staff and workers of the enterprises, foreign investors, and so on.

12. Zhang Yanning (*FBIS*, 21 February 1989), vice minister of the State Commission for Economic Restructuring, revealed in early 1989 that, in accordance with the instructions of the "leading comrades" of the Party Central Committee and the State Council, the State Commission for Economic Restructuring had begun to work in coordination with other governmental departments concerned with speeding up the formulation of "Regulation on Joint Stock Companies" and the unified procedures for setting up experimental joint stock companies. However, no results have come out of it since then.

13. According to Marx, a stock company converted private capital into social capital. It was in this sense that the establishment of a stock company was interpreted by Marx as "the abolition of capital as private property within the framework of capitalist production itself," on the one hand, and as a transitional phase toward the reconversion of capital into the property of associated producers, on the other (Marx 1966, 433–37).

14. Li Yining is an economic professor at Beijing University and is well known for his enthusiasm for Western-style stock companies as a solution for the reform of state-run enterprises. According to his policy recommendation, of the assets of the present state-owned large- and medium-sized enterprises, one part was to be reserved for state stocks and another was to be appropriated for enterprise fund stocks, which were to be sold to the work-

ers of the enterprises and to investors in society as individuals' stock. In this way, state-owned enterprises became stock companies, which were not subject to state control. They were run by general managers who were accountable only to the board of directors set up on the basis of the general meetings of the shareholders. Li recommended (*China Daily*, 16 February 1989) that the transition from state ownership to the shareholding system be broken down into three stages: In the first stage, namely before 1990, typical enterprises would be chosen to carry out experiments. In the second stage, roughly between 1990 and 1995, it would be put into effect on a large scale. In the third stage, around 1996 to 2000, government shares would be reduced, and by then the government would have appropriate controlling interests.

15. These arguments for the shareholding system are analogous to those of popular capitalism, which refers to the dispersion of ownership of the means of production in capitalist societies. Both types of argument are raised as opposed to the concentration of ownership—the arguments for the shareholding system in China are opposed to the concentration of ownership in state, whereas arguments of popular capitalism to the are opposed to the concentration of ownership in a few individual hands.

16. Yu was criticized by conservative leaders as advocating bourgeois liberalism in the Anti-Bourgeois-Liberalism campaign in 1987. Since 4 June 1989, he has become one of the main targets of attack by hardliners.

17. In a symposium held in April 1989, Guo Shuqing said that if he were asked who would be the real owners of the enterprises, his answer would be the stock markets.

CHAPTER SIX

1. According to official statistics for 1988, there were about 225,000 private enterprises in China, employing a total of 3.6 million workers, averaging 16 workers and 50,000 yuan of capital per unit. They accounted for less than 1 percent of the country's gross industrial output value (*XHS*, 28 June 1988).

2. The main purpose of this document was to systematically reassess Mao's achievements and errors, and the CCP's past policies.

3. This number did not include those who were doing individual business without licenses from the government.

4. The title of the document was *Some Decisions on Revitalizing Economy and Solving Urban Employment Problem.*

5. See the investigative report by the General Office of the State Council, 1986.

6. See the investigative report by the Research Office of the Party Committee of Wenzhou, 1986.

7. See the investigative report on individual business in Jiangsu Province, by the Jiangsu Administrative Bureau of Individual Industry and Commerce, 1986.

8. See *Investigative Report on Individual Economy in Chongqing,* by the Chongqing Administrative Bureau of Individual Industry and Commerce, 1986 in *Investigation and Study on Individual Economy,* ed. by General Office of State Council.

9. See *The Status Quo and Problems of Individual Economy,* by the Research Office of the General Office of the State Council, June 1986.

10. This coal mine used to be a sidepiece of the state-run Changgouyu coal mine. It was abandoned because the state mine saw it as uneconomical to continue exploiting it. The state mine signed an agreement with a former party official and a peasant to yield the right for exploitation. These two persons, through bank loans, became the owners of the mine.

11. From 1982 to early 1987, Zhao Ziyang was premier of the state council, which was believed to be reform oriented.

12. See The Survey on the Individual Business in Tianjing, by the General Office of Tianjing Municipal Government, 1986.

13. See the investigative report on individual business in Jiangsu Province, by the Jiangsu Administrative Bureau of Individual Industry and Commerce, 1985 in *Investigation and Study on Individual Economy,* ed. by General Office of State Council.

14. See *A Survey on the Individual Business in Shenzhen Special Economic Zone,* by the Investigative Team of Individual Business of Shenzhen Municipal Government, 1986.

15. See *An Analysis of Some Problems of the Labor-Hiring Operation,* by the Policy Research Office of the Wenzhou Party Committee, 1986.

16. See *Theories and Policies of Labor Hiring,* the Jilin Administrative Bureau of Individual Industry and Commerce, 1986.

17. See *An Analysis of Some Problems of the Labor Hiring Operation,* by the Policy Research Office of the Wenzhou Party Committee, 1986.

18. The report prepared by the General Office of the State Council cited such an argument.

19. According to an official report in 1986, 60 percent of owners of private enterprises formerly were cadres at town and brigade levels and salespersons from state, collective, and township enterprises; 15 percent of them were party members. This suggests that it was those who had more social connections, managerial skills, and access to resources that tended to become private owners first. *Investigation and Study on Individual Economy,* ed. by General Office of State Council, 1986.

20. This problem will be discussed in detail in chapter 7, which is devoted to the issues of distribution and social equality.

21. Deng expressed his "complete agreement" with Zhao's 13 May speech. (See Chen 1990).

22. This became one of the principal charges by conservatives against Zhao Ziyang after he was dismissed from power in the June Fourth Incident of 1989.

23. The new article reads: "The state permits the existence and development of private economies within the domain defined by laws. The private economies are a supplement to the publicly owned economy. The state protects the legal rights and interests of private economies, and guides, supervise and regulates private economies." Consitutional Amendment passed by the Seventh National People's Congress, 25 March to 13 April 1988. See Ma Yuping and Huang Yucong, *China's Yesterday and Today* (Beijing: Liberation Army Press, 1988).

24. Both percentages excluded foreign-owned enterprises. If they were included, the percentages would be 5 percent and 4.4 percent, respectively.

25. Although acknowldging the high degree of commercialization of China's rural economy in the coastal areas, the author believes that the larger proportion of the countryside can be characterized as the domain of the natural economy.

26. This was an estimation in 1988. The proportion of the workforce involved in the natural economy in the pre-reform period was much higher than in 1988.

27. The "many other countries" implicitly referred to the newly industrializing nations and areas in the third world, particularly such as the "four little tigers" (South Korea, Taiwan, Hong Kong, and Singapore).

28. It was reported, for example, that because of buying, selling, and reselling, the price for a ton of aluminum increased from 6,000 to 14,000 yuan in the latter half of 1988. (See *Zhongbao* [Center Daily], 20 December 1988).

29. According to surveys conducted by the China Social Survey System, for example, dissatisfaction with the government increased from 73.8 percent in November 1986 to 92.1 percent in May 1988. (See Stanley Rosen 1989, 153–70).

30. For an analysis of the crisis situation in late 1988 and early 1989. (See Andrew Nathan 1990).

31. Zhang Weiguo was the chief correspondent for the Shanghai-based *World Economic Herald* in Beijing and a well-known liberal. He was arrested after the events of 4 June 1989 and released early in 1992. Now he lives in the United States.

CHAPTER SEVEN

1. To say that Maoist ideology pursued the goal of egalitarianism does not mean that pre-reform China was an egalitarian society in all dimensions. There was a great difference between the urban and rural dimensions, and geographic inequalities were large. Mao himself never denied the existence of the "phenomena of inequality" in his revolutionary China, such as differences between urban and rural, industrial and agricultural, and mental and manual. Even though he believed that these differences stemmed from China's low productivity, and therefore could not be done away with in a short period, his ideology showed strong tendencies to mold a more egalitar-

ian society. The fact that his polices seemed more egalitarian in some dimensions than in others was, I believe, due largely to conditional constraints and technical difficulties.

2. It should be noted that unequal development due to the household responsibility system in different areas during that period might also contribute to the higher gini coefficients.

3. This refers to a period during the Great Leap Forward in 1958, when utopian illusions about the feasibility of a rapid transition from socialism to communism produced widespread tendencies to restrict commodity exchange, to expand equal distribution regardless of labor performed, to appropriate labor and productive assets without compensation, and to transform producers' collectives into bigger and more public entities.

4. For example, the Lanzhou municipal government stipulated that households that met certain conditions could be regarded as specialized hoseholds: They raised over 100 laying hens, or over two milk cows, or over fifty goats or sheep, or over ten pigs, of produced twenty cases of beer, and their income from these products constituted 60 to 70 percent of the aggregate income (Economic Research Office of the Secretariat of the CCP Central Committee 1984, 16)

5. Specialized households were engaged in a wide range of production activities. Their products included not only traditional crops, livestock, and poultry, but also fruit, lumber, silkworms, seafood, medicinal herbs, flowers, and fungi, and even scorpions, beetles, earthworms, and oysters.

6. Wan Li (in November 1983), in his report to a national conference on rural work in, cited a locally based survey regarding the issue of what kind of people got rich fast. The survey showed that among 20,989 specialized households in Ying County in Shanxi Province, 43 percent were brigade and team cadres, or peasants who used to be cadres; 42 percent were educated youths and demobilized servicemen, 9 percent were skilled craftsmen, and 5 percent were individuals who had commercial minds and were good at planning and management; fewer than 1 percent were individuals who had a record of violating the law. Wan believed that this was a representative sample of the national condition (*BR*, 27 February 1984, 9).

7. But the rate of unemployment will shoot up in the years to come. According to *China in the Year 2000*, edited by Ma Hong, vice president of the Chinese Academy of Social Science, 29 million of the 80 million employees in state enterprises could be out of work within the next ten years (*China Time Weekly*, 15 October 1992).

8. Qian Jiaju was a member of the Chinese People's Political Consultative Conference (CPCC). He was visiting Hong Kong when the June Fourth Incident occurred. He publicly condemned the CCP leadership and refused to return. He was expelled from the CPCC in 1990 and now resides in Los Angeles.

9. According to Qian, some children of high officials settled down in Los Angeles with some hundreds of thousands or even million of dollars. Citing

from some U.S. emigration officials, he claimed that most of them were relatives of high officials. He believed that they could only accumulate such a huge amount of money through "official speculation."

10. In some major cities, for example, the Exchange Center of Skilled Personnel was set up to solve the problem of the misplacement of a large number of professional people in the previous planned personnel assigning system. People who sought new jobs compatible with their professions could register in the center, which would help them find suitable employment.

11. This research project resulted in a book titled *Commodity Economy and Allocation of Human Resources: A Study of the Socialist Job Market*, in 1988.

12. In 1987–89 many articles focused on Western welfare systems, especially the model of Swedish socialism.

13. However, even in April 1989, Jiang Zemin told a conference that "gaps in the distribution of income should be widened." (See *The New York Times*, 17 November 1991.)

CHAPTER EIGHT

1. It is worth noticing that this phenomenon was also manifest in the former Soviet Union and Eastern European countries (See Sakwa 1990; Callinicos 1991).

2. It is said that Zhao Ziyang once instructed his secretary to ask the World Economic Herald to run a series of articles on this subject. Rumor had it that Deng Xiaoping once said, "This (neo-authoritarianism) is exactly my idea."

BIBLIOGRAPHY

LITERATURE IN ENGLISH

Aharoni, Yair. 1977. *Markets, Planning and Development*. Cambridge, Mass: Ballinger Publishing Company.

Allison, Graham. 1971. *Essence of Decision: Explaining the Cuban Missile Crisis*. Boston: Little Brown.

Almond, Gabriel. 1990. *A Discipline Divided: Schools and Sects in Political Science*. Newbury Park, Calif.: Sage Publication.

Amsden, Alice. 1989. *Asia's Next Giant: South Korea and Late Industrialization*. New York: Oxford University Press.

Apter, David. 1965. *The Politics of Modernization*. Chicago and London: University of Chicago Press.

Bachman, David. 1990. "Planning and Politics in Mainland China Since the Massacre." In *Issues and Studies* 26 (8):2/3):43–66.

———. 1991. *Bureaucracy, Economy, and Leadership in China: the Institutional Origins of the Great Leap Forward*. New York: Cambridge University Press.

Barnett, Doak. 1974. *Uncertain Passage: China's Transition to the Post-Mao Era*. Washington, D.C: Brookings Institute.

Bates, Robert, ed. 1988. *Toward a Political Economy of Development*. Berkeley: University of California Press.

Baum, Richard. 1989. "Beyond Leninism? Economic Reform and Political Development in Post-Mao China." in *Studies in Comparative Communism* 22 (2/3):111–23.

Berger, Peter. 1992. "The Uncertain Triumph of Democratic Capitalism." *Journal of Democracy* 3 (3):7–16.

Bienen, Henry and John Waterbury. 1989. "The Public Economy of Privatization in Developing Countries." *World Development* 17 (5):617–32.

Birnbaum, Norman. 1960. "The Sociological Study of Ideology (1940–1960)." *Current Sociology* 2:91–172.

Bogomolov, Oleg, ed. 1990. *Market Forces in Planned Economies*. New York: New York University Press.

Boudon, Raymond. 1989. "Subjective Rationality and the Theory of Ideology." In *Social Structure and Culture*, Hans Haferkamp ed. New York: Walter de Gruyter.

Brabant, Jozef. 1990. *Remaking Eastern Europe: On the Political Economy of Transition*. Dordrecht: Kluwer Academic Publisher.

Brugger, Bill and David Kelly. 1990. *Chinese Marxism in the Post-Mao Era*. Stanford, California: Stanford University Press.

Brus, Wlodzimierz and Kazimierz Laski. 1989. *From Marx to the Market: Socialism In Search of An Economic System*. Oxford: Clarendon Press.

Brzezinski, Zbigniew and Samuel Huntington. 1964. *Political Power: USA/USSR*. New York: Viking Press.

Bulletin of Concerned Asian Scholars. 1983. *China from Mao to Deng*. New York: Sharpe.

Burton, Charles. 1990. *Political and Social Change in China Since 1978*. New York: Greenwood Press.

Callinicos, Alex. 1991. *The Revenge of History: Marxism and the East European Revolutions*. Pennsylvania: Pennsylvania State University Press.

Campbell, Robert. 1991. *Socialist Economics in Transition*. Bloomington:Indiana University Press.

Carver, Terrell and Liu Jun. 1989. "Chinese 'Realism' and Marx's 'Mistakes'." *The Pacific Review*. 2:89–93.

Chan, Anita. 1990. "China's Long Winter." *Monthly Review* 41:1–14.

Chang, David. 1988. *China Under Deng Xiaoping: Political and Economic Reform*. New York: Macmillan Press.

Cheng, Tun-jun. 1989. "Democratizing the Quasi-Leninist Regime in Taiwan," *World Politics* 16 (4):471–99.

Christensen, Peer Moller and Jorgen Delman. 1983. "A Theory of Transitional Society: Mao Zedong and the Shanghai School." In *China from Mao to Deng*, ed. The Bulletin of Concerned Asian Scholars. Armonk, New York.: Sharpe.

Corrigan, Philip, Harvie Ramsay and Derek Sayer. 1979. *For Mao: Essays in Historical Materialism*. Atlantic Highlands, New Jersey: Humanities Press.

Deane, Phyllis. 1989. *The State of the Economic System*. New York: Oxford University Press.

Deng, Xiaoping. 1984. *Speeches and Writings*. New York: Pergamon.

Dernberger, Robert. 1990. "China's Mixed Economic System: Properties and

Consequences." *China's Economic Dilemma in the 1990s.* Joint Economic Committee, Congress of the United States, ed. Armonk, New York: Sharpe.

Deyo, Frederic. 1987. *The Political Economy of the New Asian Industrialism.* Ithaca, New York: Cornell University Press.

Ding, Xueliang. 1988. "The Disparity between Idealistic and Instrumental Chinese Reformers." *Asian Survey.* 28 (11):1117–39.

Dirlik, Arif and Maurice Meisner. 1989. *Marxism and The Chinese Experience: Issues in Contemporary Chinese Socialism.* New York: M.E. Sharpe.

Dittmer, Lowell. 1984. "Ideology and Organization in Post-Mao China." *Asian Survey* 24 (3):349-69.

———. 1990. "China in 1989: The Crisis of Incomplete Reform." *Asian Survey* 30 (5):25–41.

Djilas, Milovan. 1957. *The New Class: An Analysis of the Communist System.* New York: Praeger.

Dorn, James and Wang Xi. 1990. *Economic Reform in China: Problems and Prospects.* Chicago: University of Chicago Press.

Duncan, Graeme. 1987. "Understanding Ideology." *Political Studies* 4:649-59.

DuRand, Cliff. 1986. "The Reconstitution of Private Property in the People's Republic of China: John Locke Revisited." *Social Theory and Practice* 12 (3):337-50.

Eckstein, Alexander. 1977. *China's Economic Revolution.* London: Cambridge University Press.

Engels, Friedrich. 1939. *Herr Eugen Duhring's Revolution in Science.* New York: International Publisher.

Ethridge, James. 1990. *China's Unfinished Revolution: Problems and Prospects since Mao.* San Francisco: China Books and Periodicals.

Fairbank, John. 1986. *The Great Chinese Revolution, 1800–1985.* New York: Harper & Row.

Falkenheim, Victor. 1982. "Popular Values and Political Reform: The 'Crisis of Faith' in Contemporary China." In *Social Interaction in Chinese Society,* ed. Sidney Greenblatt, *et al.* New York: Praeger.

Feuchtwang, Stephan and Athar Hussain. 1983. *The Chinese Economic Reforms.* New York: St. Martin's Press.

Friedman, Edward. 1984. "Three Leninist Paths within a Socialist Conundrum." In *Three Visions of Chinese Socialism,* ed. Dorothy Solinger. Boulder, Colorado: Westview Press.

———. 1989. "Modernization and Democratization in Leninist States: The Case of China." *Studies in Comparative Communism* 22 (2/3):251–64.

Fukuyama, Francis. 1989. "The End of History?" *National Interest* (Summer):3–18.

———. 1992. *The End of History and The Last Man.* New York: Free Press.

George, Alexander. 1969. "The 'Operational Code': A Neglected Approach to the study of Political Leaders and Decision-Making." *International Studies Quarterly* 13:190–222.

Gilison, Jerome. 1975. *The Soviet Image of Utopia*, Baltimore and London: Johns Hopkins University Press.

Gill, Graeme. 1987. "The Single Party As An Agent of Development: Lesson From the Soviet Union." *World Politics* 28 (4):566–78.

Gong, Ting. 1993. "Corruption and Reform: An Analysis of Unintended Consequences," *Crime, Law and Social Change* 19:311–27

Gong, Ting and Chen Feng. 1990. "Neo-Authoritarian Theory in Mainland China," *Issues and Studies* 27 (1):84–98.

Gouri Geeta, ed. 1991. *Privatization and Public Enterprises: The Asia-Pacific Experience*. New Delhi: Oxford & IBH.

Graham, Cosmo and Tony Prosser. 1991. *Privatizing Public Enterprises*. Oxford: Clarendon Press.

Grindle, Merlee and John Thomas. 1991. *Public Choices and Policy Change: The Political Economy of Reform in Developing Countries*. Baltimore: Johns Hopkins University Press. 1991.

Gurr, Robert. 1970. *Why Men Rebel?* Princeton, New Jersey: Princeton University Press.

Gurtov, Mel, ed. 1990. *The Transformation of Socialism*. Boulder, Colorado: Westview Press.

Habermas, Jurgen. 1975. *Legitimation Crisis*. Boston: Beacon Press.

Hall, Peter, ed. 1989. *The Political Power of Economic Ideas: Keynesianism across Nations*. New Jersey: Princeton University Press.

Halperin, Morton. 1974. *Bureaucratic Politics and Foreign Policy*. Washington, D.C: Brookings Institute.

Hamrin, Carol. 1990. *China and the Challenge of the Future*, Boulder, Colorado: Westview Press.

Harding, Harry. 1981. *Organizing China: The Problem of Bureaucracy*. Stanford, California: Stanford University Press.

———. 1987. *China's Second Revolution: Reform after Mao*. Washington, D.C: Brookings Institute.

He, Jianzhang and Zhang Weimin. 1982. "The State of Ownership: A Tendency toward Multiplicity." In *China's Economic Reforms*, ed., Lin Wei and Arnold Chao. Philadelphia: University of Pennsylvania Press.

Heilbroner, Robert. 1990. "Reflections: After Communism." *New Yorker* (September):91–100.

Helm, Dieter, ed. 1989. *The Economic Borders of the State*. New York: Oxford University Press.

Hinton, William. 1983. *Shenfan*. New York: Random House.

———. 1984. "Transformation in the Countryside." *US-China Reviews* 3:8–13.

———. 1984. "A Trip to Fengyang County: Investigating China's New Family Contract System." *Monthly Review* 35:1–28.

Hoffmann, Erik, and Robbin Laird. 1982. *The Politics of Economic Modernization in the Soviet Union*. Ithaca, New York: Cornell University Press.

Holsti, Ole. 1970. "Study of Political Leaders: John Foster Dulles's Philosophical and Instrumental Beliefs." *Canadian Journal of Politics* 3:14–26.

Howard, Pat. 1988. *Breaking The Iron Rice Bowl.* New York: M.E. Sharpe.

Hsiung, James. 1987. "Giving Marxism a New Lease on Life in Mainland
China." *Issues and Studies* 23 (6):67–79.

Johnson, Chalmers, ed. 1970. *Change in Communist Systems.* Stanford, California: Stanford University Press.

———. 1982. *MITI and the Japanese Miracle.* Stanford, Calif.: Stanford University Press.

———. 1987. "Political Institutions and Economic Performance: The Gov-
ernment-Business Relationship in Japan, South Korea, and Taiwan." In
Political Economy of the New Asian Industrialism, ed. Frederic Deyo.
Ithaca, New York: Cornell University of Press.

Johnson, Graham. 1986. "Responsibility and Reform: Consequences of
Recent Policy Changes in Rural South China." *Journal of Contemporary
Marxism* 12–13 (Spring):144–62.

Joint Economic Committee, Congress of the United States, ed. 1993. *China's
Economic Dilemmas in the 1990s.* New York: Sharpe.

Joseph, William. 1984. *The Critique of Ultra-Leftism in China, 1958–1981.* Stanford, California: Stanford University Press.

Kaminski, Barlomiej. 1991. *The Collapse of State Socialism.* Princeton, New
Jersey: Princeton University Press.

Kaminski, Barlomiej and Karol Soltan. 1989. "The Evolution Communism."
International Political Science Review 4:371–91.

Kelley, Donald. 1986. *The Politics of Developed Socialism: The Soviet Union as
a Post-Industrial State.* New York: Greenwood Press.

Kniss, Fred. 1988. "Toward a Theory of Ideological Change: The Case of the
Radical Reformation." *Sociological Analysis* 49:29–38.

Kornai, Janos. 1990. *The Road to a Free Economy,* New York: Norton.

Kriesberg, Louis. 1983. *Social Conflicts.* Englewood, Cliffs, New Jersey: Pren-
tice-Hall.

Krug, Barbara. 1991. "Blood, Sweat, Or Cheating: Politics and the Transformation of Socialist Economies in China, the USSR, and Eastern Europe."
Studies in Comparative Communism 24 (2):137–50.

Laaksonen, Ovia. 1988. *Management in China During and After Mao in Enterprises, Government, and Party.* Berlin: Walter de Gruyter.

Lambert, Richard and Alan Heston. 1990. *Privatizing and Marketizing Socialism.* New York: Sage Publications.

Lampton, David, ed. 1987. *Policy Implementation in Post-Mao China.* Berkeley: University of California Press.

Lane, Christel. 1984. "Legitimacy and Power in the Soviet Union Through
Socialist Ritual." *British Journal of Political Science* 14:207–17.

Lane, Robert. 1966. "The Decline of Politics and Ideology in a Knowledge-
able Society." *American Sociological Review* 31: 649–62.

LaPalombara, Joseph. 1966. "Decline of Ideology: A Dissent and an Interpretation." *American Political Science Review* 1:5–16.

Lee, Yung Hong. 1986. "The Implications of Reform For Ideology, State and Society in China." *Journal of International Affairs* 2:77–90.

Leites, Nathan. 1951. *The Operational Code of the Politburo*. New York: McGraw Hill.

———. 1953. *A Study of Bolshevism*. Glencoe, Illinois: Free Press.

Lenin, V.L. 1964. "Central Features of Historical Development of Marxism." *Collective Work* 17:39. New York: International Publishers.

Li, Cheng and Lynn White. 1990. "Mainland China and Taiwan: Empirical Data and the Theory of Technocracy." *China Quarterly* 3:12–25.

Lieberthal, Kenneth and Michel Oksenberg. 1992. *Bureaucracy, Politics and Decision Making in Post-Mao China*. Berkeley: University of California Press.

Lieberthal, Kenneth. 1982. *China's Economic Reforms*. Philadelphia: University of Pennsylvania Press.

———. 1985. "The Political Implications of Document No.1, 1984." *China Quarterly* 4:15–27.

———. 1993 "The Dynamics of Internal Policies" In *China's Economic Dilemmas in the 1990s*, ed. Joint Economic Committee, Congress of the United States. New York: Sharpe. Lin, Wei and Arnold Chao.

Lindblom, Charles. 1977. *Politics and Markets*. New York: Basic Books.

Ling, Huan-Ming. "Intellectual Responses to China's Economic Reforms," *Asian Survey* 28 (5):541–54.

Liu, Alan. 1982. "Political Decay on Mainland China: On Crises of Faith, Confidence and Trust." *Issues and Studies* 24 (4):21-33.

Lowenthal, Richard. 1970. "Development vs. Utopia in Communist Policy." In *Change in Communist Systems*, ed. Chalmers Johnson. Stanford, California: Stanford University Press.

———. 1974. "On 'Established' Communist Party Regimes." *Studies in Comparative Communism* 4:335–58.

———. 1976. "The Ruling Party in a Mature Society." In *Social Consequences of Modernization in Communist Societies*, ed. Mark Field. Baltimore: Johns Hopkins University Press.

MacAvoy, Paul, W.T. Stanhury, George Yarrow, and Richard Zeckhause. 1989. *Privatization and State-Owned Enterprises*. Dordrecht: Kluwer Academic Publisher.

MacFarquhar, Roderick. 1974. *The Origins of the Cultural Revolution*. New York: Columbia University Press.

Mao, Zedong. 1958. *On Practice*. New York: International Publishers.

———. 1960. *On the Correct Handling of Contradictions among the People*. Beijing: Foreign Languages Press.

———. 1961. *One People's Democratic Dictatorship*. Beijing: Foreign Languages Press.

———. 1977. *A Critique of Soviet Economics*, trans. Moss Roberts. New York: Monthly Review Press.

March, James and Johan Olsen. 1989. *Rediscovering Institutions: The Organizational Basis of Politics*. New York: The Free Press.

Martin, Helmut. 1982. *Cult and Canon*. Armonk, New York: Sharpe.

Marx, Karl. 1966. *Capital*. New York: International Publishers.

———. 1972. *Critique of the Gotha Programme*. Beijing: Foreign Languages Press.

Marx, Karl and Friedrich Engels. 1948. *Communist Manifesto*. New York: International Publishers.

Masters, Roger. 1979. "On the Ubiquity of Ideology in Modern Societies." *Cahiers Vilfredo Pareto* 46:59–72.

McCormick, Barrett. 1990. *Political Reform in Post-Mao China: Democracy and Bureaucracy in a Leninist State*. Berkeley: University of California Press.

Meisner, Maurice. 1977. *Mao's China, A History of the People's Republic*. New York: Free Press.

———. 1982. *Marxism, Maoism and Utopianism*. Madison, Wisconsin: The University of Wisconsin Press.

Mokrzycki, Edmund. 1991. "The Legacy of Real Socialism and Western Democracy." *Studies in Comparative Communism* 24 (2)211–17.

Moody, Peter. 1983. *Chinese Politics after Mao*. New York: Praeger Publishers.

Moore, Barrington. 1965. *Soviet Politics: The Dilemma of Power*. New York: Harper & Row.

Mullins, Willard. 1972. "On the Concept of Ideology in Political Science." *American Political Science Review* 66:498–501.

Myers, James. 1985. "China: the 'Germs' of Modernization." *Asian Survey* 25:981-87.

Nagle, John. 1992. *Introduction to Comparative Politics: Political System Performance in Third Worlds*, 3d ed. Chicago: Nelson-Hall.

Nathan, Andrew. 1985. *Chinese Democracy*. Berkeley and Los Angeles: University of California Press.

———. 1990. *China's Crisis*. New York: Columbia University Press.

Nayar, Baldev. 1989. *India's Mixed Economy: The Role of Ideology and Interest in Its Development*. Bombay: Popular Prakshan.

Nee, Victor and David Stark. "Peasant Household Individualism." In *Chinese Rural Development: The Great Transformation*, ed. William Parish. New York: Sharpe.

———. 1989. *Remaking the Economic Institutions of Socialism: China and Eastern Europe*. Stanford, California: Stanford University Press.

Nellis, John and Sunita Kikeri. 1980. "Public Enterprise Reform: Privatization and the World Bank." In *World Development* 17 (5):659-72.

North, Douglass. 1981. *Structure and Change in Economic History*. New York: W.W.Norton.

Nove, Alec. 1983. *The Economics of Feasible Socialism*. London and Boston: G. Allen & Unwin.

————. 1986. *Marxism and "Really Existing Socialism."* New York: Harwood Academic.

Oi, Jean. 1989. *State and Peasants in Contemporary China: The Political Economy of Village Government*. Berkeley: University of California Press.

Onis, Ziya. 1991. "The Logic of the Developmental State." In *Comparative Politics* 23, (October):109–26.

Ozinga, James. 1991. *Communism: The Story of the Ideas and Its Implementation*. New Jersey: Prentice Hall.

Parsons, Talcott. 1982. "Evolutionary Universals in Society." In *On Institutions and Social Evolution*, ed. Leon Mayhew. Chicago: University of Chicago Press.

Pejovich, Svetozar. 1990. *The Economics of Property Rights: Towards a Theory of Comparative Systems*. Dordrecht: Kluwer Academic.

Perry, Elizabeth. 1989. "State and Society in Contemporary China." *World Politics* 41 (4):579–91.

Perry, Elizabeth and Christine Wong, eds. 1985. *The Political Economy of Reform in Post-Mao China*. Cambridge: Harvard University Press.

Post, Ken and Phil Wright. 1989. *Socialism and Underdevelopment*. London: Routledge.

Pravad, Alex, 1988. *Ideology and Soviet Politics*, New York: St. Martin's Press.

Prybyla, Jan. 1989. "Why China's Economic Reform Fail." *Asian Survey* 24 (11):1017–32.

Przeworski, Adam. 1991. "Could We Feed Everyone? The Irrationality of Capitalism and the Infeasibility of Socialism." *Politics and Society* 19:1–38.

Pye, Lucian. 1981. *The Dynamics of Chinese Politics*. Cambridge, Massachusetts: Oelgeschlager, Gunn & Hain.

————. 1988. *Mandarin and the Cadre: China's Political Cultures*. Ann Arbor: University of Michigan, Center for Chinese Studies.

Randall, Vicky and Robin Theobald. 1985. *Political Change and Underdevelopment*. Durham, North Carolina: Duke University Press.

Reeve, Andrew. 1986. *Property*. Atlantic Highlands, New Jersey: Humanities Press International.

Rejai, M. 1971. "Political Ideology: Theoretical and Comparative Perspectives." In *Decline of Ideology*, Rejai, M. ed. . Chicago: Aldine-Atherton.

Reynolds, Bruce. 1987. *Reform in China: Challenge & Choices*. New York: Sharpe.

Riskin, Carl. 1987. *China's Political Economy*. New York: Oxford University Press.

Rosen, Stanley. 1989. "Public Opinion and Reform in the People's Republic of China." *Comparative Communism* 22 (2–3):153–70.

Sakwa, Richard. 1990. *Gorbachev and His Reform: 1985–1990*. New Jersey: Prentice Hall.

Sartori, Giovanni. 1969. "Politics, Ideology, and Belief Systems." *American Political Science Review* 63:398–411.

Schmid, Herman. 1981. "On the Origin of Ideology." *Acta Sociologica* 24:57–73.

Schram, Stuart. 1984. *Ideology and Policy Since the Third Plenum, 1978–1984.* London: University of London, School of Oriental and African Studies, Contemporary China Institute.

Schurmann, Franz. 1966. *Ideology and Organization in Communist China.* Berkeley: University of California Press.

Selden, Mark. 1988. *The Political Economy of Chinese Socialism.* Armonk, New York: Sharpe.

Seliger, Martin. 1976. *Ideology and Politics.* New York: Free Press.

Seymour, James. 1980. *Fifth Modernization,* Standfordville, New York: Human Rights Publishing Group.

Shirk, Susan. 1985. "The Politics of Industrial Reform." In *The Political Economy of Reform in Post-Mao China,* ed. Elizabeth Perry and Christine Wong. Cambridge: Harvard University Press.

————. 1993. *The Political Logic of Economic Reform in China.* Berkeley: University of California Press.

Shlapentokh, Vladimir. 1986. *Soviet Public Opinion: Ideology, Mythology and Pragmatism.* New York: Praeger, 1986.

Sik, Ota. 1976. *The Third Way.* London: Wildwood House.

————. 1981. *The Communist System.* Trans. by Marianne Freidberg. New York: Praeger.

Sikkink, Kathryn. 1991. *Ideas and Institutions: Development in Brazil and Argentina.* Ithaca, New York: Cornell University Press.

Silber, Irwin. 1990. "Perestroika Revives Leninism's Flexibility. *Guardian* 21 February: 5–7..

Silverman, Lawrence. 1985. "The Ideological Mediation of Party-Political Responses to Social Change." *European Journal of Political Research* 13:69–93.

Simon, Herbert. 1976. *Administrative Behavior.* New York: Free Press.

Smith, Steve. 1988. "Belief Systems and the Study of International Relations," In *Belief Systems and International Relations,* ed. Richard Little and Steve Smith. New York: Blackwell.

Solinger, Dorothy, ed. 1984a. *Three Visions of Chinese Socialism.* Boulder, Colorado: Westview Press.

————. 1984b. *Chinese Business under Socialism: The Politics of Domestic Commerce, 1949–1980.* Berkeley: University of California Press.

————. 1989. "Capitalist Measures with Chinese Characteristics." In *Problems of Communism* 38 (January–February):19–33.

Spence, Jonathan. 1990. *The Search for Modern China.* New York: W.W. Norton.

Stalin, Joseph. 1972. *Economic Problems of Socialism in the USSR*. Beijing: Foreign Languages Press.

Staniszkis, Jadwiga. 1989. "The Dynamics of a Breakthrough in the Socialist System: An Outline of Problems." *Soviet Studies* 12 (4):560–73.

Suleiman, Ezra and John Waterbury. 1990. *The Political Economy of Public Sector Reform and Privatization*. Boulder, Colorado: Westview Press.

Sweezy, Paul, and Charles Bettelheim. *On the Transition to Socialism*. New York: Monthly Review Press.

Tidrick, Gene and Chen Jiyuan, ed. 1987. *China's Industrial Reform*, published for the World Bank. Oxford: Oxford University Press, 1987.

Tsou, Tang. 1986. *Cultural Revolution and Post-Mao Reforms*. Chicago: University of Chicago Press.

Tucker, Robert. 1969. *The Marxian Revolutionary Idea*. New York: W.W. Norton.

Ulam, Adam. 1964. *The Unfinished Revolution*. New York: Vintage Books.

Volgyes, Ivan. 1989. "The Dilemmas of Socialism: Ideology, Culture, and Society in Soviet Type Systems during the Gorbachev Era." *Studies in Communism* 2/3:278–84.

Wade, Robert. 1990. *Governing the Market: Economic Theory and the Role of Government in East Asian Industrialization*. Princeton, New Jersey: Princeton University Press.

Walder, Andrew. 1986. *Communist Neo-Traditionalism*. Berkeley: University of California Press.

Walker, Stephen. 1977. "The Interface Between Beliefs and Behavior." *Journal of Conflict Resolution* 1:129–65.

Walle, Nicolas. 1989. "Privatization in Developing Countries: A Review of the Issues." *World Development* 17 (5):601–15.

Weiner, Myron and Samuel Huntington. 1987. *Understanding Political Development*. New York: Harper Collins.

White, Gordon. 1983. "Revolutionary Socialist development in the Third World: A Overview." In Gordon White and Robin Murray, *Revolutionary Socialist Development in the Third World*. Lexington, Kentucky: University of Kentucky Press.

———. 1983. "The Postrevolutionary Chinese State." In *State and Society in Contemporary China*, ed. Victor Nee and David Mozingo. Ithaca, New York: Cornell University Press.

White, Stephen and Alex Pravda. 1988. *Ideology and Soviet Politics*. Houndmills, Basingtoke, Hampshire: Macmillan.

Whynes, David and Roger Bowles. 1981. *The Economic Theory of The State*. New York: St. Martin's Press.

Womack, Brantly. 1979. "Politics and Epistemology in China Since Mao." *The China Quarterly* 80:768–92.

———. 1989. "Party-State Democracy: A Theoretical Exploration." *Issues and Studies* 26 (3):24–37.

World Bank. 1983. *China: Socialist Economic Development.* Washington, D.C.
———. 1985. *China: Long-Term Development Issues and Options.* Washington, D.C.
———. 1990. *China: Macroeconomic Stability and Industrial Growth under Decentralized Socialism.* Washington, D.C.
———. 1990. *China: Between Plan and Market.* Washington, D.C.
Wright, Anthony. 1986. *Socialism: Theories and Practices.* Oxford: Oxford University Press.
Wuthnow, Robert. 1981. "Comparative Ideology." *International Journal of Comparative Sociology* 3/4:123–40.
———. 1985. "State Structures and Ideological Outcomes." *American Sociological Review* 50:799–820.
Zaslavsky, V. 1980. "Socioeconomic Inequality and Change in the Soviet Ideology." *Theory and Society* 9:134–48.
Zhao, Ziyang. 1982. *China's Economy and Development Principles.* Beijing: Foreign Languages Press.

LITERATURE IN CHINESE

Asian Institute. 1989. *New Asia* Vol.1 and Vol.2. Shanghai: Sanlian Bookstore.
Beijing Bureau of Industrial and Commerical Management. 1986. "Investigation of Sanlian Coal Mine." In *Investigation and Study on the Individual Economy*, ed. General Office of the State Council. Beijing: Economic Science Press: 195–202.
Bureau of Retired Cadres of Shanghai Municipal Party Committee. 1989. *Study Materials* (internally circulated). February 9.
Central Party School and the State Commission of Economic System Reform. 1987. *Reflections on Industrial and Agricultural Reforms.* Beijing: Economic Science Press.
Chang, Xiuze. 1986. "On the Reform of State Enterprises." In *Promoting Reforms*, ed. The Theoretical Research Office of the Secretariat of the CCP Central Committee, Shanghai: Shanghai People's Publishing House.
Chao, Jingqing. 1988. *On Equality.* Shanghai: Eastern China Chemical Engineering Institute Press.
Chen, Shengsheng. 1988. "On Establishment of Market Order." *Zhongguo: Fanzhan yu Gaige* (China: Development and Reform) 9:3–12.
Chen, Wenjun and Feng Rusheng. 1988. "A Few Comments on Private Enterprises." *Tansou* (Exploration) 3:18–20.
Chen, Yizhi. 1990. *China: Ten-Year Reform and the Democratic Movement in 1989.* Taiwan: Lianjin.
Chen, Yonghu and Zhu Yugeng. 1988. "The Status Quo of Private Enterprises in Shanghai and the Problems of Their Regulation." *Tansuo yu Zhengming* (Exploration and Contending) 1:33–34.
Chen, Yun. 1982. *The Collected Works.* Beijing: People's Publisher.

Chongqing Administrative Bureau of Individual Businesses. 1986. "Investigative Report on Individual Businesses in Chongqing." In *Investigation and Study on the Individual Economy*, ed. General Office of the State Council. Beijing: Economic Science Press.

Collected Documents of The CCP's 13th National Congress. 1987. Beijing: People's Publisher.

Deng, Xiaoping. 1983. *The Selected Works of Deng Xiaoping*. Beijing: People's Publisher.

———. 1987. *Building Socialism with Chinese Characteristics*. People's Publisher.

Development Institute. 1988. *Reforms Faces Institutional Innovations*. Shanghai: Sanlian Bookstore.

Dong, Nan. 1988. "A Summery of Contending Views on the Leasing System." *Tansuo yu Zhengming* (Exploration and Contending) 4:61–63.

Du, Runsheng. 1985. *Chinese Rural Economic Reform*. Beijing: Chinese Social Science Press.

Economic Research Office of the Secretariat of the CCP Central Committee. 1984. *On Specialized Households*. Beijing: Economic Science Press.

Editorial Department of Philosophical Study. 1979. *Practice is the Only Criterion for the Truth: Collected Essays*, Vol.1 and Vol. 2. Beijing: Chinese Social Science Press.

Fang, Gongwen. 1988. "On the Private Economy at the Preliminary Stage of Socialism." In *Essays on the Preliminary Stage of Socialism*, ed. Zheng Bijianand Jian Chunfeng. Beijing: Chinese Youth Press, 1988.

Gao, Fang. 1988. "Two Theoretical Issues on Socialism in Underdeveloped Countries." *Qiushi Xuekan* (Seeking Truth) 4:1–7.

Gao, Shuanping and Sheng Xing. 1986. "On the Separation of Ownership and Management in State Enterprises." *Tansuo* (Exploration) 3:1–3.

Gao, Xilan, ed. 1989. *China's National Situations: Questions and Answers*. Beijing: Chunqiu Press.

General Office of the State Council. 1986. *Investigation and Study on the Individual Economy*. Beijing: Economic Science Press.

General Office of Tianjing Municipal Government. 1986. "The Survey on the Individual Business in Tianjing." In *Investigation and Study on the Individual Economy*, ed. General Office of the State Council. Beijing: Economic Science Press.

Gu, Changchun and Wu Li. 1989. *A Survey of China's Ten Year Reforms*. Beijing: Zhanwang Press.

Gu, Shutang and Chai Xiaozhen. 1987. *Socialist Economic Theory and the Study of the Economic System*. Shanxi: Shanxi People's Publisher.

Gu, Yan. 1989. "An Investigation on the Experiment with Shareholding System in Shanghai." *Shanghai Gaige* (Shanghai Reform) 4:36–40

Guo, Zhengying. 1986. *Questions and Answers Regarding the Shareholding Economy under Socialism*. Beijing: Beijing Aeronautical Institute Press.

He, Bo. 1989. *The China on the Mountain: Problems, Predicaments and Painful Choices*. Guizhou: Guizhou People's Publisher.

He, Jianzhang. 1989. "On the Issue of State-Owned Enterprises." *Zhongguo Gongye Jingji Yanjiu* (Studies of Chinese Industrial Economy) 5:3–9.

He, Shenggao. 1988. "Guiding the Reform of the Enterprise System to a Higher Level." *Shangai Jingji* (Shanghai Economics) 9:3–7.

He, Wei. 1988. "On the Socialist Nature of Labor Commodity." In *Commodity Economy and the Allocation of Skilled Labor Resource*, ed. Shanghai Municipal Personnel Bureau. Shanghai: Shanghai Academy of Social Science Press.

Hua, Shen. 1986. "Prospects and Strategy of China's Reform." *Zhongguo: Fazhan yu Gaige* (China: Development and Reform) 2:4–8.

Institute of Industrial Economy. 1980. *Policy Documents Since the Third Plenum of the CCP* (internally circulated). Beijing Academy of Social Science Press.

Investigative Team of Individual Business, Shenzhen Municipal Government. 1986. "A Survey on Individual Business in Shenzhen Special Economic Zone." In *Investigation and Study on the Individual Economy*, ed. General Office of the State Council.Beijing: Economic Science Press.

Ji, Xiaopeng, Jiang Sidong and Yao Gang. 1987. "Clearly Defining Property Rights: A Historical Necessity of Deepening Reforms." *Zhongguo: Fanzhan yu Gaige* (China: Development and Reform) 5:4–15.

Jiang, Chenlong. 1988. "Labor as a Commodity in Socialism." In *Commodity Economy and the Allocation of Skilled Labor Resources*, ed. Shanghai Municipal Personnel Bureau. Shanghai: Shanghai Academy of Social Science Press.

Jiangsu Administrative Bureau of Individual Business. 1986. "Investigation on the Status of Individual Businesses in Jiangsu." In *Investigation and Study on the Individual Economy*, ed. General Office of the State Council. Beijing: Economic Science Press.

Jiang, Tiezhu. 1989. "On The Separation of Two Powers in All-People-Owned Enterprises." *Shanghai Gaige* (Shanghai Reform) no.9:21–23.

Jiang, Xuemo. 1986. "Several Points of View on the Reform of the System of the Means of Production." *Jingjixue Dongtai* (Economic Information) 2:4–7.

Jiang, Zhaoyi and Hu Liping. 1983. *On Socialist Revolution of Our Country*. Beijing: Hongqi Press.

Jilin Bureau of Industrial and Commerial Management. 1986. "Some Views on the Hiring of Workers." In *Investigation and Study on the Individual Economy*, ed. General Office of the State Council. Beijing: Economic Science Press.

Jing, Sidong and Song Guoqing. 1988. "Theoretical Debate on the Reform of Enterprise System." *Zhongguo: Fanzhan yu Gaige* (China: Development and Reform) 4:38–48.

Lei, Tao. 1989. *A Reflection on Equality.* Beijing: Chinese Women Press.

Li, Honglin. 1988. "We Uphold What Kind of Marxism." *Makesizhuyi Yanjiu* (Studies in Marxism) 3:1–9.

Li, Ming. 1989. *China's Crises and Reflections.* Tainjin: Tianjing People's Publisher.

Li, Wei. 1988. "A Survey on Income Differentials of Different Social Members in Shanghai and the Recommendation for Adjustment." *Tansuo yu Zhengming* (Exploration and Contending) 3:50–54.

Li, Xueman. 1988. "A Reflection on Exploitation in Economic Operation." *Zhongguo Jingji Wenti* (China's Economic Issues) 3:48–52.

Li, Yining. 1989. *Where Is the Chinese Economy Heading?* Hong Kong: Shangwu Publishing House.

Li, Zhongfan. 1987. "The Law and Model of Socialist Commodity Economy." In *Reflections on Rural and Urban Reforms,* ed. Central Party School and the State Commission of Economic System Reform. Beijing: Economic Science Press.

Lin, Jingyao and Zhu Shuxian. 1987. *Understanding the Preliminary Stage of Socialism and Speeding Up Reforms and Openness.* Beijing: Beijing Normal University Press.

Lin, Ling. 1986. *An Inquiry Into the Reform of China's Economic System.* Sichuan: Chongqing People's Publishing House.

Lin, Shulin. 1984. "The Roles of Specialized Household in China's Rural Areas." In *On Specialized Households.* ed. Economic Research Office of the Secretariat of the CCP Central Committee. Beijing: Economic Science Press.

Lin, Zili. 1983. "On Production Responsibility System with Output-Related Contracts." *Zhongguo Shehui Kexue* (Chinese Social Science) 6:3–32.

Liu, Guangdi. 1987. "On the Experience of CSIC." In *Reflection on the Industrial and Agricultural Reforms,* ed. Central Party School and the State Commission of Economic System Reform. Beijing: Economic Science Press.

Liu, Guoguang, ed. 1983. *A Study on China's Economic Development Strategies.* Shanghai: Shanghai People's Publisher.

Lu, Fanzhi. 1985. *Chinese Economic Reforms and Adjustments.* Hong Kong: Yingcheng.

Lu, Yingling and Fang Li. 1988. *The Productive Forces and Socialism.* People's Army Press.

Lu, Zhengyu. 1988. "An Inquiry into the Theory of the Reform of State Ownership." *Tansuo* (Exploration) 10:5–8.

Ma, Hong. 1988. *The Road and the Prospecct of Chinese Socialist Modernization.* Shanghai: Shanghai People's Publisher.

Ma, Yuping and Huang Yucong, ed. 1988. *China's Yesterday and Today.* Beijing: Liberation Army Press.

Mo, Guogiang. 1986. "How to Treat the Phenomenon of Labor-Hiring." *Tansuo yu Zhengming* (Exploration and Contending) 12: 23–24.

Propaganda Department of the Shanghai Municipal Party Committee. 1990. *Socialist Education Reference Materials.* Shanghai.

Qing, Ping. 1986. "On the Openness to the Capitalist World." *Qingnian Pinglun* (Youth Commentary) 5:12–19.

Qiu, Jingji. 1988. "The Essence and Purposes of the Shareholding System in China." *Zhongguo Gongyu Jingji Yanjiu* (Studies in Chinese Industrial Economy) 4:38–41.

Research Office of the State Council: "Survey of Individual Business in China." In *Investigation and Study on the Individual Economy,* ed. General Office of the State Council. Beijing: Economic Science Press, 1986.

Research Office of Secretariat of the CCP Central Committee. 1982 and 1987. *Important Documents Since the Third Plenum.* Beijing: People's Publishing House.

Research Officce of Party Committee of Wenzhou. 1986. "Analysis of the Labor Hiring." *Investigation and Study on the Individual Economy.* ed. General Office of the State Council. Beijing: Economic Science Press, 1986.

Rural Policy Research Office of the Secretariat of the CCP Central Committee and the Center of Rural development of the State Council. 1987. *The Progress in Agricultural Reforms.* Beijing: Agricultural Press.

Shanghai Municipal Personnel Bureau. 1988. *Commodity Economy and the Allocation of Skilled Labor Resource.* Shanghai: Shanghai Academy of Social Science Press.

Shanghai Party School. 1989. *Cadre Study Documents.* Shanghai: Party School.

Sheng, Hong. 1989. "On Modernization of Institutions." *Zhongguo: Fanzhan yu Gaige* (China: Development and Reform) 5:3–11.

Song, Yangyan. 1988. "The Separation of Two Powers: The Manifestation of a Self-Perfection of Socialist System in Our Country." *Zhongguo Jingju Wenti* (Issues of China's Economy) 4:11–17.

State Education Commission. 1990. *The Evolution and Prospect of the Situations of Eastern Europe.* Beijing: Higher Education Press.

State Statistic Bureau. 1989. *A Statistical Survey of China: 1989.* Beijing: Chinese Statistical Press.

Su, Chengding and Jiangxin. 1989. "The Dual Constraints on the Enterprises into Markets." *Zhongguo: Fanzhan yu Gaige* (China: Development and Reform) 8:28–33.

Su, Ya and Jia Lushang. 1990. *Who Is Able to Contract?* Guangdong: Huacheng Press.

Sun, Changjiang. 1989. "From the Practice Criterion to Productive Criterion." *Makesizhuyi Yanjiu* (Studies in Marxism) 22:7–15.

Sun, Xuewen, 1982. "We Must Correctly Carry Out Enterprise Responsibility System." *Caimao Jingji* (Financial Study) 4 :12–19.

Tang, Zongkun. 1980. "The Grounds for the Long Existence of City/Town Collective Ownership in Our Country and Its Future," *Studies on Collective*

Economy, ed. Research Group of Agricultural Reform. Beijing: People's Publishing House, 1980.

Theoretical Bureau of the Propaganda Department of the Central Committee of the CCP. 1988. *Theory of the Preliminary Stage of Socialism and Party's Fundamental Lines*. Beijing: Hongqi Press.

Tian, Yuan and Zhu Yong. 1988. "On Property Rights System Reform." *Zhongguo: Fazhan yu Gaige* (China: Development and Reform) 12:3–13.

Wan, Hao. 1988. "Does Private Economy Necessarily Lead to Exploitation?" *Tansuo yu Zhengming* (Exploration and Contending) 6:7–14.

Wang, He. 1988. "The Reform of Property Rights and Re-establishment of the Socialist Ownership System." *Tansuo* (Exploration) no.4:3–8.

Wang, Hongmo and Zhang Zhanbing. 1989. *The Course of Reform and Openness*. Henan: Henan People's Publishing House.

Wang, Kezhong. 1990. *A Study on China's Current Private Economy*. Shanghai: Fudan University Press.

Wang, Kezhong and Li Guorong. "On Capitalist Private Ownership at the Current State of Our Country." *Tansuo* (Exploration) 3:23–27.

Wang, Yizou. 1988. "Re-understanding Capitalism." *Qiqihaoer Shehui Kexue* (Qiqihaoer Social Science) 3:82–86.

Wen, Guanzgong. 1989. "The Defects of China's Current Land System and Their Solutions." In *China's Crises and Reflections*, ed. Li Ming. Tainjin: Tianjing People's Publisher.

Wenzhou Municipal Government Investigate Team. 1986. *The Wenzhou Model*. Zhejiang: Zhejiang People's Publisher.

Wu, Jiaxiang. 1986. "Rich First and Common Prosperity." *Promoting Reforms*, ed. Theoretical Research Office of the Secretariat of the CCP Central Committee. Shanghai: Shanghai People's Publishing House.

———. 1987. "On the Theory of the Preliminary Socialism." In *Understanding the Preliminary Stage of Socialism and Speeding Up Reforms and Openness*, ed. Lin, Jingyai and Zhu Shuxian. Beijing: Beijing Normal University Press.

———. 1988. "Options for Property Rights Reform." In *Zhongguo: Fazhan yu Gaige* (China: Development and Reform) 4:32–37.

Wu, Qi. 1988. "The Role of Government in Economic Take-Off." *Zhongguo: Fazhan yu Gaige* (China: Development and Reform) 9:45–57.

Xie, Zifen and Zhou Tao. 1982. *The Road to Prosperity for Eight Hundred Million Peasants*. Shanghai: Shanghai People's Publisher.

Xin, Geng. 1988. "The Formation and the Basic Contents of the Theory of the Preliminary Stage of Socialism." *Shehui Kexue Pinglun* (Social Science Review)1:24–31.

Xinhua News Press. 1988. *The Chronicle of Chinese Reforms: 1978–1987*. Beijing: Xinhua News Press.

Xu, Yaojun. 1988. "On the Principle of Socialist Distribution and the Law of Value." In *Commodity Economy and the Allocation of Skilled Labor Resource*, ed. Shanghai Municipal Personnel Bureau. Shanghai: Shanghai Academy of Social Science Press.

Xue, Muqiao. 1981. *China's Socialist Economy*. Beijing: Foreign Languages Press.

Yang, Xiao and Xue Xingxing. 1989. "The Relationships and Power Distribution between Government and Enterprises." *Zhongguo: Fazhan yu Gaige* (China: Development and Reform) 8:19–27.

Yang, Xinpei. 1987. "The Speed, Efficiency, and the Road of the Capital Steel Corporation." In *Reflections on Rural and Urban Reforms*, ed. Central Party School and the State Commission of Economic System Reform. Beijing: Economic Science Press.

Ying, Ming and Geng Yuan. 1989. *The Social Problems of Contemporary China*. Neimenggu: Neimenggu People's Publisher.

Yu, Guangyuan. 1985. *The Fundamental Issues on The Reform of China's Economic System Reforms*. Nanchang: Jiangxi People's Publisher.

Yuan, Enzheng ed. 1987. *The Wenzhou Model and the Road Toward Prosperity*. Shanghai: Shanghai Academy of Social Science Press.

Yuan, Xunzhong and Zhao Li. 1989. *The Key To The Historical Transformation*. Beijing: People's Army Press.

Zhang, Guangsheng. 1989. "A Preliminary Inquiry of the Transfer of State Property Rights in Shanghai." In *Shanghai Gaige* (Shanghai Reform) 1:26–31.

Zhang, Guangzhu. 1988. "Reflections on Unequal Economic Relations at the Socialist Stage." In *Tansuo yu Zhengming* (Exploration and Contending) 5:1–5.

Zhang, Xianyang. "Seriously Studying the New Development of Marxism in China." In *Makesizhuyi Yanjiu* (Studies in Marxism) 21:15–34.

Zhao, Mao and Zhang Yuelei. 1989. "A Preliminary Inquiry on the Relations of Income Distribution between the State and Enterprises." In *Shanghai Gaige* (Shanghai Reform) 3:32–35.

Zhao, Rulin. 1986. "On The Principles of Income Distribution in Reform of the Economic System." In *Tansuo yu Zhengming* (Exploration and Contending) 6:28–30.

Zhao, Juncheng. 1987. "Inquiry on the Potential Problems of the Experiment of Shareholding with State Enterprises." *Tansuo* (Exploration) 9:15–18.

Zhao, Ziyang. 1987. *Political Report to the 13th National Congress of the Chinese Communist Party*. Beijing: People's Publisher.

Zheng, Bifeng and Jia Chunfeng. 1988. *On The Preliminary State of Socialism: Essays*. Beijing: Chinese Youth Press.

Zheng, Gang and Shu Guang. 1987. The Methods of Revitalizing Sate Enterprises." In *Jingji yu Guanli Yanjiu* (Studies in Economics and Management) 1:6–9.

Zhou, Guanwu. 1987. "The Key of the Reform is to Stir Up the Enthusiasm."

In *Reflections on Rural and Urban Reforms*, ed. Central Party School and the State Commission of Economic System Reform. Beijing: Economic Science Press.

Zhou, Qiren. 1988. "A Revolution of the Property Relations in China's Countryside." In *Reform Faces Institional Innovations*, ed. Development Institute. Shanghai: Sanlian Book Press.

Zhou, Shulian. 1985. *Inquiry into Chinese Socialist Economy*. Shangyang: Liaoning People's Publisher.

———. 1987. *Selected Work of Zhou Shulian*. Shangxi: Shangxi Economic Press.

INDEX

Marx, K.
on public ownership 23
Marxism 4, 14, 16, 198, 199, 203, 205, 212
Marxism-Leninism Mao Zedong Thought
Marxism-Leninism Mao Zedong Thought
14
Means of production 27, 29, 30, 32, 33, 66,
67, 70–73, 75, 76, 83, 127, 132, 134, 145,
154, 161, 162, 168, 171, 175, 178, 181,
184, 187–90
Middle class 194
Mmeisner, M. 19
Moore, B. 11
Mullins, W. 212

Nathan, A. 7
Nationalization 91, 92
Natural economy 143, 144, 147
Negative legitimation 155
Neo-authoritarianism 148, 206, 208, 222
New conceptualization of socialism 62
Nove, A. 200

Official speculation 182, 222
Open door 15
Optimal combination (youhua zuhe) 181
Organization Department 157
Ownership by the whole people 29, 30
Ownership rights of the land 83, 89, 91,
92
Ownership system 21, 22, 24, 25, 32, 33,
65, 66, 202, 205, 212

Pakistan 164
Perceptional change 9
Petty bourgeoisie 33
Philippines, the 164
Plundering production 111
Polarization 169, 172, 175, 176, 194
Political criteria 45–47
Political primacy of production 55, 56, 58,
59
Political primacy of the criterion of pro-
ductive forces 35
Politics in command 15
Popular capitalism 218
Post-Mao leadership 18, 19, 21, 22, 58, 59,
62–65, 199

Power struggle approach 6–9
Practice criterion 22, 35, 36, 42–47, 50–54
Preliminary Stage of Socialism 58, 59, 61,
184, 186
Price scissors 72
Private economy 185, 186
Private enterprises 128, 131–34, 137–39,
141, 142, 146, 147, 149, 155, 157, 158,
176, 178, 179, 184, 185, 189, 200, 201
Private ownership 76, 81, 84, 88, 89, 91–93,
127, 128, 136, 137, 145, 149, 152, 153,
156
Private plots 72
Privatization 128, 139, 148, 150–153, 155,
156, 177, 178, 200, 202–5
Problem solving 5, 6, 9, 10, 12, 14, 15, 48,
64, 87
Production brigade 66
Production team 66
Profit contract 103
Profit retention 103
Property rights 108, 113–20, 122–25, 167,
176, 183, 184, 192, 203–5, 207, 208
exclusivity 115
transaction costs 116
transferability 115
Property rights economics 114, 115, 117
Public ownership 15, 21, 23–27, 29, 30,
32–34, 66, 82, 93, 94
Pure ideology 11
Pye, L.

Quasi commodification 89, 90, 92
Quasi private ownership 83, 84

Rational choice approach 6–8
Rationality crisis 19
Red Guard Movement 49, 213
Regime transformation 1
Relations of production 40, 53, 54, 56, 57,
63
Relative deprivation 191
Relativism 48
Responsibility system 15
Restricted capitalism 138, 139
Returned students 43, 213
Rural decollectivization 22, 65, 75, 76, 84
Russian Revolution 24, 44